Turning Points

ALSO BY LOUIS BALDWIN

Jesus of Galilee

Oneselves
(McFarland, 1984)

Edmond Haley and His Comet

Portraits of God
(McFarland, 1986)

The Pope and the Mavericks

One Woman's Liberation

The Loves of Their Lives

Triumph Over the Odds

Intruders Within

Women of Strength
(McFarland, 1996)

WITH VIRGINIA BALDWIN

To Marry, with Love

Turning Points

Pivotal Moments in the Careers of 83 Famous Figures

by

LOUIS BALDWIN

McFarland & Company, Inc., Publishers
Jefferson, North Carolina, and London

To Ginnie, with love

Cover photograph of Rosa Parks used by permission of Photographs and Prints Division, Schomburg Center for Research in Black Culture, The New York Public Library, Astor, Lenox and Tilden Foundations.

Library of Congress Cataloguing-in-Publication Data

Baldwin, Louis
    Turning points : pivotal moments in the careers of 83 famous figures / by Louis Baldwin.
      p.   cm.
    Includes index.
    ISBN 0-7864-0626-7 (sewn softcover : 50# alkaline paper)
    1. Celebrities—Biography.   2. Biography—20th century.
    3. Life change events. I. Title.
    CT120.B23 1999
    920'.009'04—dc21   99-29852
                                                  CIP

British Library Cataloguing-in-Publication data are available

Manufactured in the United States of America

McFarland & Company, Inc., Publishers
  Box 611, Jefferson, North Carolina 28640
    www.mcfarlandpub.com

CONTENTS

Introduction	1	Ella Fitzgerald	63
		Henry Fonda	66
Muhammad Ali	3	Jane Fonda	69
Woody Allen	5	Clark Gable	72
Maya Angelou	7	Bill Gates	75
Yasir Arafat	10	George Gershwin	77
Louis Armstrong	13	Newt Gingrich	80
Fred Astaire	15	Whoopi Goldberg	82
Lauren Bacall	17	Cary Grant	84
Lucille Ball	20	Katharine Hepburn	87
Mikhail Baryshnikov	22	Bob Hope	89
Leonard Bernstein	24	Edward Hopper	91
Humphrey Bogart	26	Lena Horne	93
Ben Bradlee	28	John Huston	95
David Brinkley	31	Jesse Jackson	97
Tom Brokaw	33	Michael Jackson	100
George Burns	35	Peter Jennings	102
George Bush	38	John Paul II	104
Michael Caine	40	James Earl Jones	107
Jimmy Carter	43	Barbara Jordan	109
Ray Charles	45	Gene Kelly	112
Bill Clinton	47	John F. Kennedy	115
Hillary Rodham Clinton	50	Larry King	117
Sean Connery	53	Martin Luther King, Jr.	119
Marlene Dietrich	56	Spike Lee	122
Bob Dole	58	Maya Lin	124
Clint Eastwood	61	Madonna	126

Nelson Mandela	128	Janet Reno	170
Thurgood Marshall	131	Pat Robertson	173
Grandma Moses	133	Paul Robeson	176
Rupert Murdoch	136	Jackie Robinson	179
Ralph Nader	139	Ginger Rogers	181
Laurence Olivier	141	John Steinbeck	183
Rosa Parks	144	Mother Teresa	186
Luciano Pavarotti	147	Margaret Thatcher	188
I. M. Pei	149	Spencer Tracy	190
Ross Perot	151	Harry Truman	192
Pablo Picasso	153	Lech Walesa	195
Colin Powell	155	Barbara Walters	197
Elvis Presley	158	Oprah Winfrey	200
Leontyne Price	160	Malcolm X	202
Yitzhak Rabin	163	Boris Yeltsin	204
Dan Rather	166		
Ronald Reagan	168	*Index*	207

INTRODUCTION

A mixed bag, did you say? Yes, indeed—Lauren Bacall and Mikhail Baryshnikov, Marlene Dietrich and Bob Dole, Madonna and Grandma Moses, Lech Walesa and Barbara Walters. But then people generally are a mixed bag, and so are people with notable careers. Those treated in the following pages of course constitute only a sampling.

Not all people with notable careers have "pivotal points" in those careers. Luciano Pavarotti clearly had one in his, Placido Domingo evidently didn't. Most do, however. Indeed, each of us in our career, notable or not, may well have experienced some such turning point.

Or be hoping for one.

MUHAMMAD ALI

The months of May and June 1967 were not the happiest in the life of Muhammad Ali, recently the 25-year-old heavyweight boxing champion of the world. Recently, because he was now the ex-champion, having been deprived of his title by the chauvinistic World Boxing Commission in April after his refusal to be inducted for military service. ("I ain't got no quarrel with those Viet Cong, anyway," he had explained, eloquently adding, "They never called me nigger." In addition, he did have a quarrel with a Selective Service System that favored the privileged, such as educated whites, as against the underprivileged, such as undereducated blacks. In any case, the bottom line was that, like others of his generation, he refused to be forced into the indiscriminate killing of people who had done him no discernible harm.)

It was for such insolence that he had been imperiously declared ex-champion. (Boxing commissions, wrote Howard Cosell, "are nothing but a bunch of politically appointed hacks.") In May he was indicted, photographed, fingerprinted, and released on bail of $5,000 with the admonition not to leave the country. In June he was convicted by an all-white jury, after 20 minutes of soul-searching deliberation, and sentenced by an equally conscientious judge to the maximum five years' imprisonment and a fine of $10,000. (The judge would later confess that he was favorably impressed by the way the defendant had behaved in court, saying "yes, sir" and "no, sir" in a colorfully deferential manner.) To add injury to insult he also ordered confiscation of Ali's passport lest he accept offers from abroad. The prisoner was then reluctantly released, pending an appeal.

After a few months of puzzled unemployment—despite his unwillingness to injure others with whom he had no quarrel, prizefighting was all he knew—he discovered that his tireless tongue could be as talented as his fist and even reasonably lucrative. On a lecture tour of colleges, according to the practiced orator Julian Bond, he was "fantastic." By being "just himself," with his self-centered volubility he would have his mostly white audiences "in the

3

palm of his hand," generally including those who disagreed with his readily available opinions on any topic presented to him. Because of his membership in the close-to-the-vest Nation of Islam, his lectures were monitored regularly by government agents.

In December 1968, in Florida's celebrated Dade County, he was given a taste of what the future might have in store for him when he was arrested for driving without a valid license and sentenced to ten days in jail. Jail, he discovered, "is a bad place," and his confinement there "was terrible." It was enough to give him some pause, yet only some, and briefly. "A man's got to be real serious about what he believes to say he'll do that for five years. But I was ready if I had to go."

The Fifth Circuit Court of Appeals had already affirmed his conviction, and in April 1969 he was discreetly suspended from the Nation of Islam. His income from lecturing wasn't enough to pay the lawyers continuing his appeal. In some desperation, with the help of friends he made a couple of pugilistic documentary films and even did the title role in an ill-starred Broadway musical, *Buck White*. Still intent on returning to boxing, he ignored advice to the contrary. To some friends, despite his quips and shrugs and general cheerfulness, he seemed a pathetically quixotic dreamer. "Tell Muhammad to get out of boxing," Rocky Marciano begged his young wife Belinda. "Get him out of boxing and forget the whole thing."

Not a chance, she replied. As it turned out, her husband didn't have that much longer to hold on. In June 1970 the U.S. Supreme Court reversed his conviction, and in the fall a lower Federal court denounced the revocation of his boxing license as "arbitrary and unreasonable." Back in business, he was to find that, as the fight manager Jim Jacobs put it, "In some ways the exile from boxing was the best thing that could have happened to Ali. In terms of his skills, it was a tragedy, but in terms of his earning power, it was a plus." His new reputation as a gritty underdog enormously enhanced his reputation and the attendance at his fights, especially among blacks. It helped his opponents, too, including his first one, Jerry Quarry, who despite his defeat earned a purse of $300,000. Ali's purses soon would rise to seven figures.

He would have to wait through three years and sixteen fights, but after the seventeenth in October 1974, with the defeat of George Foreman, he would once again be the heavyweight champion of the world.

Or, to use his demure description, "The Greatest."

WOODY ALLEN

In the fall of 1960 Woody Allen at 24 was painfully contemplating a career change. His current career was that of comedy writer for such television shows as Sid Caesar's and Garry Moore's. By and large it gave him a lot of satisfaction, even pleasure, as well as an outrageously gratifying income about 40 times that of the average wage earner. Occasionally, especially after reverently watching Bob Hope or Mort Sahl, he had hankered wistfully for a career as a performer but had quickly dismissed the idea as not only improvident but terrifying.

Earlier in the year a friend had persuaded him to seek a new agent and had recommended the partnership of Jack Rollins and Charles Joffe. At the meeting that ensued, he asked with his customary diffidence if he could do some comedy writing for their clients Nichols and May but was summarily told that the team wrote their own material. Well then, he asked, could he read one of his sketches aloud? They agreed, he began his reading, lost his shyness, and utterly captivated them. This fellow can *deliver* this material, they both thought—he should be a performer.

To their suggestion to this effect he responded with an unqualified *no*. He wanted them to represent him as a writer. But we represent performers, they protested, not writers. We haven't had the necessary experience—we really don't know *how*. Yet his pleas, and talent, were irresistible, and they agreed to give it a try over the next few months.

They were too modest. During those months they managed to get him quite a few lucrative writing assignments. Yet the more he read for them, the more solidly convinced they became that here was that rarity, a talent who could write, perform and, probably, direct. It was their turn now to enter pleas, that he give some thought to becoming a performer. And it was his turn to agree, reluctantly, to give it a try.

After he had written an act, in October 1960 Rollins got him a Sunday night audition at The Blue Angel, a minuscule, crowded, smoky show-biz mecca in Manhattan. Following an act by Shelley Berman, who gave him a warm introduction, he conquered his stage terror and launched into his act. He fully kept Berman's promise that he'd be funny. Indeed, although the terror ceased when he started talking, the audience began laughing immediately and kept on laughing so hard and often that he grew nervous and almost withdrawn before he finished. He was nonetheless an instant success. Offers began coming in.

Rollins advised rejecting them, every one. Allen wasn't ready, he needed experience, seasoning in the small comedy club environment in which audiences were less formidable and even appreciative. For instance, there was that club in Greenwich Village, The Upstairs at the Duplex, which could pack in about 50 people but where the usual weeknight audience consisted of only eight or ten. Maybe audiences that small would prove less frightening.

They didn't, at least at first. Most of the time he had to be shoved forcibly onto the little stage before going into his act. And it indeed turned out that he needed seasoning. Rather than use a prop like Berman's stool, he simply stood in front of the audience, looking stiff and uncomfortable. Sometimes, particularly when the audience failed to react properly (his humor at times could be very special), the nervousness that had evaporated at the start reasserted itself. It also began to show itself in various ways—fevered scratching, hands over face, entanglements with the microphone cord, awkward delivery of lines.

So there were times when he badly needed reassurance from Rollins and Joffe, and their advice. With that advice he began to recognize that his attitude toward performing was that it was simply an exhibition of his writing skills, to be gotten over with as quickly as possible, rather than an extended effort to relate to the audience, indeed to like them. ("There was no reason the audience wouldn't like me—they had paid to see me.") He learned to "luxuriate in the performance and want to stay on longer." Not that the learning was easy—his post-performance repair sessions with his ever solicitous agents often lasted until three in the morning, when exhaustion took over.

They became less and less exhausting, and less and less necessary, as the weeks of performing drifted into months and into years and as audience rapport slipped at times into downright affection. And then one night in 1964 the audience during his performance at The Blue Angel included a highly risible Shirley McLaine, who was there with a movie producer, Charles K. Feldman. Amid the laughter Feldman detected an opportunity to solve a problem. He needed a comedy writer to spruce up a movie to be eventually entitled *What's New, Pussycat?* He offered Allen $60,000 and a role in the film. The performer accepted, and the movie, in which he took no great pride artistically, made untold heaps of money.

Well, so far, so good. One is reminded of the title of his 1971 movie, *Take the Money and Run.*

MAYA ANGELOU

In 1935 the seven-year-old Marguerite Annie Johnson was living in St. Louis with her divorced mother, a live-in male companion, and her year-older brother Bailey—who somewhat possessively called her Maya." The two children had been shunted earlier from St. Louis, where they were born, to California for three years, then (after the divorce) to their Grandmother Henderson's home in the minuscule burg of Stamp, Arkansas, and now back to Mother & Co. in St. Louis. Their resultant feelings of insecurity, aggravated by their three years of living in the literally dread-full and hate-full atmosphere of Southern segregation, evidently brought on a severe though temporary case of stuttering for Bailey and frequent, terrifying nightmares for her. To calm her, her mother took to letting her sleep with her and her bedfellow, evidently unaware that this might lead to a much worse nightmare.

It did. On occasion her mother would get up early, leaving daughter and bedfellow in intimate togetherness. This led one morning to whispered coaxing, titillating touching, furtive fondling, his sexual gratification, and then a period of tender embrace that the little girl, who had experienced so little tenderness, found very gratifying. In the weeks after the incident he neglected her, except to warn her that he'd kill Bailey if she ever told "anybody what we did." After a while they did it again, and she almost welcomed it in her loneliness. During the next long period of neglect she assuaged that loneliness with books obtained from the local library with her first library card.

That period of neglect ended when he reentered her life, this time to rape her. She told Bailey, who told their grandmother, who told the police, and the fellow was arrested. His trial, however, was a painful trial for her. Fearful that she'd be accused of enticing him if she admitted to their early encounters, she lied, testifying that the rape was their first occasion of intimacy. Although convicted and given a year's sentence, he contrived to be released within hours, yet only to be "stomped to death" that evening. The stompers were never found, but she did have some very vindictive uncles.

7

The man's death was a paralyzing shock for her, since she was convinced that her testimony had been the principal cause. Thus convinced, she determined literally to keep her mouth shut, and that's essentially what she did for the next five years, burying herself in her beloved books. Her mother interpreted this as sullen, obstreperous behavior, and soon the two children once again found themselves entrained, this time on their way back to their grandmother.

In Stamps the people, the black people, quietly habituated to racist misery and rural boredom, welcomed the children as big-city celebrities. Familiarity with misery helped them to understand what the little girl had been through and why she remained mute, and to accept her odd behavior. Even her teachers were understanding, especially since she and Bailey were conscientious students far ahead of their age groups academically.

And then into her state of withdrawal came Bertha Flowers, the little town's black aristocrat, elegantly affluent, gloriously educated, graciously dignified, and empathetically perceptive. During a visit one day to the grandmother's general store to buy some groceries, she asked if Marguerite could accompany her home because "I've been meaning to talk to her." Quickly changing into clothes more fitting for such company, the little girl followed shyly and respectfully several paces behind the great lady until gently urged to walk side by side.

In the elegant parlor, fortified with cookies and iced lemonade, she was given a friendly lecture on the embarrassment she had shown over her grandmother's lack of education and sophistication, and on the intelligence and sterling character often displayed by the untutored. And then she was treated to a reading from Dickens' *A Tale of Two Cities*, as well as a gift of some books to carry home with her (and a bag of cookies for Bailey). Thus began a series of literary lessons, starting off with a poem for her to recite, gently forcing her to break her silence. Not only was her love of reading reinforced, but the fond solicitude shown her made her feel special. "I was liked," she wrote later, and "respected not as Mrs. Henderson's granddaughter or Bailey's sister but just for being Marguerite Johnson."

This new self-confidence fortified her against the slings and arrows of outrageous Southern racism until her grandmother extricated her from that infernal land by sending her back to her mother, now in San Francisco. There, in 1943, the racism was mild enough to be overcome by persistence—and by lying about her age of 15, since her six-foot height now made her look adult. With the help also of the war shortage of young males, she became the city's first black and first female streetcar conductor.

This gave her some financial independence and an opportunity to take advantage, in the evenings, of a scholarship in drama and dance at the California Labor School. (This later kept her from enlisting in the U.S. Army after the School was listed as "subversive" by congressional ferrets.)

Through the next quarter-century she lived restlessly, had sex, a baby, and a series of jobs as waitress, cook, madam (briefly), restaurant manager, chauffeur, clerk, and singer and dancer (the last as Maya Angelou, after a marriage gave her the name of Angelos), as well as some lovers and a drug habit. In the 1950s she toured the world with the chorus of *Porgy and Bess*. In the 1960s, after a few years in Africa with a new husband, she returned to L.A., appeared in Anouilh's *Medea*, wrote a play for local production, and created a long series of programs on African culture for national public television.

The influence of Bertha Flowers on Marguerite Johnson was finally beginning to manifest itself in the career of Maya Angelou. It really took hold after Angelou, urged on by James Baldwin and Jules Feiffer, wrote her first autobiographical book, *I Know Why the Caged Bird Sings*, published in 1970. The enthusiasm of its critical reception inspired her to write five more such life-story books and six volumes of poetry, firmly establishing her literary credentials and leading to the request from her fellow Arkansan, Bill Clinton, for her reading, at his inauguration as President, of a poem she had written for the occasion.

With Bertha Flowers doubtless beaming down upon her from above.

YASIR ARAFAT

"There can be no compromise or mediation," declared a defiant Yasir Arafat, the 42-year-old leader of the Palestine Liberation Organization in 1970. "Peace for us means Israel's destruction and nothing else." A couple of years later, for instance, the 1972 Olympic Games in Munich were grimly interrupted by the symbolic murder of 11 Israeli athletes. Sixteen years later, in the spring of 1988, after Israel had invaded Lebanon and ousted Arafat and the PLO headquarters from that shattered country, scattering his 15,000 soldiers among eight Arab nations on two continents, Israel's feisty Prime Minister Yitzhak Shamir defiantly declared that the relationship remained unchanged: "For us Arafat is like Hitler. He wants to see every one of us dead." Yet only about six months later, in November 1988, Arafat announced that the PLO had forsaken terrorist tactics and now recognized Israel's right to exist.

This wasn't a sudden change. As early as the fall of 1974 he had ended a celebrated speech to the assembled delegates of the United Nations in New York with tentatively softer words wrapped in a challenge: "I have come bearing an olive branch and a freedom fighter's gun. Do not let the olive branch fall from my hand." In response the delegates voted UN observer status for the PLO and formally recognized the right of the Palestinians to self-determination.

This didn't do all that much for them. During the civil war in Lebanon elements of the PLO made life in northern Israel as hellish as possible with raids from southern Lebanon, rendering Arafat's olive-branch approach irrelevant. As a result of this harassment, aggravated by the wounding of the Israeli ambassador in London, Israeli armed forces invaded Lebanon in June 1982 and, among other things, dispersed the PLO.

Arafat and his principal associates became fugitives, repulsed not only by Israel but by the militant Arab states as well, and indeed even assiduously hunted by Israeli security agents and by Palestinian terrorists, forcing them to keep ever on the move, furtively and unpredictably. Among Arab militants he was despised for his talk of an olive branch. Desperate to find a location for his PLO headquarters, he was forced to go as far west as Tunis, capital of a Tunisia willing but by no means eager to receive him. Shortly thereafter he further enraged Arab radicals by meeting with one of their favorite targets, King Hussein of Jordan, in an effort to coordinate a joint Jordanian–PLO administration in Palestine. In April 1983 the PLO executive committee summarily rejected his effort, and shortly thereafter the Jordanian representative in the negotiations was assassinated. Hussein ended the talks, leaving the Palestinians to their own devices.

After the bitter dissatisfaction with his soft approach split the PLO into rival factions, he found himself at the head of a minority besieged by radicals egged on by Assad of Syria. During a meeting in 1984 of the Palestine National Council, he responded to strident criticism by suddenly resigning as chairman, gambling that the Council wouldn't find anyone with enough support to replace him. He was right. Not only did the Council reelect him chairman, but it also voted surprising approval of his negotiations with King Hussein. The revived negotiations, however, failing to solve the insoluble, ended in 1986 when Hussein once again opted out.

As grisly PLO–Israeli warfare continued, he became ever more "softly" realistic. To a reporter interviewing him in 1987 he conceded that there were only two options open, either "to continue in this very tough military confrontation" or "to find a solution through the UN." But in December of that year, rebellion against Israeli rule in Palestine took on a new form in local, stone-throwing attacks. The tough Israeli general Yitzhak Rabin, able to contain this persistent uprising (the "Intifada") but not to suppress it entirely, concluded that "you can't rule by force over one and a half million Palestinians." An effort to do so would mean endless warfare.

This general idea was gaining ground. In the fall of 1988 King Hussein announced the end of his claim to the West Bank as part of Jordan, and the PLO formally accepted Arafat's insistence on the acknowledgment of Israel's right to exist and the renunciation of terrorism. Yet, although the idea was gaining ground, it was by no means a universal commitment. The truce that followed was an uneasy one indeed, marred by sporadic violence and mutual suspicion. Even after the intransigent Shamir was replaced as Prime Minister by the less rigid Rabin in a mid–1992 election and peace feelers looked ever more genuine (despite Arafat's ruinous support of Iraq's Saddam Hussein), fundamentalists on both sides continued the homicidal battling.

Nevertheless, Arafat had in Rabin someone he could talk to, at least through intermediaries, someone who would listen and respond. From secret negotiations by their representatives in Oslo there arose the possibility of some sort of peace agreement—such as the draft agreement signed in Washington in September 1993 establishing progressive degrees of self-rule in Gaza and in expanding areas of the West Bank. For all its precariousness, this limited peace at least contrasted well with what had gone before. "Things will work out," explained Arafat, "if not this time, then next time. There is no alternative. Wars are an impossibility for everybody."

LOUIS ARMSTRONG

One day in January the 12-year-old Louis Armstrong was a very sad and rueful boy indeed, miserably spending his first day in a New Orleans reformatory, wondering if he'd ever see his mother and little sister again.

Until New Year's Eve things seemed to be going along pretty well. True, the three of them lived rather huddled in a tiny flat. True, his father had long ago taken off for a life less burdened with responsibility. But lately he had teamed up with three buddies to sing for their suppers, and their families' as well. The four mellifluous voices could be heard on street corners, outside bars, near hotel entrances, wherever coins could be expected from passersby and where police patrols were infrequent and reasonably casual.

The boys' incomes consisted only of pennies, nickels, dimes and occasionally quarters, but these coins were a welcome supplement to their families' meager resources when even a mere penny was more than superfluous change. One part of their habitual route that gave him enormous pleasure was near a saloon featuring a jazz band. On, how he loved that jazz! And oh, how he loved listening to the cornet player, the celebrated King Oliver. Somehow he felt that he could play the cornet too, if only he had enough money for one.

New Year's Eve in New Orleans was, among other things, a very noisy affair. He knew his buddies would have a supply of firecrackers, torpedoes, iron pipes (for clanging), and other roof-raisers for giving 1913 a properly uproarious welcome. But he had recently come across something at home that would put them all to shame. He had found an old trunk, and at the bottom he had secretly discovered, under some clothes and wrapped in newspaper, a .38 revolver that must have been his father's. This, he figured, would be a *real* noisemaker.

It was indeed. It satisfactorily overwhelmed the general racket, attracting the rapt attention not only of startled revelers but also of an apprehensive policeman. Although the gun was loaded with blanks, the cop took a very

13

dim view of his merrymaking technique and hauled him off to the nearest house of detention, where he spent a night devoid of merrymaking.

The next morning in juvenile court, despite his mother's pleading, he was dispatched to the Colored Waifs' Home for Boys, where he would have to stay "until those in charge decide you are ready to be released." Here he swiftly learned about rules and regulations and punishment for failure to observe them. He gave up thoughts of escape after being forced, along with his fellow inmates, to watch the severe whipping of a runaway who had been caught and returned.

Since the home included a school, he received some basic training in reading, 'riting and 'rithmetic. Other activities, such as woodworking, failed to interest him, with one outstanding exception. The school had a music section and even a Waifs' Home Band, consisting of a bass drum and about a dozen horns. He yearned to be selected for it. Maybe he'd even be given a chance to play a cornet in the band. But the music teacher, Peter Davis, had no use whatsoever for boys from his section of town, and so his only attention from Davis was punitive. Avoiding the man, he nonetheless managed to listen avidly to most of the band's practicing sessions.

He had plenty of other things to do—serving food, doing dishes, scrubbing floors, laundering clothes. Yet he also did some entertaining. After singing lessons conducted for the boys by a lady volunteer, he'd do some of his own singing and dancing as an encore. His performances greatly amused his fellow residents, who in honor of his expansive grin began affectionately called him Satchelmouth. He would be Satchmo for the rest of his life.

His performances apparently also caught the eye of music teacher Davis, in addition to his exemplary following of the rules and regulations. One day he felt, hopefully, that Davis was smiling at him. Soon thereafter he was honored with a greeting, "Mornin', Louis." That made his day until the evening, after supper, when Davis approached him without any reassuring smile. The words were reassuring, however, to say the least. Unlike some others from his district, Davis had concluded, he was well behaved. Further, he liked music, obviously liked it a lot—would he like to join the band? The answer of course, with much gulping and heart-throbbing, was *yes!*

After a few weeks of learning to read music and to play a bugle and an alto horn, and then some more weeks playing in the band, he was again approached by an unsmiling Davis, who, remarking that he probably was ready for this now, handed him a cornet.

It was of course this type of horn, and its close relative the trumpet, with which he would earn his reputation not only for technical mastery but also for his imaginative genius. Along with his unique singing voice and style and his unflagging geniality, it would make him an international star. Perhaps the most gratifying result of his fame during his career was that he and his band, when booked to play in a Southern hotel, were no longer refused accommodations.

FRED ASTAIRE

In mid-summer 1933 Fred Astaire at 34 had reason to be anxious about his future, as indeed he was. His talented sister Adele was now Lady Cavendish. Fred and Adele Astaire had been dancing together in musicals on both sides of the Atlantic since 1917. By 1932 they'd been in 10 shows, most of them resounding, lucrative hits, especially the Gershwins' *Lady Be Good* in 1924 and *Funny Face* in 1927. By 1932, however, Adele, thoroughly fed up with the strain of show-biz life, opted for a career less harrowing as the wife of Lord Charles Arthur Cavendish, thereby leaving her brother without a partner for the first time in his career. He was alone yet by no means destitute, nor utterly devastated. Among his consolations were such doodads as his spiffy Park Avenue penthouse, luxurious Rolls-Royce limousine, and a dazzling wardrobe. And his racing forms.

Not among his consolations was the critical response to his dancing without Adele. His first show without her was the Broadway production of *The Gay Divorce*, with music and lyrics by Cole Porter. It was Porter's "After You, Who?" that convinced him to do the show, although it suffered from an asthmatic dog of a script and included another song, "Night and Day," which he was sure he couldn't sing and which no one liked very much anyway. The Boston tryout was a dismal flop not only because of the anemic plot but also because of Adele's absence, although Claire Luce, his partner for the show, was quite a hoofer.

The New York opening, despite some strenuous efforts at overhaul, fared no better, provoking yawns and chit-chat in the audience and smirks from the critics. His singing of "Night and Day" was received with no better than listlessly polite applause. (The song was thereafter transformed into a radio hit by the valiant work of indomitable song pluggers.) As for the critics, one pontificated that "two Astaires are better than one," and another maintained that poor Fred seemed to be looking searchingly into the wings in the hope that Adele "would come out and rescue him."

Porter, Astaire & Co. nevertheless refused to throw in the theatrical towel. After considerable restaging and a *lot* of rewriting, the show began to evoke happier audience reactions and more fragrant critical notices. It was a romantic but unsentimental musical comedy now, with a straightforward love story, bright dialogue and frisky dancing, all promising a good run until at least the end of the season.

Yet he was feeling a westward urge. Sound had come to Hollywood, pretty reliable sound in fact, and performers were dancing, even *tap*-dancing, on the big screen. For someone like him this obviously had its intriguing aspects. How about putting out some feelers? He asked his agent Leland Hayward. And so it was that before long David O. Selznick, RKO's VP-producer, sent a memo to the suits upstairs asking them to look at an audition that he'd filmed with this fellow Astaire. He confessed to some doubts because of the "enormous ears and bad chin line," yet pointed out the "tremendous charm" that shone "through even in this wretched test." The fellow was "a magnificent performer," he added in defense of his rashness, and "unquestionably the outstanding young leader of American musical comedy."

Although the suits' reactions were generally tentative at best—one of them (according to Astaire) responded, "Can't act. Slightly bald. Also dances."—he was signed up for RKO's *Flying Down to Rio*. To his chagrin, as soon as he was free from his stage commitments and was ensconced in Hollywood with his new wife Phyllis, RKO lent him to MGM for a role in *Dancing Lady*. It was only a secondary role—one MGM producer had seen his test and reportedly sniffed that the studio could "get dancers like this for seventy-five bucks a week"—yet it gave him a chance to work with the costar Clark Gable and dance with the costar Joan Crawford. It also showed him that he could perform without the stimulation of an audience, and that doing a dance over and over, plus editing, could bring him close to his ever elusive goal of perfection.

It wasn't until he returned to RKO from *Dancing Lady* that he learned of the turmoil over the casting of *Flying Down to Rio*. At contract signing he had been promised the lead, yet during his MGM hiatus incessant rewriting and recasting had created a different movie. Now it was centered on Dolores Del Rio, with Astaire relegated to the status of half of the dancing team, the other half being Dorothy Jordan. (Indeed, he was given fifth billing, after Jordan.)

Yet the studio did do a couple of things to make up for this shabby treatment, however inadvertently. For one thing, when dance director Dave Gould became preoccupied with the memorable finale of chorus girls on airplane wings, he casually assigned Astaire to his assistant Hermes Pan, a terpsichorean soulmate who helped his fellow dancer enormously in this new and unfamiliar environment. And for another thing, after Dorothy Jordan abruptly quit to get married, the studio replaced her with a lissome lass whom Astaire had worked with briefly and even dated once some three years earlier. Her name was Ginger Rogers.

LAUREN BACALL

In the spring of 1943 Betty Bacall was in Hollywood. Although only 18, she'd had considerable experience in such jobs as garment worker and theater usher, besides a lot of "pounding the pavement" (as she later described it, without relish) in search of work. More recently she'd had a couple of minor roles in forgettable plays in New York, her home town, and for the past several months she'd been busy in the fateful and much more rewarding role of photographer's model.

After her pictures in *Harper's Bazaar* stirred some interest in Hollywood, she received nibbles from Columbia, Howard Hughes, and Howard Hawks. Hawks especially, prodded by his wife who was intrigued by the pictures, was interested enough to ask Charles Feldman, his agent, to make her an offer. All offers were limited, of course, to doing some testing, but she was thrilled at the thought of being even tentatively sought after, as well as nervous over having to make a choice. In a toss-up decision, but certainly a consequential one, she chose Hawks.

On the day after her arrival in Hollywood she and *her* new agent Charles Feldman had lunch with Hawks at the Brown Derby. She was "terrified" (a favorite word, for all her laid-back demeanor on the silver screen) despite the imposing Hawks' gentle but noncommittal friendliness. All he wanted, he assured her, was a simple test. Feldman suggested some cosmetic dental work, but Hawks dismissed the idea rather summarily, perhaps disappointingly (would that come later, only if the test panned out?). After lunch the two men strolled down the street at a leisurely, almost languid pace, lost in animated conversation, while Betty followed meekly, hopefully behind. That evening Feldman called her with the news that Hawks liked her, however inscrutably, and that the test was scheduled for the end of the week.

It was postponed, of course, but the delay afforded her a couple of get-acquainted visits with Hawks during which, besides having lunch, she read for him and he educated her with anecdotes of his directing experiences with

17

actresses. On the day before the test the make-up genius Perc Westmore set about making her over but she summoned up enough gumption to protest to Hawks, and he reined in Westmore with the admonition that he wasn't looking for another Marlene Dietrich—he wanted Betty "exactly as she is." And that, of course, in spite of Westmore's misgivings, wasn't bad at all. Especially after Westmore stubbornly added a few minor touches the next day, before the test.

She was so terrified as she entered the sound stage that the sight of a girl being tested for the lighting made her afraid that she had already been replaced. (The rumor was that in Hollywood only one girl was tested out of 10,000 who wanted to be tested.) The test was indeed simple, and successful enough to bring her a standard contract (seven years, $100 a week to start, $1,250 at the end, when $10,000 a year was a respectable business salary).

What ensued wasn't a movie role but rather was several months of impatient waiting, eased considerably by her mother's arrival from the East to live with her (protectively—she turned 18 just that summer). Although both Feldman often and Hawks occasionally kept in touch, she couldn't help wondering if Hawks really had anything in mind for her. How long was she going to be kept on hold? Would she ever stand in front of a camera again—even though, at his instance, she had changed her first name to Lauren?

At one point he did talk to her vaguely about her doing a film with Cary Grant or Humphrey Bogart. Her reaction to the Grant idea was "Terrific!" but as for Humphrey Bogart: "Yucch!" About a year earlier she and her aunt Rosalie had seen the movie *Casablanca*, and Rosalie had been "mad about" the sexy Bogart. Betty, although she'd enjoyed his performance and appreciated him as an actor, wasn't very impressed with him as a man. She rather favored the Leslie Howard type. From his roles, Bogart seemed an illiterate mug.

Toward the end of 1943 Hawks doubtless had something specific for her in mind, for he began having her take singing lessons along with her other training. He was fond of Ernest Hemingway's *To Have and Have Not* and considered it—or a version of it, à la *Casablanca*—eminently filmable. William Faulkner was in Hollywood and available to help with the script, and as music man Hawks had his eye on Hoagy Carmichael. Now if he could just get Betty—no, Lauren—to lower her voice, the change would help her singing as well as her speaking.

Shortly after Christmas he finally gave her the news. He felt sure she'd fit the part and wanted to test her for it. She was disheartened on learning that Bogart would be her leading man, but for such a juicy part she could certainly live with *that*. The scene Hawks chose for the test turned out to be the now celebrated whistle scene ("You just put your lips together, and blow."), a remarkable and rather trying scene for a young actress who knew not man. Since Bogart was on a USO tour of North Africa, she would make the test with a young actor named John Ridgely, a selection that rendered the prospect less nerve-racking.

A week or so later she was called in to view the screening of the test. She watched it with growing horror, but it wasn't her low opinion of it that counted. Hawks like it, Feldman liked it, and, most important, Jack Warner had seen it and liked it. Further, Bogart had generously agreed to appear with someone so unknown—unknown to him, to the profession, and to the public, and indeed of unknown quality.

Production was scheduled to start in February 1944, after Bogart's return. Soon after his return she met him coming out of Hawks' office just as she was about to enter. "I just saw your test," he said with a friendly smile. "We'll have a lot of fun together."

That they surely did, for the next 13 years.

LUCILLE BALL

In late 1949 Lucille Ball at 38 was frustrated because in none of her work—movies, radio, television—was she ever given a satisfactory chance to display her talent for comedy. Oh, there were those two films she did with Bob Hope, but it wasn't *her* comic talent that was really on display. Nor could she see any doors opening on a brighter future.

But then the CBS management suggested that she might be interested in doing a television version of her recent radio show, *My Favorite Husband.* Yes, indeed she was interested, especially if Desi Arnaz could play the part of her husband. Nonsense, the network moguls responded—who could believe that a woman so all–American could be married to a Cuban conga-drum "Babalu" band leader? Preposterous! Her answer was obvious: they had been married for the past ten years! And, she hoped, working together would help to keep them married.

After talking over the CBS reaction, the odd couple came up with an idea for testing it. They'd go on tour together during the summer as a married couple and test audience reaction to their togetherness. He handled the financing, setting up Desilu Productions, organizing a cast of supporting players, scheduling the tour. He set up a sketch for her that had her wearing baggy pants, applauding like a seal, and struggling with an obstreperous cello that seemed more like a bottomless portmanteau. She was in her element. So was he. Besides his Cuban crooning and exercising his considerable financial acumen, he joined her in comedy sketches, to her great delight.

And to their audiences'. After they opened in Chicago in June 1950, *Variety* welcomed their routine as "top fare for vaude houses and niteries." Their investment of time and money (it cost them about $20,000) had been more than worth making. Despite the tour's success, it was interrupted in late June by the discovery that she was pregnant. Although the pregnancy thereafter assumed first priority, it was not to end happily. Late in July, during a party at the Desilu ranch, she was seized with severe pain and rushed to a

20

hospital. (The wild ambulance ride included a comic yet potentially tragic scene when the intern fell through the unaccountably open back door and Desi desperately held on to his feet until they arrived.)

Their grief over the miscarriage could be somewhat assuaged by absorption in their plans for their hoped-for TV series, and that's the route they chose. Their initial idea of playing themselves was shelved in favor of fiction, keeping his band-leader image as background and presenting her as the little woman at home trying to cope with uncooperative household items and seeking to introduce variety into her life with schemes just short of dementia. Her love for her husband would keep her amenable to his insistence on having only one professional performer in the family. When the pilot episode, for instance, called on her character to fill in for an absent clown, she relished doing the act but rejected a show-biz offer to keep her husband happy.

When CBS distributed a kinescope of that pilot episode to judiciously selected ad agencies on Madison Avenue, their first response was judiciously negative. Indeed, there was a good deal of nose-wrinkling even in the hallowed halls of CBS management, as in the case of the programming nabob who disdained it as "the worst thing I've ever seen" and as utterly unmarketable. Even after the series was sold to Philip Morris, the odd couple were deluged with similarly expert opinion. Philip Morris insisted that their plan for a biweekly series was unacceptable, that it had to be weekly. This meant that he would have to give up touring with his band and she would have to give up movie work, but they decided to "gamble everything" on the series. That was when they were flooded on all sides with "you're crazy" admonitions.

Other snags kept cropping up. Philip Morris, for instance, insisted on their doing the show live on the East Coast for the benefit of its teeming potential audience, and then distributing it by kinescope to the scattered viewers in the hinterland. The odd couple refused to leave their cherished California. The confrontation ended in a compromise based on the superiority of film over kinescope: the shows would be filmed in Los Angeles and the films sent East. This doubled the cost of production, however, and neither Philip Morris nor CBS was willing to cough up the additional money. The rapidly growing Desilu Productions nonetheless found enough coughers to get started—and in the process kept control of the films just in case they might be of some use later.

Meanwhile she was joyfully producing a daughter; Lucie was born in mid–July 1951. Four months later the long-awaited series went on the air, complete with Vivian Vance and William Frawley to provide a touch of reality. A month later it would be in the Top Ten and then would go on for 180 episodes, as well as reruns and spinoffs, apparently for all eternity. *I Love Lucy* is still a regular entry in *TV Guide*.

MIKHAIL BARYSHNIKOV

In 1960, when he gave up soccer for the ballet, Mikhail Baryshnikov at twelve was already a bit long in the tooth to be launched into professional dancing. (The conventional age was nine, sometimes ten.) Nevertheless he took to it like a gazelle to leaping. Within a couple of years after his admission to a Riga school of dance he was promoted to an advanced class in which the students were more nearly his contemporaries. One of these, the now celebrated Alexander Godunov, marveled at this "wonderboy whose phenomenal physical equipment [was] combined with extreme zest and conscientiousness."

In 1964 the wonderboy switched teachers, moving to Leningrad to study under the master Alexander Puskin, who among many other things helped him to perfect his stratospheric jump. Three years later he made his debut with the Kirov ballet company. There the pooh-bahs observed his work with some misgivings, since it was puzzling: conventional, yet unconventionally energetic and precise. In this debut performance he danced the peasant pas de deux with an aplomb that apparently was considered a kind of effrontery. Efforts to keep a good man down gradually proved ineffective, and in 1967 he was given the juicy role of Mercutio in Igor Tchernichov's *Romeo and Juliet*. His performance so brilliantly and spectacularly expressed that character's flamboyance as to leave the audience stunned. The ballet was canceled after its premier performance, however, as erotically offensive to Kremlin Puritans, those arbiters of Soviet morality.

Over the next two years he began being assigned to leading roles and even having ballets created particularly for him to perform. One of these, Leonid Takobson's *Vestris*, was designed for an international ballet competition to be held in Moscow in 1969. Baryshnikov danced his heart out so splendidly and dramatically that one of the judges gave him thirteen points out of a possible twelve. His performance earned him a gold medal. (He was seen in *Vestris* on American television seven years later, in October 1976, during a program entitled *Baryshnikov at Wolf Trap*.) Later that year he also received the Nijinsky award. Toward the end of 1973, indeed, he would be given the title of Honored Artist of the Republic.

In the meantime, however, he was becoming increasingly distressed by the Kirov's gradual yet painfully detectable deterioration in quality, a distress aggravated by his melancholy over the death in 1970 of his "artistic father" Alexander Pushkin. Nor was he encouraged by the persistent oversight of KGBunglers and the gimlet-eyed dimwittery of Kremlin critics. He could not have been unaware that his colleague, the celebrated Natalia Makarova, had fled that oppressiveness in 1970 and sought asylum in the West. But he was also acutely aware that his KGB overseers were not about to let him perform outside the Soviet Union.

He was wrong. His KGB overseers can't have known of his tentative question, in the spring of 1974, to his friend Gennady Smakov—"Do you think that if I worked in, say, New York, I'd be successful?"—or they never would have relaxed enough to allow him in June to join a ballet troupe going to Canada under the wary supervision of Party factotums. Because he had been so restricted, rumors of his impending departure created quite a stir among balletomanes in Leningrad and Moscow.

His arrival in the West created a similar stir among Canadian devotees. Would he stay or would he return? He didn't know himself. In the USSR, after all, he was a star with a comfortable living and with good friends and fellow performers, people with whom he shared a love of country as well as a love of dancing.

Yet he had friends on this side of the Atlantic too, and some of them in Toronto had made arrangements to accommodate him should he choose to stay. By matinee time on June 29 they were ready if he was. He was, or at least would be after that evening's performance of the *Don Quixote* pas de deux. He would meet them, he promised nervously, at a restaurant from which they could then eagerly transport him to safety.

The time for his arrival at the nearby restaurant came and went while his friends waited apprehensively. A defective curtain mechanism at the theater had caused a delay. After the performance his overseers had insisted on his attending a theater party, but he eluded them by rushing out of the front exit and losing himself in a crowd of fans. Trouble was, the crowd followed him when he headed for the restaurant and he could get there only by outrunning them. Although he did outrun them, fortunately he was met in the street by a worried friend who bundled him into a taxi and raced to an out-of-the-way apartment where he'd be safe. After his other worried friends arrived there from the restaurant, they had their own theater party.

And he managed to get a call through to London, to his good friend Natalia Makarova, who assured him of a warm welcome at New York's American Ballet Theater, where they could dance together.

And did they ever!

LEONARD BERNSTEIN

In November 1943 Leonard Bernstein at 25 had only just emerged from a period of depression, or at least of discouragement severe enough for regular visits to an analyst. Because of an asthmatic condition he had been rejected for military service, and the rejection had aggravated his depression. He had come to New York about a year earlier seeking employment, but, despite his obvious gifts, had found nothing better than tedious and ill-paid work copying scores for a music publishing house. Artur Rodzinski, recently appointed music director of the New York Philharmonic Orchestra, had heard of his predicament and reportedly "felt bad that so gifted a young man should be earning his living copying manuscripts."

And so in August Rodzinski, after agonizing over his list of candidates for the position of his assistant musical director, resorted (he said) to divine inspiration for the selection of the so gifted young man—who thereafter, among other things, would have to be prepared to fill in for a sick boss on the podium or for any guest conductor who failed to appear. Although this was a rather daunting prospect, it didn't seriously concern the young man, since Rodzinski gave every indication of being in splendid health, and guest conductors were reassuringly well known for reliability. He was so happy about his appointment and so sure of his ability to handle the job that he sent a pertinent newspaper clipping and an accompanying photo to a woman friend with a marginal note reading, "Here we go! Love, Lenny."

What he didn't know was that, at least in the memory of any of the Philharmonic players, no assistant conductor had ever had to fill in. The list of assistants was thus one of bitterly frustrated people, musically all dressed up with no place to go. But what he also didn't know was that this wouldn't be his fate. Quite the contrary.

The orchestra was scheduled for a matinee performance, to be broadcast on CBS radio, on a Sunday in November when Rodzinski was vacationing at his farm, contentedly too far away to get to New York through the deposit of snow from an early winter storm. Bernstein had been carrying on, musically and otherwise, at a Saturday all-night party, and had just gotten into bed at dawn that Sunday when he was abruptly startled awake by a deafening phone bell and informed that he would "have to conduct at three this afternoon." Bruno Walter, the guest conductor, had come down with the flu and was "all wrapped up in blankets at the hotel." He would, however, "be happy to go over the score with you for an hour or so."

Bernstein was awake now, fully enough to get dressed and take advantage of that hour or so with Walter. Not that he got much out of it, what with his hangover and gnawing apprehension—all that earlier self-confidence had dissolved into sheer terror. When he stopped at a drugstore after the Walter visit the pharmacist, alarmed at how he looked, gave him a barbiturate to calm his nerves and an amphetamine to see him through his pending ordeal. (He never did take them.) He did have the presence of mind to call his visiting family and suggest that they postpone their planned departure until tomorrow if they'd like to see him that afternoon conducting the New York Philharmonic Orchestra, for better or worse. He'd leave the tickets at the box office. They eagerly agreed.

As he stood in the wings "all atremble" (his words), he was afforded an opportunity to hear how well known he was when the associate manager announced from the stage that Bruno Walter was ill and would be replaced by the assistant conductor, and the announcement was greeted with widespread groans. Thus fortified, he strode onto the stage, mounted the podium and assumed the position only to recall that the first selection, the overture from Schuman's *Manfred*, is formidably tricky at the start, on the first beat, beginning on a syncopation in the middle of the bar, "and if they misunderstand, then the whole thing is over." He gave the beat, and "they came in like angels." He never could recall the rest of the performance. But he does remember receiving a wire from his friend and mentor Serge Koussevitzky during the intermission, "Listening now. Wonderful." And a like one from Rodzinski. And treasured praise from his heretofore skeptical father.

One of the violinists later recalled that the orchestra members, who had rehearsed the program with Walter, had expected to do the leading, a la Walter, rather than be conducted by this young whippersnapper, yet their performance under the whippersnapper's baton "had nothing to do with Bruno Walter." At the end the stunned players "stood up and cheered." And so did the audience. Indeed, there was stamping and cheering, with call after call for him to return to the stage and acknowledge the adulation.

The Philharmonic management formally announced that he would be seen on the podium very often in the future, by anticipated popular demand. The media had a field day polishing his image. He had a reputation now, and there would be no more groans.

HUMPHREY BOGART

In the latter part of 1934 Humphrey Bogart was already 35 and seemed to be getting nowhere. His father's recent death had left him depressed as well as burdened by a debt inherited from his father, who as a doctor had been more interested in healing than in fee collection. A friend later described the son as "desperate" and as feeling that "his acting career was finished, although he kept beating on producers' doors with all the other out-of-work actors."

He couldn't see Leslie Howard coming up over his horizon. Nor did he realize that his selection for the role of a villain in a play called *Invitation to a Murder* was more than a lucky break—it was *the* lucky break. Shortly before the final curtain had rung down on *Invitation*, he heard that someone would be needed to play a somewhat similar part in a forthcoming Broadway production of Robert Sherwood's *The Petrified Forest*. It promised to be a juicily similar part indeed, modeled more or less on John Dillinger, the notorious criminal of the early 1930s labeled by the FBI as "Public Enemy Number One." He asked to read for this now famous part of Duke Mantee, and did so with nervous anticipation. Although Sherwood wanted him for another role (Boze Hertzlinger, the football player!), the star, Leslie Howard, sitting in the orchestra and hearing the weary menace in Bogart's voice coming from the stage during the audition, called out eagerly, "That's the man!" This was just the actor they needed for the part, he insisted, and promised to help him get it just right.

That he did. Bogart let his beard grow to give him the appropriately unshaven look, lowered his voice to give it a rather menacing rasp, and with Howard's help managed to suggest seething emotion under a mask of hard impenetrability. Even his irrepressible lisp seemed to fit the character. (During World War I he had been guarding a prisoner, a fellow sailor, who unceremoniously smashed him in the face with his manacled hands and ran off. Although Bogart managed to drop him with his .45, wounding him, the

26

manacles had nearly torn off his upper lip, which was sewn together well enough to be passable, cosmetically and phonetically—and, of course, histrionically.)

The play opened and ran for a couple of weeks in Boston for remedial touch-ups and then opened in New York. Although Howard got the rave reviews, Bogart received some flattering notices, quite enough to justify Howard's confidence in him. Even Alexander Woollcott, who a few years earlier had described his portrayals of "Tennis, anyone?" characters as "what might mercifully be described as inadequate," completely reversed himself on the subject of Duke Mantee. Indeed, Bogart's three-day growth of beard became a conversation piece among theatromaniacs, with some ticket-buyers asking for seats close enough to see it clearly.

And then there was all that highly palatable money. He made enough of it to clear up all his father's debts as well as his own, with enough left over to keep him alive *and* enable him to turn down parts he didn't want—his F.Y. money, he called it.

In 1936 he heard that Warner Brothers had signed up Howard for a movie version of the play. Remembering that Howard, known to be a man of his word, had promised him the role of Duke Mantee in any movie version, he took off for Hollywood (with his second wife, Mary Philips) in eager anticipation. Warner Brothers, however, didn't share his anticipation, which turned into severe disenchantment when he was told that they wanted Edward G. Robinson for the role. Robinson declined it—eager anticipation again. But the Warners kept on casting about without casting, auditioning other actors for the part—and Howard was vacationing in Scotland.

Counting on Howard's reputation, he cabled Scotland. Immediately a cable arrived from Scotland at Warner Brothers demanding that, if they wanted Howard, they'd have to take Bogart as well. Years later Bogart would name his daughter Leslie.

Hollywood wasn't a new experience for him. Between 1930 and 1934 he'd appeared in 11 movies, more or less unnoticeably, until he returned in discouragement to the stage as a possible alternative to, say, hotel clerking. Although he now had a 40-week contract at $400 a week in mid–Depression dollars, he and his wife avoided the expense of ostentatious living, opting for a bungalow at the Garden of Allah, a modest conglomeration of such bungalows which nonetheless provided a swimming pool, and importantly, a 24-hour bar service. He rented, assuming that his employment in Tinseltown was a very temporary thing.

It wasn't, of course. Although he had to spend several years typecast as Mantee-style heavies, he had many a notable film in his future, starting in the early 1940s with *The Maltese Falcon* and *Casablanca*. Also, there was another person that he didn't see coming up over his horizon. Not Leslie Howard this time, but Lauren Bacall.

BEN BRADLEE

In late October 1972 Ben Bradlee, 51, felt professionally forlorn. Or, as he wrote years later, "It was lonely out there." For the past five months, as executive editor (and vice-president) of *The Washington Post*, he'd been supervising the gradually unfolding story arising out of a bit of bungled burglary at the headquarters of the Democratic National Committee—and the story's political implications. It had been almost exclusively a *Post* story, and now it seemed more exclusive than ever. Other papers and the newsmagazines were neglecting it for steeplechase coverage of the Nixon-McGovern Presidential campaign.

The five months had been arduous, replete with both frustration and exhilaration. It had all started in June with the burgling of the main offices of the DNC by five bunglers furnished with tools of the trade and a goodly supply of $100 bills. After hearing from the DNC that the burglars were already in jail awaiting arraignment, the *Post* editors (Bradlee was briefly out of town) assigned a couple of reporters to follow up on this local story. During the arraignment one of the five, James McCord, was asked whom he had worked for before his retirement, and he replied in a whisper, "The CIA."

One of the reporters, Bob Woodward of subsequent celebrity, heard the whisper. "No three letters in the English language," Bradlee has explained in his autobiography, "arranged in that particular order, and spoken in similar circumstances, can tighten a good reporter's sphincter faster that C-I-A." This provided the first clue to the source of those $100 bills. Local story indeed.

The next clue was a name in an address book ruefully forked over at the jail by one of the bunglers. It was that of Howard Hunt, a White House factotum. A phone call to his office there rang without answer, but a White House phone operator suggested that he might be in Mr. Colson's office— and Charles Colson was assistant to the President! A Colson phone operator

suggested that Hunt might be at a local public-relations firm. When Woodward finally reached him there and asked why his name was in that address
book, Hunt's only response, after a long pause, was a horrified "Good God!"
Shortly thereafter McCord was found to be an employee of the Committee
to Reelect the President, a.k.a. CREEP.

By now Bradlee was breathlessly supervising the investigating and
reporting—this was clearly no mere burglary but a major story, and the *Post*
would have to stay ahead of the competition (as of course it did). One help
in this respect was reporter Carl Bernstein's discovery that some of the bunglers' money had come ultimately from a fund-raiser for the Nixon campaign
through CREEP. Soon the *Post*'s provocative reporting was eliciting responses
from the White House (Ron Ziegler) and Washington Republicans (led by
Senator Bob Dole)—responses that included threats culminating in a deli-
cately phrased and resonant warning from CREEP's campaign manager, John
Mitchell, that *Post* publisher Katharine Graham, Bradlee's firm backstop, was
"going to get her tit caught in a big fat wringer."

Soon Woodward was getting guidance from that anonymous, cautious
dispenser of lowdown information thereafter known as "Deep Throat." And
meanwhile Bernstein was getting a lead from a similarly anonymous source
on the activities of one Donald Segretti in a dirty-tricks campaign conspir-
acy. Woodward extracted confirmation from Deep Throat: "They were playing games, all over the map," with Mitchell lamenting, "If this all comes out,
it could ruin this administration. I mean ruin it." And him. And so, from the
White House and the Republican National Committee, came denial after outraged, splenetic denial.

Then came the *Post*'s mistake, the first mistake really in all that tortu-
ous time. In late October Bradlee & Co. ran a story linking the bunglers still
more closely to the Oval Office. Unfortunately, it was based on an ambiguous answer from a reliable source, and the political egesta hit the fan. "The
denials exploded all around us all day like incoming artillery shells." And of
course it was chiefly the denials that the competition was only too happy to
headline in its campaign sweepstakes reporting. The *Post* was isolated, belea-
guered—"it was lonely out there."

A phone call, however, made it less so, quite unexpectedly. It was from
a former colleague from Bradlee's days as a reporter for *Newsweek*, announcing that he and that celebrated model of journalistic integrity, Walter
Cronkite, had "gotten CBS to agree to do two back-to-back long pieces on
the 'Evening News' about Watergate. We're going to make you famous."

That they did. After the reelected Nixon's failed attempts to punish the
Post (e.g., nonrenewal of its TV station licenses), and after the bunglers' con-
victions, the Senate Watergate hearings, the ruinous tapes, the conviction
and imprisonment of more than 40 political intriguers, and the bitter resig-
nations of a Vice President and a President, this relatively obscure editor of

a Beltway newspaper became famous enough to be portrayed in a four-star movie by Jason Robards.

Maybe his most gratifying experience was a phone call from "Clark Clifford, then at the height of his power and influence, [who,] in that dramatic, triple-breasted basso profundo of his, spoke for much of Washington: 'Mr. Bradlee, I would like to tell you something. I woke up this morning, put on my bathrobe and my slippers, went downstairs slowly, opened the front door carefully, and there it was. The sun was already shining. And I looked up to the heavens, and said, "Thank God for *The Washington Post*."'" To this day, despite some down times, as David Remick testified in a September 1995 *New Yorker*, "it is still the only real competitor of the *Times*." He meant, of course, *The New York Times*.

DAVID BRINKLEY

In early 1956 David Brinkley at 35 was stationed in Washington, D.C., and "doing little stories" for NBC, as he has drily put it. One such story to which he was assigned was about the big new computer, SEAC, at the U.S. Bureau of Standards. Since he wasn't allowed to have a picture taken of it and since no one could explain its operation intelligibly, the story was dropped. That's about how things were going.

Meanwhile NBC had been sending talent scouts around the country in a desperate search for a newscaster who could give CBS's Edward R. Murrow enough competition to give NBC newscasts a boost in the ratings. In Los Angeles they came across a local newscaster, Chet Huntley, who had the requisite looks, voice and experience, and so they lured him to New York. There the network brass concluded that it would be safer to cover the imminent 1956 political conventions with two correspondents rather than one in an effort to counter the experience accumulated by Cronkite, who had been reporting political meetings since—was it the Constitutional Convention? It took some time to find a partner for Huntley, since Brinkley was in Washington and brass horizons extended no further south than lower Manhattan. Finally someone pointed out that Brinkley had been reporting on politics in the nation's capital, such as they were, for some time now and knew a great many of the conventioneers and a great deal about them. Why not Huntley and Brinkley?

And so that was the decision, with deep misgivings all around. So deep, indeed, that a song-and-dance man was hired to give lessons in liveliness, and scarlet, embossed NBC blazers were offered in place of ordinary suit coats. Thanks, but no thanks. Instead, Brinkley prepared by preparing notes, scads of "ad-libs" likely to be usable in the conventional milieu. This approach "worked so well that on the third day of the convention there was a newspaper column that changed my life forever." The formidable TV critic Jack Gould of *The New York Times* hailed him as someone new in TV news com-

31

mentary, "with a dry wit and a heaven-sent appreciation of brevity" who "contributes his observations with assurance but not insistence"—and so on and so on. It comforted him to know that Gould was quite regularly read Upstairs.

After the convention word came from Upstairs that the conventional two were to take over the evening news broadcast and that the format was to be *different*. How different? Well, for one thing Huntley would be in New York and Brinkley in Washington, with emphasis as appropriate. How about a name? Somebody came up with *The Huntley-Brinkley Report*, and no one else came up with anything better. Flashier maybe, but not better.

The program was introduced on Monday evening, October 29, 1956, only to encounter a world scene inconsiderately jam-packed with major news events. The Suez Canal was attacked by Israeli troops while France and Britain made menacing noises. Hungary was invaded by Soviet tanks while the Hungarian Red Cross begged for help in treating the 50,000 wounded. At home the Presidential campaign heated up, with Adlai Stevenson exhibiting uncharacteristic vehemence in attacking Eisenhower. And so on. It was just too much for the news program to handle. He remembers it as "the worst evening news program in the history of American network television." As it ended he was "filled with abject despair."

The next few months did little for his morale. Or for that of Huntley, a farm boy at heart who, in anticipation of being dropped, bought some farmland on the other side of the Hudson River, stocked it with cattle and started a silage business. Brinkley, being without a similar alternative, made no such emergency plans on the assumption that They'd have to have *someone* deliver the news, and who better than someone highly praised by Jack Gould?

Amid the gloom a ray of hope unexpectedly appeared when the mail grew more flattering and the ratings rose—high enough, indeed, for Texaco to buy up all the program's advertising time. It was now that someone came up with the celebrated sign-off, "Good night, Chet—Good night, David." They detested it, but the audience loved it, and who would gainsay *them*?

Within a couple of years theirs would be television's top-rated news program, and it would remain so during most of its 14 years. They'd both become so well known that one of his favorite stories is of a woman who came up to him in an airport while he was waiting for a flight and said, "Oh, you're Chet Huntley, aren't you?" He said yes, not wishing to embarrass her or prolong the conversation (or maybe because he's part pixie), and she added, "Oh, I like you on the news, but I can't stand that idiot Brinkley!"

TOM BROKAW

Tom Brokaw was 18 when he graduated from high school in Yankton, South Dakota, in 1958. During the preceding years he hadn't been exactly a bookworm or scholarly grind. Goof-off was more like it—at least that was his word for the rambunctious Tom who "pushed the edge of the envelope." For example, on a memorable visit to Deadwood, across the state from Yankton, he and some buddies, thoroughly sauced, tried sobering up in a laundromat. Yes, a laundromat. He maintains to this day that he holds "the record in downtown Deadwood for riding the dryers for the most revolutions. I'd be inside the dryer, with a friend on the outside holding the door so I didn't bake to death." The process attracted a crowd of spellbound spectators large enough to create something of a disturbance. "And so when the gendarmes arrived at the front door, we ran out of the bathroom window." Soberly, no doubt.

As has often happened in other lives, after graduation from high school came "a two-year period in which I lost all the points of my compass." He enrolled at the University of Iowa, where the academic demands proved too much for his high spirits. Returning home, he tried the University of South Dakota while making ends meet with a job reading news reports for the local radio station. Again college proved too demanding and work too confining. At the university a professor recommended that he purge "all the wine, women and song" out of his system, and at the radio station he was simply fired. Then he found a job in southwest Minnesota, working the four-to-midnight shift at a small radio station. It did little for his general composure, especially since he and the contentious manager were almost continuously in a state of open warfare. Before his first week was up he was on his way back to Yankton.

Despite his deep discouragement, he decided to give the University of South Dakota another try. The university was guardedly willing, and this time he did better, especially in his major, political science. Not splendidly, but better. After all, he was burdened with long working hours. In this he also did better. Far from getting fired, he was promoted from radio to television, appearing during his senior year on NBC's outlet in Sioux City, Iowa, some 30 miles away.

He became quite fond of political science, particularly since it provided so much opportunity for discussions conducted with spirit but without implacable hostility. By the summer of 1962 he had his bachelor's degree in that discipline, if that's the word for his concept of it. (He's described himself as "a political junkie.")

Later that summer, in August, he was married and moved with his new wife Meredith Lynn to Omaha, Nebraska, where he'd lined up a job with the local NBC-TV affiliate. Assigned to the early-morning shift, he quickly discovered that at this little station he was expected to do everything—not only to report on labor troubles, crime, crop yields, whatever, but also to handle the camera work and the writing and editing, and even to apply his own makeup. He couldn't have asked for a period of more rigorous training in the details of television news broadcasting. He probably *wouldn't* have asked for it, but he got it, and it served him well.

It lasted only three years, after which he received, with grateful relief, an offer to do the anchoring for another of NBC's couple of hundred affiliates, this one a large and important one, Atlanta's WSVB-TV. His reports on the South's mounting racial turbulence, often aired on *The Huntley-Brinkley Report*, brought him his first national attention as well as some nods of approval at network headquarters.

As a result, within a year he was in Los Angeles, reporting and anchoring the late-night news show for KNBC-TV, no mere affiliate but a station owned and operated directly by the network. Although he knew approximately as much about California as about the moon, he absorbed strenuously and learned fast about such things as the state's tumultuous politics, earthquakes, assassinations (Robert Kennedy's) and border problems. A competitor, Richard Threlkeld of CBS, after first dismissing him as "just a pretty face," soon discovered otherwise the hard competitive way.

He met with similar attitudes of dismissal when, in 1973, he was moved east as NBC's Washington correspondent, but again he won respect with his genial yet implacable competitiveness. Soon he was giving Dan Rather a run for his money. Three years later he took over as host of the network's morning show, *Today*. It wasn't until August 1983—after a year of awkward coanchoring with Roger Mudd in Washington—that he became sole anchor of the evening *NBC Nightly News*, partly if not mainly because of his talent for ad-libbing. That's how comfortable he, and the network for that matter, had become.

GEORGE BURNS

It was 1922, and the vaudeville career of Nathan Birnbaum was getting nowhere. He had been a performer for 19 of his 26 years, having sung in a "PeeWee Quartet" of seven-year-olds on street corners, in backyards, and even on the Staten Island Ferry. (On the ferry they were given money by busy lovers *not* to sing.) A dancing school that he helped to organize at 14 was abruptly closed down by suspicious police.

On approaching adulthood he barged into vaudeville as George Burns, performing with seals and dogs and on roller skates, doing "anything I could think of to stay in show business." This even included a brief marriage to a girl whose father adamantly opposed her going with him on a 36-week barnstorming tour without the explanatory license, although he apparently did not object to the divorce that immediately followed the tour and the dissolution of the partnership 36 weeks after it was formed.

George Burns was by no means committed to George Burns. Indeed, as he tells it, he had to change his name continually to keep booking agents from recognizing him readily and remembering his act. On one occasion he became Eddie Delight when Eddie suddenly left not only show business but also a thousand printed business cards behind. At other times he was Cap'n Betts, Buddy Links, Jimmy Malone, Billy Bierce, Jed Jackson, until George Burns was relatively safe again.

He also sought success in occasional partnerships. He was Williams of Brown & Williams, singing more or less precariously on roller skates—precariously as much because of audience reaction as hazardous equilibrium. He also was one of a trio, "Glide" of Goldie, Fields & Glide because, when it came to the light fantastic, gliding was his specialty. By 1922, still stubbornly in show business and now courageously back to George Burns, he had graduated to first billing in an act called "Burns & Lorraine." The act was doing all right when Billy Lorraine unexpectedly deserted him. So he needed a new partner.

35

Meanwhile Grace Ethel Cecile Rosalie Allen at 16 was also looking for a partner, at least subconsciously. She had show biz in her blood. Her father, a song-and-dance man, taught vaudeville dancing at home. His pupils included his four daughters. His youngest, introduced in the local paper as "la petite Gracie," at the age of three sang an Irish ballad on stage while dressed in an ill-fitting costume of top hat and tails. A year later, having developed an extraordinary skill in her highland flings, she performed in a sword dance that won her a prize.

Later she spent most of her afternoons and most of her allowance on trips downtown, where she could visit theater lobbies and gawk at the posters, yearningly. If her mother wanted her to get something from a store, she'd locate it for her by saying that it was so many blocks from the Orpheum Theater.

In her mid-teens she managed to combine school with vaudeville, joining her sisters on the stage of theaters in their home town, San Francisco. After graduation she joined them in a traveling company, warbling her lilting Irish ballads in a brogue that later plagued her with its adhesiveness. It may also have given her something of an Irish temper, for when the owner of the company flatly refused to add "& Company"—meaning the Allen Sisters—to the marquee sign, she quit. Not merely the company, but show biz.

Since she quit when they were playing, or were about to play, in Hoboken, she had a short and easy trip to New York City, where she began learning shorthand and typing at a secretarial school. The urge to revert to show business evidently was going to take some time returning, although its return surely was inevitable. Before it could do so on its own, a friend induced her into coming with her to a town in New Jersey to see a show that happened to include a comedy act, laced with song and dance, by a team called Burns & Lorraine. During the performance she was told that the act was breaking up, that Lorraine was leaving. After the show she went backstage, just on the outside chance. As Burns reported it later, she had "a choice of secretarial school, teaching dancing back home in San Francisco, or me. She didn't have the train fare home and hated to type, so my irresistible charm won out."

Their arrangement was that he would be the comic and she would play it straight, feeding him lines. In those days his talent, however, was in writing comedy more than in delivering it, and he soon discovered her straight lines were getting them more sympathetic laughter than his funny ones. The audiences loved her, maybe almost as much as he did. Okay, from now on she delivers the jokes and I'll play the straight man. That way I'll be able to afford those good cigars.

After a couple of years of the inevitable ups and downs that normally accompany new acts, in 1925 they opened in San Francisco, at her own Orpheum Theater no less. Yet fate intervened, and she was rushed to a hospital with acute appendicitis. His constant, tender solicitude was so overwhelming that it brought tears to her eyes. After she recovered he proposed marriage, and despite a tie elsewhere, she accepted. After all, she told him, "if you could make me cry like that, I must be in love with you."

They were married in January 1926, and six weeks later they were headliners at New York's Palace Theater. Ahead of them lay movies, televison, and an undying love till death did them part.

GEORGE BUSH

At one point in July 1980 George Bush, 56, then in Detroit for the Republican National Convention, was in a considerably less than upbeat mood. The month before, as Ronald Reagan was clearly about to secure the 998 votes needed to capture the Party's nomination for President, Bush had ended his own campaign for the nomination with a bit of realistic rue. "I'm an optimist," he had remarked to reporters, "but I know how to count to 998."

He'd been on the campaign trail for 14 arduous months, since May 1979, waving, glad-handing, mixing, enduring rubber-chicken orgies and unruly band music here, there and everywhere. After his big win in the Iowa caucuses in January 1980 the race had narrowed into a Bush-Reagan competition, yet after the New Hampshire primary the following month it had reversed into a Reagan-Bush competition. Especially after that nationally televised incident preceding the nationally televised debate.

What he didn't know was that the Reagan campaign had put up the money for the debate, which was scheduled as a Reagan-Bush confrontation. When the four other candidates unexpectedly but resolutely arrived ready to join in, the moderator invited them to leave, explaining that this was a two-candidate event, as advertised. Bush, a play-by-the-rules man, said nothing. But as resentful murmurs in the audience grew into shouts of protest against the unfairness, Reagan evidently saw, and seized, a golden opportunity. He grabbed a microphone and added his protest, insisting that the debate be open to all. When the moderator imperiously cut off his mike, he shouted sternly that he had paid for it and expected to use it. Although the moderator won *that* debate and the other candidates in the end weren't allowed to participate, many a voter was left with the impression of a weak Bush competing with a strong Reagan. He garnered 20 percent of the New Hampshire vote to Reagan's 50 percent and never fully recovered.

Perhaps as a result—desperation can be a powerful source of adrenalin—he lambasted Reagan quite forcefully during the rest of the campaign,

38

ridiculing his supply-side ideas, for instance, with a memorably disdainful term, "voodoo economics." Yet his experience as Congressman, UN ambassador, chair of the Republican National Committee and CIA director failed to match Reagan's executive experience during his eight years as governor of the mammoth state of California. Besides, he was up against one of nature's, and Hollywood's, personality kids.

Once the magic 998 votes, and more, were clearly in his opponent's pocket, there was talk of his chances to be picked as running mate. But they evaporated, ironically, as he was on his way to the speakers' platform at the convention to give his speech introducing the nominating process. As he was "walking up the long ramp to the convention podium," he has reported, "a backstage worker came by, patted me on the back and said, 'I'm sorry, Mr. Bush, really sorry. I was pulling for you.'" When Bush asked what he was sorry about, he explained, "'You mean you haven't heard? It's all over. Reagan's picked Ford as his running mate.'"

Indeed, during the earlier gossip Reagan-Ford had been called a "Dream Ticket," although that wasn't the way his family described it when he returned to their hotel suite that evening, after his wife and children had spent hours "hearing their father written off by the network analysts." When he told them that it was simply all over, he felt sure that he was talking about his political career.

The hotel phone rang. Campaign manager Jim Baker answered it and, after a brief conversation, put his hand over the mouthpiece and announced that the thing might be coming apart. It was. As it turned out later, ex–President Ford's price was too high—evidently he didn't hanker after being No. 2, seemed to want something like No. 1½. In reaction to the news, Bush shrugged wearily. After all, there were plenty of people eager to be No. 2.

But then the phone rang again. This time a Secret Service agent was on the line, reporting that his group had taken a room two floors below the Bush suite and would be available "in case you need anything." It was all very mysterious until the phone rang once again. This time the caller asked specifically to speak to George Bush, who thereupon heard a familiar voice say, "Hello, George, this is Ron Reagan. I'd like to go over to the convention and announce that you're my choice for Vice President—if that's all right with you."

It was all right, perfectly all right. And voodoo economics would be all the rage, with him as well as others, for many years to come.

MICHAEL CAINE

It was March 1933, early in the Great Depression, when a baby boy was born in London named Maurice Joseph Micklewhite, Jr., later to be internationally known as Michael Caine. At the very outset of his life he needed a turnaround, for his father had just before lost his fish-market job and was now on relief while his mother scrubbed floors and sewed at a clothing store for a measly ten shillings a week. Six months later the family was relocated in a slum-clearance drive into a tiny, shabby, soot-stained apartment without electricity. There they lived, if that's the word, for the next six years.

And then came World War II. His father, briefly reemployed, departed for army service, leaving his mother and younger brother to the assiduous visitations of the German air forces until the boys were hastily evacuated to a farm further north. There they spent a relatively idyllic six years, especially after their mother took a job in the area and joined them, but after the war they had to return to devastated London. Their apartment building having been bomb-demolished, they were housed in a prefab in London's sooty slums—for the next ten years.

The boy was twelve now and could read, and this offered him escape. Further, the family's fortunes gradually improved enough for him to go to the movies, and he quickly became addicted to their realms of reverie. Although he had done a little acting for a youth club, being *in* a movie was an idea far beyond any horizon that he could even imagine.

After a stint in the army in the early 1950s, preferably forgettable, and a brief job in a meat market, he rather desperately decided to take a chance on the theater after a friend brought him an ad in *The Stage* for a stage-manager's job with a repertory company in Sussex, an ad that promised "occasional walk-on parts." The job proved exhausting, up to 100 hours a week as what he called "a general dogsbody—errand boy, shifting scenery, painting, decorating," and furniture-renting or -borrowing. Yet he reveled in it, especially after the manager gave him one of those occasional walk-on parts, this first one as a policeman in a mystery story, with a line to say, firmly: "Come along with me, sir!" He changed his name from Micklewhite to Scott, for professional reasons. Next he played a butler ("Dinner is served"), and after that his roles gradually grew more demanding.

But a bout of malaria, from his grueling service in Korea, interrupted his career, and after his discharge from the hospital he could pursue it only by taking various kinds of incidental menial jobs for eating purposes. His live TV acting proved short-lived when he forgot his lines and in frustration appeared in "this unforgettable shot of me coming right up to the lens and saying: '*Oh bugger it!*'" His discouragement was deepened after his father died and his foredoomed marriage with a competitive actress fell apart. He was so obviously depressed that his ever supportive mother gave him the 25 pounds from his father's insurance and urged him to leave London, if only to just get away. He chose a trip to Paris. He was, he said later, at "my absolute all-time rock-bottom low."

Not that his six months in Paris lifted him to any giddy heights. He found that one "can live very cheaply in Paris," and that's what he did, partly by cadging coffee and sandwiches at a snack bar, partly by sleeping in an airport seat with an old suitcase beside him to suggest a passenger waiting for a flight, and so on. But at least he looked and felt much better on his return home. And he took up his old career with a new name, Michael Caine, lifted rather casually from a film about mutiny. (He had long been a fan of Humphrey Bogart.)

He appeared a few times on the London stage and in some movies but he grew busiest, surprisingly and courageously, in television shows, well over 100 during the next seven years without serious mishap. He got plenty of work, and plenty of experience, simply by never refusing any offer. Nevertheless, the early 1960s were a time of discouragement, not so deep as before, but pervading and growing. He borrowed later from Thoreau in describing this as a period "of quiet desperation." His roles were getting neither bigger nor better, and his reputation—well, he really didn't have much of a reputation. Nor was he affluent enough to pay the alimony that his ex-wife demanded, at least regularly enough to avoid frequent arrest. Arrest, indeed, sometimes was welcome, since it afforded him an opportunity to do some eating at government expense. About the only break in his sullen skies was his unexpected acquisition of an agent, Dennis Selinger, who had at first turned him down but more recently, impressed by his perseverance, had begun to sense a certain potential in him.

And so it was Selinger who called his attention to a big-budget African adventure movie being planned and who even sent him a copy of the screenplay, which he read eagerly and longingly. Although his screen test was, in the director's opinion, "the worst I've ever seen," and although he didn't get the part he wanted, he did get a good one, and he played it well enough to earn him rave notices in the English-speaking world, including a Toronto critic's prediction of "a brilliant film future" for him. The movie was 1964's *Zulu*.

The next two years would bring him leads in *The Ipcress File* and *Alfie*, roles that would introduce him to stardom and to the successful film career that he had hoped for during so many daunting years. Not that it was invariably successful, but then he made quite a lot of movies, avoiding role refusals on the principle that bad notices of even many failures "would be drowned out by the occasional success." His successes have been frequent enough to earn him a luxury apartment in London and an estate on the Thames with some 600 feet of frontage on the river.

JIMMY CARTER

In October 1953, shortly after his 29th birthday, Jimmy Carter resigned his commission and left the United States Navy after serving seven years and four months.

The decision wasn't an easy one. His yen for naval service reached back to the age of six and to his enchantment with the bewitching post cards that a maternal uncle, a Navy tar, kept sending the family from exotic ports around the world. After learning to read and write he employed these new skills in requesting catalogs from the U.S. Naval Academy and then eagerly poring through them while dreaming of a naval career. His life as a farmboy in Plains, Georgia, was by no means an unhappy one, yet for Plains the adjective "exotic" wasn't the first that came to mind.

In high school his yearning grew more sophisticated. His further goal now was to be Chief of Naval Operations. In junior college he made a point of taking courses that seemed relevant to naval operations, as indeed they later proved to be—chemistry, for instance, and engineering. The school also provided him as a freshman with some mild extracurricular hazing which also would prove relevant, as preparation for the diabolical fun and games of his plebe year at Annapolis.

Before Annapolis, however, he spent a year at the Georgia Institute of Technology in Atlanta, and in its Navy ROTC for a taste of nautical regimentation, while waiting hopefully for his Congressman, under some pressure from his father, to get him an appointment to the Academy. His appointment came through in 1943. He entered the Academy that June while millions of other young Americans with less affluence and influence were being shipped out to very uncertain fates.

Not that his three years at Annapolis were all that cushy. He suffered not only through the fun and games but also through the traditional regimen of instilled subservience. Perhaps because he was temperamentally unsuited to educational abuse, his record, though quite respectable, wasn't outstanding. When he graduated in 1946 he was in about the top tenth of his class.

His first couple of years of sea duty were neither satisfying nor very promising. The first he spent on the *Wyoming*, a battleship so old and decrepit that it was declared unsafe and scrapped almost immediately after his year was up. His second year, on the newer and more respectable *Mississippi*, he spent largely, as training officer, in a small office in the bowels of the ship, with relatively little chance to see the sea. When the two years were up he lost no time requesting assignment to the submarine service, prepared as he was by all that below-decks duty.

In December 1948, after six months of training, he was assigned to a sub as electronics officer. Even after being washed overboard—by an enormous wave that considerately deposited him back on deck as it receded—he enjoyed sub duty, partly because the extraordinarily close living inspired a genuine team spirit in the crews.

The sub duty he *really* wanted, however, was with Hyman Rickover's celebrated atomic submarine division of the Bureau of Ships. He applied and late in 1952, after a grueling interview with the granitic Rickover that left him almost too weak to walk out of the room, he was accepted, assigned to the prototype atomic sub *Sea Wolf*, and enrolled in graduate-level courses in nuclear physics and reactor technology, which proved almost as difficult as the Rickover interview. The work was challenging and occasionally dangerous, as when he and some others were inadvertently exposed, as he has put it, to "a year's maximum allowance of radiation in one minute and 29 seconds. There were no apparent aftereffects from this exposure—just a lot of doubtful jokes among ourselves about death versus sterility."

Although he found the work stimulating and was delighted when he was made chief engineer of the *Sea Wolf*, he also was made pretty uncomfortable by the zealous Rickover's severe and often psychologically brutal treatment of subordinates (and superiors, but that's another story). And so it was that, when his father died of cancer in July 1953, he faced a turning point not merely in his career but in his life. The friendly, caring behavior of his father's many friends in Plains during his illness and after his death brought home to the son the importance of community—and the relative lack thereof in Navy service.

And so, despite mild objections from his wife Rosalyn, who rather enjoyed Navy life and was leery of loving parental interference back home, they returned to civilian life in Plains in October 1953. Before long he was, like his father, an active, respected, popular member of the community.

That sort of status leads rather naturally into politics.

RAY CHARLES

"It was in the middle of May that my life suddenly changed." Ray Charles Robinson (he later dropped the Robinson to avoid any confusion with Sugar Ray) was only 14 when word arrived at his school in 1945 that his mother had died, apparently from food poisoning. Her death was quite a shock. She was only 32 and had been a wise and caring mother who had imbued her son with a spirit of independence despite his blindness from early childhood. As a result of her solicitude and his determination, he learned to walk the street of Greenville, Florida, alone, and even to ride a bicycle.

For the past seven years he had been enrolled at the St. Augustine School for Deaf and Blind Children, where he had learned to play the piano, organ, sax and clarinet, as well as to compose music, including various arrangements, in Braille. He had developed unusual talent: he needed only to hear a piece of music played once to reproduce it perfectly. He had done well at the school, had obtained his high-school diploma, and enjoyed the environment. But now, with his beloved mother gone, he wasn't sure that he should go back.

He didn't. "Those summer months after Mama's death were a turning point for me." Or at least the beginning of a turning point. By autumn he was in a train headed for Jacksonville, responding to the rhythmic clatter of the wheels. In that city he was taken in by kind friends of his family who happened to live near the headquarters of the musicians' union. He soon memorized the way there so that he could play the piano in the meeting hall whenever possible. On his arrival other pianists would call out, "Here comes that kid!" as a warning against letting him do his perfect imitations of their favorite pieces.

But before long they were asking him to play for their entertainment, and paying him—to the point where he was considered a professional and induced to join the union, Local 632. Soon offers to perform at various gigs began to come his way, occasionally with one of the big bands. He was versatile, adaptable, "doing piano boogie here or playing big-band swing there—

depending on what the boss wanted." Indeed, not long after this he found himself in Tampa playing with a white hillbilly band. *That*'s adaptable!

But first there was a move to Orlando, where a prospective gig was abruptly canceled and he faced impending malnutrition while seeking work in a highly competitive job market. A big-band job that finally came his way proved especially stimulating when the leader asked him to do some original arrangements. By and large, however, Orlando had little to offer, and so it was on to Tampa and that white hillbilly band. He played his favorite instrument, piano, and enjoyed the music. He played well, of course—acceptably despite his color.

It was in Tampa that he started wearing sunglasses. He'd been told that sometimes his eyes didn't look right—on occasion tearing and caked. Sunglasses have been a kind of trademark ever since.

Although he was earning, even saving, some money now, he'd had all he wanted of Florida. The travel bug began to bite. After a friend had spread out a map of the United States, he asked him to find the big city farthest from Tampa, and soon he was on his way to Seattle. After five gruelingly tedious days and nights his bus arrived in Seattle at five in the morning. Finding a hotel room, he slept until three or so the next morning. On awakening, he asked the room clerk where he could get some breakfast and was told that probably the only place open would be a nearby nightclub, The Rocking Chair.

There he found a talent show in progress and, of course, joined in, singing the blues to rounds of enthusiastic applause. After his performance he was asked if he could get a trio together for a gig at The Elks Club night after next. Could he ever! After raiding the union hiring hall for talent, he formed a trio with enough staying power to play The Elks Club and then The Rocking Chair. Meanwhile he was composing arrangements for some of the city's big bands. In 1954 he organized a seven-piece band with himself on piano and alto sax. It was this combo that introduced his "I Got a Woman," an unprecedented combination of gospel and blues, his "first real smash" that brought him an international audience, black and white, and gave his career the impetus it needed. Some years later he would be hailed by Frank Sinatra as "the only genius in our business."

BILL CLINTON

In December 1978 Bill Clinton was only 32 but, having been an effective attorney general of Arkansas for the past two years, he was now awaiting his January inauguration as the country's youngest governor, recently elected by a vote margin of two to one. Yet a little more than two years later, in February 1981, he was the country's youngest, and perhaps most thoroughly depressed, ex-governor.

Perhaps it was his youth that had impelled him into trying to do more than Arkansas voters could handle comfortably, and certainly more than the rather torpid legislature could readily accommodate. His dozens of ideas had apparently lacked focus, adding up to a program that his aide and pollster Dick Morris described as "admirable but indescribable. There was a bit of everything. Like a kid in a candy store, he wanted to do it all."

In two areas his efforts had been especially unpopular, aggravated by growing voter unease with the Carter administration in Washington: his attempts at consolidating the state's schools had angered admirers of the status quo, and his raising of taxes on cars and trucks for highway improvement had alienated the closefisted. In addition, there had been abrasive problems with restless Cuban refugees detained at Fort Chafee, and many lips were pursed over the disquieting fact that he was married to Hillary Rodham rather than to Hillary Clinton. His 1980 campaign opponent, Frank White, although a bank official new to politics, used this ammunition effectively during the Ronald Reagan landslide. And maybe there was a mystical factor involved, since White, a "creation science" enthusiast, reverentially described his election as a "victory for the Lord."

Clinton was thoroughly discouraged, sporadically resentful of voter ingratitude, press insensitivity and campaign scurrilities, but just as often of his own failure to make hay while the sun shone. His wife was similarly disheartened—had she come to darkest Arkansas for *this*? They both were engaged in private law practice now, she more or less contentedly, he miserably.

47

Before long, however, they both were planning a comeback. Soon Dick Morris was commuting from New York to help with such ideas as the now celebrated ad offering the judgmental voters an abject apology for past administrative sins.

As the primary campaign, a three-way race, got under way, Morris the pollster rather abashedly reported that Morris the campaign adviser's apologetic television ad had been followed by a sharp drop in Clinton's poll ratings—but explained, hopefully, that it would prove to be a form of immunization, foresightedly stealing the thunder from any opponent's attack on the Clinton record. To his and the Clintons' surprise, this did indeed seem to be the case, especially as Clinton, in his anxiety for rehabilitation, resorted uncharacteristically to what *The Arkansas Gazette* referred to as "low road" tactics. (No lower, however, than those of his final opponent, Frank White again, or than the record in office of Gov. White, whom the more alliterative members of the local press corps had taken to calling "Governor Goofy.") After a similarly anxious Hillary began referring to herself as "Mrs. Bill Clinton," he won the election with 55% of the vote.

This second time around things were going to be different. Less emphasis on youth, with a gramps executive assistant and a granny receptionist. More sympathetic attention to Bible-thumpers, with an aid assigned to join in precautionary prayer with visitors bearing the word of God Almighty. More important were his efforts to reach out to contrary legislators in addressing such serious problems as the peril in the state's economy and the neglect of education. (Arkansas was spending less on education than any other state.)

At the level of politics he vowed with Morris to avoid the press as a medium for communicating with voters, relying instead on advertising, mailings, and radio and TV commercials. And for listening to those feckless voters' concerns he would rely on Morris's incessant polling, to permit conformance in policies and rhetoric. After deciding that his first priority should be raising the schools from deepest mediocrity, he organized a committee, Arkansas Partners in Education, to raise money ($130,000) and spend it on radio and television ads to sell his reforms to a public who would have to pay the cost of an extra cent in sales tax. Another committee handed out booster ribbons and a quarter of a million brochures.

With the support of most thus educated voters and against the opposition of most teachers, and with considerable wifely cooperation, he also introduced competency testing to do something about such teachers as the one who was found enlightening students about World War Eleven because of perplexity over the meaning of "II." Not instant dismissal, but at least rehabilitation. The program proved effective enough to win the praise, eventually, of the Arkansas Education Association.

Indeed, this second term was exhilaratingly better than the first, so much so that Arkansas' voters kept reelecting him to office through 1990. After "absolutely, positively" promising that year to serve his full four years, he was elected for an unprecedented fifth term. In 1992 he appealed to the voters for extrication.

During his first term *The Washington Post*'s star newsman David Broder, in an article in *Parade*, had touted him as a likely prospect, some day, for the Presidency.

HILLARY RODHAM
CLINTON

In August 1974 Hillary Rodham, a couple of months short of her 27th birthday, was rather at loose ends. Her stimulating staff work for the Watergate Committee having been abruptly terminated by the Nixon resignation, she had a directional decision to make. A highly competent and extraordinarily bright lawyer, as well as an ardent feminist with a defiant confidence in her recognized abilities, she could stay comfortably north of Mason-Dixon to pursue a probably successful legal or even political career. Or she could launch into a career of social service, with emphasis on an aspect of it dear to her heart, assistance to disadvantaged children. Or she could join her true love Bill Clinton and take her chances in enigmatic Arkansas.

On visits to Arkansas she had been beguiled by the scenery, but living there might be quite another thing. Would the people there accept a woman with aspirations beyond dutiful homemaking? She doubted it, apprehensively. Shortly after their graduation from Yale, in proposing marriage he'd admitted that his commitment to Arkansas made her choice a difficult one, and she'd agreed. A quarter of a century later she would tell an interviewer from *The Arkansas Gazette*, "Suppose I'd sat down and tried to map out my life. Do you suppose I would have said I'd be married to the governor of Arkansas and practicing law in Little Rock? No way!"

Now, in 1974, she didn't know that he'd be governor, although during their days at Yale she had jollied a friend with her lightly considered opinion that Bill would be President someday. On balance, Arkansas hardly seemed to be a land of opportunity, at least for such as Hillary Rodham. Should she make the gamble? "No way!"

Still, she wasn't entirely unfamiliar with U-turns in her life. There was one especially, not a turnaround in career but rather in political ideology. Her affluently Republican family in Park Ridge, Illinois, had exerted an influence

50

that impelled her into working for the neanderthal Barry Goldwater in the 1964 election, and that's about as maniacally Republican as anyone can get. About a year later, however, a minister in her Methodist church conducted a class in social realism, leading his comfortable suburban students to the eye-opening slums of south Chicago, for example, to expose them to how the other half, or quarter, or tenth had to live. He also took them to a lecture by Martin Luther King Jr. and introduced each of them to that Christian martyr-to-be. Her sympathetic reaction to this experience was reinforced intellectually in her years at Wellesley College, during which she supported the primary campaign of the ultraliberal Eugene McCarthy, and in her years at Yale, during which she campaigned for the similarly liberal George McGovern.

What she particularly did for McGovern in that 1972 campaign was to register Hispanic voters in Texas, where his campaign was being run by that attractive fellow Bill Clinton, to whom she had been forgettably introduced by his friend Bob Reich and whom she had met more directly and less forgettably in a celebrated encounter in the Yale library. (Essentially: "If we're going to sit in here staring at each other, we should introduce each other.") As they got to know each other thereafter, he had found her considerably smarter than any paint he knew about, and she'd been delighted to see that he wasn't in the least intimidated by that discovery. From this time on they had been sporadically inseparable until his addiction to home politics and her absorption in Watergate intervened to keep them a thousand miles of telephone lines apart.

Watergate—that was 1974, the year in which Bill Clinton ran for Congress. If he won, her reservations about a life and career in Arkansas would become irrelevant, for he'd be living in Washington. But because he lost, as she put it later, "I had to make a decision. What was I to do? I could have gone to work for a big law firm in a place like Chicago or New York. I could have gone back to work for the Children's Defense Fund, stayed on that career path for whatever series of motivations I had been moving toward all my life." But there was something else to consider. "I also knew that I had to deal with a whole other side of life—the emotional side, where we live and where we grow and, when all is said and done, where the most important parts of life take place." Further, as she remarked on that same occasion, there was "something very special about Bill."

There was also something special about the University of Arkansas, where Bill was teaching law in addition to his private practice. When she had visited him there in Fayetteville early in 1974 he had introduced her to, among others, Dean Wylie Davis of the School of Law. The dean, among others, had been greatly impressed, so greatly that he suggested that, if she'd ever consider teaching there, she should give him a call.

And so she gave him a call—was the job offer still open? Indeed it was. Soon she was on her way with a friend in a car encumbered with her clothes and books and ten-speed bike. Once in Fayetteville, unfortunately, they encountered a vast herd of overstimulated University football fanatics sporting pig hats in honor of the Razorbacks and shrieking, "Sou-eee! Sou-eee! Pig, pig, pig!" Nevertheless she felt committed. She joined Bill and then reported for work. After their marriage the next year, the die would be irretrievably cast.

Four years afterward he would be the Governor and she the First Lady of Arkansas. Two years later she would be the ex–First Lady having some understandable second thoughts. And two years after *that* she would be the First Lady again in the second of her husband's five terms. From then on it would be, on balance, gangbusters.

SEAN CONNERY

In the fall of 1956 Sean Connery was a young, aspiring Scottish actor of 26, handsome in a burly, hairy way and more ambitious than experienced. He had done bit parts in two or three utterly forgettable movies when the director Terence Young offered him a minor role with one significant scene, featuring a disconcertingly unsuccessful sexual attack. *Action of the Tiger* starred the American Van Johnson in one of his more wooden performances, an uninspired British cast, and a soporific script.

Before it was in the can director Young knew that it was ungarnished turkey, and audience reaction, after its release in 1958, soon confirmed his dismal view. He had been impressed, however, with Connery's performance—strong in more than one sense. So when the insecure young actor asked how he'd done, Young encouraged him, apologetically confessing to the film's rancid odor, assuring him that it was no fault of his, and promising to "make it up" to him some day. The promise doubtless was perfectly sincere, but they both must have realized, given the unpredictability of fate, what a slender reed it was.

And so they went their separate ways, Young more successfully than Connery. About five years later Young attended a play in a West End theater and discovered Connery, clad only in an insignificant loincloth, displaying his manly charms on the boards, offering a strong stage presence to at least a portion of the audience and exhibiting, to others, an acting talent beyond wholesale dishabille. Young was aware that Ian Fleming's James Bond bestsellers were going to be filmed and that the prospective producers were searching for someone to play Bond—preferably not a celebrated star, since they felt that the Bond name and character would prove strong enough to carry the day. He was in no position, however, to influence the choice. He was busily preoccupied with his own directing work, which had nothing whatever to do with James Bond.

And then, quite unexpectedly, he was neither busy nor preoccupied. At the last moment a movie that he was about to direct was abruptly canceled because its star, Ava Gardner, refused to work without two limousines at her beck and call. (Such big-studio luxuries as *two* limos were beyond the means of the new independent producers.) Meanwhile the two prospective Bond producers had also been looking for a director, had been turned down by two or three, and had left a message at his hotel, perhaps at the very moment he was being informed of his unemployment. Would he be interested?

Absolutely, he replied in his return call, provided that he could select the books to be filmed—*Dr. No, From Russia with Love*, and *Thunderball*. No problem, they responded. Furthermore, he told them, if you're still looking for someone to play Bond, I'm sure I've got just the man for you, an unappreciated actor with some stage, movie and television experience, and a lot of potential. Well, they replied, we still have a few possibilities in mind—Roger Moore, for instance, and Patrick McGoohan—but, okay, let's have a look at him.

And so Young set up a meeting, urging Connery to wear a conventional suit and behave himself, to be undemanding, cooperative, and as near to obsequious as he could bring himself to be. And so an unshaven Connery arrived in slacks, an open shirt, and a nondescript lumber jacket. During the conversation he forcefully made his demands. He insisted on being free to find work in non–Bond movies as well, and he was especially vigorous concerning the Bond image that he expected to bring to the screen. The two producers, rather nonplussed, mentioned a bit hesitantly that they were testing some others for the role. That's your privilege of course, answered Connery, but I'm not playing any competitive supermarket games—take me or leave me, as is. And out he strode.

Their worries about his accent lessened considerably as they watched him from their window while he sauntered across the street and through the traffic with his catlike grace. They could surely take the rough edges off the accent, and would they be likely to find anyone else who naturally walked and moved like that? No, they decided after running a series of screen tests on other candidates. And so they announced their selection publicly, and were immediately overwhelmed by a chorus of complaints.

Among the complainants were addicts of the Bond novels who couldn't abide the thought of this roughneck with the burr-laden voice, a typical saloon-dweller, playing their suave, aristocratic patron of elegant cafés. Author Fleming apparently shared their jitters, or so the equally jittery Hollywood columnist Sheila Graham maintained (although both later recanted, overpowered by what one critic later praised as Connery's "abounding sexuality"). United Artists executives also protested, urging the two producers to find someone better. Fortunately it was too late for that.

It was fortunate, too, that Terence Young had an opportunity to exercise his considerable literary talent on the scripts prepared for him, restoring

Fleming's wit and humor, inserting some of his own, and leaving openings for Connery to add his sardonic touches. Having gotten Connery assigned to the role, he now helped to fashion an image that would carry his protégé through his Bond period into an enormously successful film career of gratifying variety.

MARLENE DIETRICH

In the fall of 1921 Marlene Dietrich was a very unhappy, bitterly disappointed 19-year-old Berliner gazing forlornly at her swollen left hand. The cast had just been removed, and the hand looked and felt so convincingly abnormal that she hardly needed the doctors' opinion that it would never again be reliable in playing the violin. Her dreams of becoming a celebrated concert violinist were shattered.

She had been playing the violin since early childhood, as well as the piano—and, later, even the guitar, although the violin always rated first. Through the ravages of World War I, including the death of her stepfather in battle, she had practiced faithfully, persistently, enriching her repertoire, sharpening her skill under the tutelage of her mother, a fine amateur musician, and of a succession of teachers.

After a year or so at boarding schools in Weimar, in the summer of 1921 she returned to Berlin and its Music Academy. There her new teacher "accepted me only after I had played hours on end for him." He seems to have had a fondness for the "hours on end" regimen. And for Johann Sebastian Bach. "It was Bach, Bach, Bach, always Bach. My mother and I almost lost our minds."

Her left hand, particularly the ring finger, began giving her intolerable pain. Tendon inflammation, that was the diagnosis, and enclosure in a cast, that was the therapy. That doubtless eliminated any chance of full recovery. Whatever the reason, the hand would never again be adequate for Bach.

It was a time for considering alternatives. One appealed to her immediately. She had recently fallen utterly in love with Rilke's poetry, and it occurred to her that only the acting profession, despite her mother's disdain, offered any opportunity to give voice to such golden lines. Maybe an audition at Max Reinhardt's drama school would give her a start.

At the school, where someone rather summarily warned her "that Rilke was not a 'theater author,'" she nonetheless auditioned, quite uncomfortably, and was ultimately accepted. Since Reinhardt managed four theaters in Berlin, students at his school had sound reason to hope for at least minor roles in occasional plays, but it was the movies that first used her talents. A film called *The Tragedy of Love* was being produced in Berlin, and the assistant producer came to the school looking for some extras, especially some "demimonde ladies." Even at her still rather tender age, she fit that bill quite satisfactorily. Still merely an extra, she did her first movie work as one of the crowd. (All this against a backdrop of Germany's postwar devastation and political upheaval, to which the focused young actress was essentially oblivious.)

So much for the cinema. She kept on at the drama school, making the rounds of the four theaters for multivarious bit parts with a single line here, maybe two or three lines there. It was a demanding routine yet enjoyable training, with rarely a dull moment as she passed rapidly from one bit part to the next. Variety was the spice of her life.

The young assistant producer of demimonde requirements, Rudolf Sieber, didn't forget her. After he offered, and she accepted, a one-line part in one of his movies, she soon realized that she was in love. At the time he was preoccupied with a weakening entanglement, but as soon as he became disentangled he began giving her more than bit parts in his films—candy, for instance, and invitations to dinner. After a year of this they were married. And about a year after that she gave birth to their daughter Maria.

Although this was a happy event in her personal life, her career, when she returned to it, seemed to be stuck on hold. She did some movie work (Sieber was no Jack Warner)—"but the films I was making were nothing special." So she returned to the Reinhardt grind, incessantly traveling on buses and trolleys from theater to theater to say a few lines here, a few other lines there. It became a pretty grueling and pretty dispiriting routine.

"Yet one day my luck changed." It did so while she was playing, for the umpteenth time, an American woman in a forgettable play with a single line, "May I invite you all to dine with me this evening?" Whatever the response was to that invitation in the play, there evidently was something irresistible in it for the Austrian, now American, movie director Josef von Sternberg, who happened to be in the audience. Not long thereafter she was asked, during a von Sternberg audition, "to climb on top of the piano, roll down one of my stockings and sing a song." When the film clip was shown to the producers, they were not impressed, but he threatened to return to America forthwith if they refused to hire her. They hired her. After all, she was an unknown and came pretty cheap.

And so it was that she played the immortal Lola in the similarly immortal *The Blue Angel*. That performance transformed the frustrated concert violinist into a famous movie actress with many a mesmerizing performance ahead of her. Hollywood was in her immediate future, and she'd be anything but cheap.

BOB DOLE

In the fall of 1941 Bob Dole, at the age of 18 and just out of high school, confidently anticipated breezing through Kansas University and then medical school on his way to a reasonably prosperous career as a country doctor. With a little bit of luck, that is, for a war was on, with U.S. entry imminent, and high school athletes were eminently draftable.

As time passed it looked as though he'd have that little bit of luck at least, on the theory that the later you wound up in combat, the greater your chances of surviving intact. After entering the Army Enlisted Reserve Corps in December 1942, he was given until June 1943 to complete his sophomore year at Kansas University and then, after some basic training, another half year to study engineering at New York's Brooklyn College. Next came some training as an antitank gunner and then acceptance into Officers' Candidate School.

As a result of all this he was finally assigned to a combat unit in late February 1945, only about ten weeks before the end of the war in Europe. But what a combat unit! It was a company in the celebrated 10th Mountain Division, a tough, battle-scarred unit then operating formidably in Italy's Apennine Mountains. The records show that this company lost, merely in those early months of 1945, five of its six officers, 181 of its 188 enlisted men, and all four of its medics. Dole later called it, the whole company, a suicide squad, with good reason.

Despite a minor leg wound suffered in March, he doggedly continued to lead his platoon in the division's heavy attack on enemy positions in the Po Valley. Caught in an ambush, targeted by machine-gun and rifle fire, mortars, and even a new German rocket, the platoon was taking untold casualties when something lethally unfriendly hit him hard in the back and right shoulder. Although the platoon achieved their objective before the day was over, they had to do so after leaving behind a leader heavily dosed with morphine and on the edge of death. (The European war ended about three weeks later.)

58

If left there on the ground for very long, he surely wouldn't have lived. But then his luck returned. A soldier herding a gaggle of seven German prisoners through the now quieter battlefield happened to notice him as he lay huddled there in a half-conscious daze, breathing but paralyzed, his right arm thoroughly mangled. He was severely wounded and a long way from any medical unit. And so it was that he was carried in a litter by Germans (who very nearly drew some friendly fire) to an ambulance center, from which he was taken to a medical aid station. He had been courageous, but what lay ahead of him would require a grittier, more sustained courage than what he had exhibited in the excitement of battle.

After preliminary stays in a Casablanca, Morocco, base hospital and then an army hospital in Florida, he was shipped to a general hospital in Topeka, Kansas, where his mother could be, and was, a constant visitor and where he would spend the next seven months in agonizing, and agonizingly slow, partial recuperation—and where he lost a kidney to an infection caused by expert neglect. (In recompense the Army promoted him to captain.)

Unable to use either hand, he was still helpless when, as 1945 drew to a close, he was shipped, crated as it were in a body cast, to the Percy Jones Army Medical Center in Battle Creek, Michigan, a facility far from home but ostensibly equipped to provide more advanced treatment. For the next 30 months he would battle against the odds to regain control of his bodily movements (his right arm would forever be practically useless, but there was some hope for his left arm and his legs), maintaining his morale with omnivorous reading and exercising his wit and humor with his fellow patients.

He desperately needed special surgery to give him at least some very limited use of his right arm and hand, but the Army, having awarded him two Purple Hearts and a Bronze Star with Clusters, refused to provide it, forcing him to resort to the private sector. A skillful and much more generous surgeon in Chicago agreed to operate without charge, giving him the ability to keep the arm reasonably steady and to hold a pen or roll of paper in the hand. By June 1948 he was in good enough shape to marry his first wife, and by that fall he was enrolled at the University of Arizona, slowly, painfully and stubbornly learning, among other things, how to write notes with his left hand.

Since mid–1945 he had known, of course, that a medical career was no longer a practical possibility, but a legal career looked like a good bet, especially if it could get him into the excitement of politics. That option opened up to him before he graduated. He had moved to Washburg University in Topeka, Kansas, for health reasons, and there he was offered a chance to run as a Republican for the state's House of Representatives. Since the House met only in the mornings and only for three months a year, he was able, by attending afternoon classes as necessary, to earn a B.A. and a law degree from Washburn by 1952.

The law degree made him eligible to run for county attorney, and so he did. (His private practice was never more than an uninspiring sideline.) And he did so again and again, serving in that office through 1960, when he was elected to the U.S. House of Representatives. After four terms there, in 1968 he was elected to the Senate just in time to act as Richard Nixon's exuberantly partisan supporter, lavishly praised by G.O.P. guru and fellow Senator Barry Goldwater as "the first man we've had around here in a long time who will grab the other side by the hair and drag them down the hill." Easily reelected in 1974, he was even more easily elected in 1980 with the experienced, savvy help of his devoted second wife Elizabeth. After 1984, when he became the majority leader, he took his leadership responsibilities most seriously, growing ever more unpredictable ideologically. Although his several efforts to occupy the White House proved a source of perennial frustration, he gained a solid reputation as a politician who could get things done.

CLINT EASTWOOD

In 1953 he was a business-administration student on the GI Bill at Los Angeles City College, but Clint Eastwood, 23, was also checking out various movie studios for casting opportunities. At Universal his six-foot-four ranginess and nicely chiseled features brought him a contract at the bit-player level.

Work at that level—with Francis the Talking Mule, for instance, and in *Revenge of the Creature*—proved alarmingly anesthetizing. Perhaps because he evinced a growing disillusionment with this sort of thespian doldrums, he was fired after a year and a half of what he called "this junk" (on the same day as Burt Reynolds, and by the same functionary). He moved for a while to New York and did a little work on live television, yet the bit-playing there proved no more stimulating. Back he came to Los Angeles, where he became an excavator of swimming-pool sites for more affluent actors. Occasionally he'd be tapped for a role in some inconsequential movie (not so much B as Z, in his opinion).

Although commercial television in the latter 1950s was offering loads of Z material, the most popular shows generally were Westerns, and these often were of better quality. One summer day in 1958, during a visit to a friend at CBS, he was noticed by a network executive who happened to know that a new Western series about cattle drives was in the planning stages and that its producer was looking for someone to play Rowdy Yates, leathery deputy trail boss, in *Rawhide*. After the hurried introductions it seemed clear that he could be Rowdy enough for the part, and he was hired.

After the pilot and the first ten episodes were in the can he had to wait through the rest of 1958 while scheduling problems were laboriously solved, but in December he received a welcome wire informing him that the series would start in January 1959. It did, and continued for another 244 episodes well into 1966. He stuck with it. It provided him with experience, solid pay, some celebrity, and much more security than "all those months without work."

61

His chief misgiving arose from his feeling that his television experience wouldn't be readily transferable to movies, or so cinematic history suggested. After the series petered out, as it surely would some day, would he be just another Hollywood TV has-been?

On the other hand, there were James Garner from TV's *Maverick* and Steven McQueen from TV's *Wanted Dead or Alive*, so such transfers weren't impossible. Still, he wasn't getting any nibbles—until 1964, when James Coburn turned down a role in a foreign spaghetti Western based on a Japanese Samurai film and to be casually shot in Spain on a ludicrously low budget by an Italian, indeed an Italian-speaking, director. Would he like to take over from Coburn, even though his pay of $15,000 would amount to maybe ten, maybe twenty dollars an hour? Sure he would, since this was the only offer on his horizon. Also, the timing was fortunate: the shoot would take four months, and there happened to be a four-month gap in the *Rawhide* schedule. And so it was off to Spain.

He arrived to find director, cast and crew in a state of boisterous disorganization. A few days later he spent some hours, for instance, being heavily made up amid "the sticky heat and the flies and the dust" only to emerge in time to learn that the camera crew had huffily departed and would return only after receiving some pay. Since this was a culmination of "just one foul-up after another ... I'd had it." He announced that he would be found at the airport awaiting a flight home.

Luckily, he was caught at his hotel and persuaded otherwise with promises of reformation. After that "things ran a little smoother." Only a little, but "we got through the film."

The character that he was to play, he discovered from the script, had a great weakness for long-winded garrulity. Taking advantage of the director's inability to understand English, he played the character as mysteriously closed-mouthed, leaving the characteristics and motivations of his avenging stranger more to the audience's intelligent divining. It was a wise decision: the film's title, *A Fistful of Dollars*, could hardly have been more fitting. Throughout Europe the movie appealed to millions, and made millions. Hastily the director, Sergio Leone, hired him to make a couple more movies in the same vein, *For a Few Dollars More* in 1965 and *The Good, the Bad and the Ugly* in 1966, by which time he was being paid a more flattering salary: a quarter of a million and a percentage per picture.

In 1967 the three movies were released in the United States, in a triple punch that brought him burgeoning celebrity. His next picture, courtesy of Malpaso, his own production company, was *Hang 'Em High*, funded by and released in 1968 through United Artists, which recovered its investment in less than three months and went on to enjoy one of its highest grosses ever.

Meanwhile, in January 1968, he flew to England to star with Richard Burton in *Where Eagles Dare*, for which he received equal billing and $750,000. A fistful of dollars indeed.

ELLA FITZGERALD

The year was 1934, deep in the Great Depression, and in the New York city of Yonkers about half of the black population was on relief. Ella Fitzgerald was either 16 or 18, depending on the applicable child labor regulations of the time. She lived there with her stepfather—she never knew her biological father—and her mother, who earned a supplementary living as a cook and laundry manager and who relaxed at home to the music on the radio and in her record collection, usually with her daughter.

It was from her mother that the daughter learned to sing along with performers from Broadway musicals and vocalists with the popular bands. Especially with her favorite, her "first singing teacher," Connee (sic) of the famous Boswell sisters. With money that she earned as a numbers messenger and as a lookout for what she called "a sporting house," she had enough wherewithal for visits to the Apollo Theater in Harlem, where various performers, old and young, amateur and professional, talented and not so talented, displayed their vaudevillian wares to wearily critical audiences who had already seen everything.

It was there that she became entranced by the routine of a dancer named Snakehips Tucker. A lissome lass, energetically nimble, she loved dancing, did a lot of it, and grew very adept at it—"hep" was the operative word at the time. Singing at home was fun, but dancing, there and elsewhere, was what she found really exciting. Her skill was such as to justify her saying later, "Everybody in Yonkers thought I was a good dancer." Even beyond that, "I really wanted to be a dancer, not a singer." For a dreamy while she thought of taking the name of Snakehips Fitzgerald, presumably until someone older filled her in on the proprietary implications.

And so it was that she found herself one day on the stage of the Apollo Theater, which offered regular amateur nights for young, untried performers to do their thing. Hopefuls were asked to write their names, addresses and phone numbers on one of the small cards provided and leave it in a box in the

63

lobby. Those whose cards came up in an ostensibly random drawing would be notified of the date for their nerve-racking performance.

On a bet with a couple of friends she had dropped her card in the box with never a thought of being struck by lightning. Yet lightning does strike, and this time, to her incredulous astonishment, it struck her. She was expected to do a dance number. Her stomach began churning with butterflies, and by the time of the big night the butterflies were in nearly complete control. As she waited in the wings, watching the end of the theater's regular program, she realized that she'd be following the Edwards Sisters, "the dancingest sisters around," as she later described them.

Her "legs turned to water." How could she possibly follow those sisters with an amateur dancing act? When her helpful friends pushed her out onto the stage, she was greeted with a less than friendly but certainly challenging shout from the audience, "What's *she* gonna do?" She froze. Not a muscle was movable. It was time for someone, anyone, to take pity on her, and it was the emcee who did so. Seeing her terror and suspecting that it was the thought of following the Edwards Sisters that held her immobile in its grip, he asked, how about a song instead? He even got the audience to give her some encouragement.

She remembered knowing the lyrics of a Hoagy Carmichael song, "Judy." Did the theater's band have, or know, the music? They did, and so she broke out into song, à la Connee Boswell, less and less nervously with every line. The audience's reaction was so enthusiastic that she had to sing an encore. Was it "Believe It Beloved" or "The Object of My Affection"?—well, it was whichever song was on the flip side of "Judy." More hearty applause. She walked on air out of the theater with her first prize of $25 and glowed all the way home. This was life's "turning point," as she described it later—"I knew I wanted to sing before people the rest of my life."

After an introduction to Fletcher Henderson proved a bust—he myopically just didn't "see much in her," and presumably didn't hear much either—she began entering Harlem's many other amateur contests without lightning-stroke entry requirements. Her phenomenal success in such talent shows finally earned her a professional engagement, a $50 booking for a week with a band at the Harlem Opera House and an honest-to-goodness press notice of her appearance.

Chick Webb's band was scheduled to follow her final performance, and as a result Webb caught her act on her last night. So did Bardu Ali, who led the band while Webb, with his partly paralyzed legs, did his virtuoso thing on the drums. We oughta hire this girl, suggested Ali, but Webb felt he didn't need a girl singer. So Ali brought her backstage and persuaded Webb to hear a few of her songs. Still reluctant, he compromised, offering her a trial run with his band at Yale the next day—if she scored, he'd give her a job.

She did, and he did. The job paid $12.50 a week, and shortly thereafter, when the band was hired for an indefinite engagement at the Savoy Ballroom, she received a raise to $15 a week. Ahead of her was a long life full of performances with symphony orchestras as well as with notable bands like those of Count Basie, Louis Armstrong and Duke Ellington, more than 200 recordings (a dozen of them Grammy winners), and the honor of being named by *Down Beat* as female singer of the year 21 times, including the unheard-of 18 times between 1953 and 1970.

It would indeed all be enough to make a dancer say, "I love to sing."

HENRY FONDA

In the fall of 1933 Henry Fonda at 28 was still in a state of depression brought on by his boisterous divorce from the fiery Margaret Sullavan, especially since her theatrical success contrasted sharply with his current career of supernumerary stage business. In December he and his buddy Jimmy Stewart had a brief revival of spirits when both were offered small roles in a Broadway play which, however, opened just before Christmas and closed just after New Year's Day 1934.

The theater managers held a wake in the form of a closing-night party that lasted well into the early morning. On their way home to the hovelish accommodations they were sharing during this low tide in their thespian affairs, Fonda stopped in the middle of Times Square and proposed that Stewart, who had his accordion with him and knew how to finger it if not to play it, discover whether he could attract an audience. Sure enough, the ensuing recital attracted an audience—out of curiosity, sympathy or grinning appreciation—and "the next thing I saw," Stewart reported later, "was Fonda passing the hat." Their take, depending on which of them you believe, ranged from twelve to thirty-six cents.

The performance ended abruptly, however, when an irate policeman expressed his opinion with a nightstick on Stewart's backside. "He said, 'It's taken me three or four hours to get all these people asleep in those doorways, and you come along and start that noise!'" Stewart was offended by the musical critique: "I've always thought he could have used a kinder word."

A few months later Fonda was mentioned by a friend to the impresario Leonard Sillman, then mounting a revue in New York, as "an actor who needs a job." Sillman agreed to an interview, at which he asked the still fairly young man if he could sing. "No," the fellow answered. "Do you dance?" Again, "No." Impatiently, Sillman asked, what *could* he do? The answer was that he did "imitations of babies from one week to one year." (He had done a lot of this at parties, usually without much urging.) Skeptically, Sillman suggested he give it a try, and so Fonda launched into a routine pantomiming a man driving a car while at the same time trying to change a diaper. Sillman, after recovering from a laughing fit, hired him to do his thing in the revue and promised that he'd have him singing and dancing soon as well.

Trouble was, Sillman didn't have any money. When he called affluent acquaintances with an offer to get in on a real good thing, he was asked who was playing in the revue and his answer, bereft of a single celebrated name like Astaire or Crosby, was greeted with a thanks anyway. But after he got the idea of calling the real good thing *New Faces* (ultimately *New Faces of 1934*, for it would start a trend), the money began to roll, or at least dribble, in. Although he couldn't accumulate enough to pay for heat in the theater during rehearsals, the cast made do with winter wear. Imogene Coca huddled in a camel's hair coat capacious enough for her *and* the camel—or for her and Fonda, an arrangement with the "adorable little clown" that he would (and may) have hugely enjoyed. She and he both received good notices, and he at least had reason for feeling "discovered," especially now that he was making a stupefying hundred bucks a week.

The discovery was real enough for him to be offered the part of leading man in a summer-theater production of *Coquette*, opposite none other than Margaret Sullavan. Although he shared only frost with her offstage, he managed the love scenes onstage with enough warmth to impress a particular someone in the audience, the drama agent Leland Hayward, who looked him up after the curtain and offered to sign him up for Hollywood. He was sure that he could get him a contract.

Nope, Fonda replied, protesting that he wasn't about to leave the theater for that celluloid route. He shrugged as Hayward shrugged and left for Hollywood. About a week later he had a wire from Hollywood, from Hayward explaining in three pages of laborious detail all the glories of a movie career. Again, *no*. Next came a phone call—come on out here at my expense, see some things and meet some people, and then see how eager you'll be to stick with your stupid theater! I'm sending you a plane ticket and will meet you at the airport. And that's just what he did.

He went further than that of course. He introduced Fonda to producer Walter Wanger of later fame, insisting, "Walter, you'd better sign this kid because he's going places." After some more sweet talk along this line, Fonda unexpectedly found himself shaking hands on a deal that would permit him to act on the stage *and* make movies—two in 1935 for starters. At $1,000 a week! After leaving Wanger's office, all he could ask Hayward was whether that handshake was really binding.

He returned to the New York stage and did very well in *The Farmer Takes a Wife*. By March 1935 he was again in Hollywood, where a film version of the play was about to go into production. After Gary Cooper and Joel McCrae both turned down offers to play his role, the producers courageously decided that maybe they ought to give him a try. So they rented him from Wanger for $5,000 a week, of which Wanger gave him $2,000. So this was Hollywood.

For the rest of his life he did indeed continue to do theater work, successfully, but it was movies which of course made his name a word in households worldwide. His movie credits occupy all of one of the fine-print columns in Leonard Maltin's *Movie & Video Guide*, ending of course with *On Golden Pond*, which his formerly estranged daughter co-produced so that he could finally win the Academy Award that he so richly deserved.

JANE FONDA

In the summer of 1958 Jane Fonda, at 20, was living in a Malibu beach house next door to the Strasbergs. She and Susan soon became good friends, being about the same age and both daughters of all-too-famous fathers. To Susan, Jane confided her feelings of aimlessness, her uneasiness that she had done many things to no purpose. She was at loose ends, to coin a phrase yet to be hallowed by Merriam-Webster.

She had never wanted to play theatrical heir or copycat to her father Henry. Although as his teenaged daughter she had been pressured by teachers and classmates into a few roles in high-school plays, these experiences had done nothing to interest her in a career on stage and screen. On the contrary, by her 16th birthday she had decided that she would study ballet or art at Vassar College. During the summer after her first year there she did agree to appear with her father in an Omaha production of *The Country Girl*, in one scene of which she "entered weeping"—a strenuously challenging bit of acting that she handled with an aplomb that left her father marveling. The next summer found her on the stage with her father again, in Cape Cod, yet still indifferent to acting as a career.

Since her studies at Vassar seemed to have little meaning for her, she asked to continue her study of art in Paris, a request that her father, a successful artist among other things, was happy to grant. At L'École de la Chauviere, however, she still seemed at those loose ends. At Vassar she had launched on a program of persistent partying, and Paris and its cavaliers provided an ideal milieu for continued indulgence of her more frolicsome instincts. (In her defense it should be added that she could speak and understand French, but not at the furious pace of her art instructors.) Evidently on to her, Henry brought her back and enrolled her in the Art Students League.

This had little effect. She seemed to do more studying in the dilettante mode, blending languages, music, and even modeling with irrepressible partying. At about this point 1958 arrived, and Malibu, and Susan Strasberg, whose response to her friend's uneasy murmuring about lack of purpose was to suggest acting. After all, Susan's father Lee was also father of Method acting and a celebrated drama coach. Maybe a visit with him wouldn't hurt anything.

It certainly didn't. Lee Strasberg said later that "there was such panic in her eyes" that he couldn't turn her away or not give her the best, most solicitous advice in his power. Their conversation was long and intense. She had talent, he insisted, lots of talent, and she should put it to good use. It was the first time, by her account, that anyone had ever told her that she "was good at anything." (Her father was of the laconic persuasion, whether because or in spite of his profession.) The visit "absolutely changed my life." Or as Brooke Hayward, a lifelong friend, put it, she had given not a sign "that she would ever become an actress. Suddenly there it was—her life."

And so she joined Strasberg's famed Actors Studio, although her father's reluctance to utterly lose himself in a role made him thoroughly hostile to Method acting. Perhaps in a declaration of independence, she returned to modeling, but this time to professional modeling, with a sensual vengeance that easily earned her tuition wherewithal. At the Studio she was subjected to much communal soul-searching and seemed to thrive on it. Strasberg, who was unlikely to have been impressed by her genealogy, apparently showed enough special interest in her ability to arouse some envy among other newcomers.

After about a year at the Studio, she received a call from Hollywood, from Joshua Logan, an old friend of her distantly doting father. After a screen test Logan offered her the customary seven-year contract, and she accepted. Her first role, in a cutesy movie *Tall Story*, was that of a cheerleader drooling over basketball crackerjack Tony Perkins. It wasn't something that she'd look back on with unalloyed pride. About the best that she got from the few critics who noticed her was condescension.

Although her performance in an unsuccessful play about a young rape victim was greeted with critical enthusiasm, her uptight resistance to her uptight father and her fear of inheriting her mother's suicidal bent kept her in a state of emotional suspense, eased only partially through a succession of liaisons and analysts, and in frequent returns to more professional distractions at the Actors Studio. Her personal turmoil received plenty of tabloid-type media coverage, which she encouraged enough to thoroughly alienate her reserved father ("Daughter? I don't have a daughter!") After doing a couple more forgettable movies and a catastrophic play that critic Walter Kerr greeted as one of the five worst plays of all time, she fled to France.

There she proved saucily and tirelessly sexy enough, cinematically and otherwise, to garner not only a reputation as another Brigitte Bardot but also Bardot's husband, director Roger Vadim. During the next five years she provided Vadim with film histrionics and domestic tranquility. In 1968 she not only gave him a daughter but even turned down offers for the leading roles in *Bonnie and Clyde* and *Rosemary's Baby* to take the title role in his *Barbarella*. Although that film had a sophisticated tongue-in-cheek flavor, its reliance on nudity and titillating eroticism smacked of sexual exploitation. Her growing acquaintance with the political views and activities of women like Joan Baez and Vanessa Redgrave, as well as some encounters with Far Eastern mysticism and the psychoanalytical transcendentalism of Herman Hesse's *Steppenwolf*, had swayed her to a viewpoint resulting in considerable feminist resentment. After some solemn consideration of a contemplated film about sibling incest starring her with her brother Peter, she and Vadim parted company.

There had already been one turning point in her life, at the Actors Studio, but fate, abetted by her own personality, had a couple more in store for her. This was one, resulting in her taking more serious roles, and taking her roles more seriously, in more serious movies. For her performances in *They Shoot Horses, Don't They?* (1969), with its cynical dance-marathon view of life, and in the detective thriller *Klute* (1971) she won an Oscar nomination and an Oscar, respectively. She also indulged in a great deal of high-profile political activism in support of African-American and Native American causes and especially in opposition to the bloody idiocy in Vietnam. Soon her movie career entered a period of doldrums until Watergate and the withdrawal from Vietnam permitted her another turning point, when she returned to the silver screen, embarking on a period in which she not only got to appear with her valued friend and fellow rebel Vanessa Redgrave (*Julia*), but even became one of Hollywood's most profitable stars. Besides maintaining her political conscience with the help of her husband Tom Hayden, she became a health-conscious best-selling author of "workout books."

And then there was the touching reunion, a turning point in its own way, in 1981's *On Golden Pond*, which brought her father his first best-actor Oscar— just as co-producer Jane Fonda had expected.

CLARK GABLE

As summer was ending in 1917 the 16-year-old Clark Gable skipped his last year in high school and left the farm for Akron, Ohio, 60 miles away. He had been asked by a buddy to join in the trip to the big city, where they could expect to find plenty of war-stimulated jobs and where Clark could finish that last year before enrolling at the University's medical school. He was eager to escape from the farm and was able to do so, despite his father's stern objections, only because of his mother's intervention. "If it hadn't been for her," he later reminisced, "I'd probably still be farming in Ohio."

In Akron he quickly got a job as timekeeper in a tire plant and not long thereafter signed up at a nearby night school. But then, during a fateful dinner at a neighborhood cafe, he met a couple of actors who fascinated him with their unfamiliar theater talk. After seeing them in a play, his first such experience, he was hooked—so inextricably that he quit his job and the night school for an unpaid job as callboy at the theater. With tips earned by running errands and doing other extra odd jobs, he managed to continue eating. Showering at the local YMCA during the day, he worked evenings and slept nights at the theater.

He was being given a bit part now and then when his mother died and his father, who had sold the farm and was now drilling oil in Oklahoma, demanded that he give up this foolishness and join him in man's work. Not a chance. The son was set on going to New York, where he could try his luck on that fabulous Broadway.

Thousands of highly capable young actors were already there. The best work he could get, after a period of odd-jobbing, was as callboy for a Broadway play. After a couple of hundred performances the play closed, and he found his situation so desperate that he decided to take that fatherly advice after all. This eventually proved to be a lucky decision, for the hard physical work in the oil fields gave him the broad-shouldered, muscular, athletic look that would later become something of a trademark.

That physique proved valuable also only a year later, when he quit the oil business to join a traveling repertory company in Kansas City as a utility man for $10 a week and a promise of at least occasional bit parts. Hired, as he later put it, "for my muscles," he not only helped put up the tent at site after site but also handled props, played whatever he could in the orchestra, and generally made himself useful—onstage too, in those occasional bit parts.

With 1922's harsh winter forcing a disastrous drop in receipts, the company had to disband on reaching Butte, Montana. Hopping a westbound freight train, he made it to Bend, Oregon. There, wary of being arrested for vagrancy, he applied for a job at the nearest office of a lumber company, was hired, and spent the next dozen weeks cross-sawing lumber, with a power-house Swede, on the other end of the saw, competitively providing him with muscle-building exercise.

On to Portland, where he made connections with an amateur theater group and traveled with it through Oregon. He played several minor roles, including one in blackface as a cook and another dressed in ill-fitting baby clothes and ensconced in an enormous crib. When this troupe also folded, he took whatever work he could find, as a lumberjack, auto parts salesman, classified-ad solicitor, telephone lineman. It was as a lineman that he encountered Portland's new Little Theater, where, after repairing the phone line, he watched the director, Josephine Dillon, as she worked with the actors.

And it was she who, as a drama coach 12 years his senior, spent the next year or so improving his voice, his speech, his breathing, his deportment, his timing, his stage presence, and even his health by persuading him to give up his lineman's work and getting him a job on a farm for the summer. After leaving Portland for Los Angeles for better drama-coaching opportunities, she wrote him, urging him to come to L.A. for some practical experience in acting as preparation for an assault on Broadway. He did, and they were married in December 1924.

The marriage lasted only about four years, with her on the West Coast and him playing whatever roles he could stir up in Houston and then in New York. Although she had urged him to return to California, he was convinced that his career, if any to speak of, would be on the Broadway stage, certainly not in those silent things called movies.

He played in a few minor roles, but the work was unreliable. He spent late 1929 and early 1930 mostly in balconies watching others do their thing. ("All that winter I was on the outside looking in.") That spring, however, he was in a leading role and attracted the notice of a couple of producers who thought he'd be just right for the role of Killer Mears in their projected West Coast production of *The Last Mile* (a role then being filled, definitively, in New York by Spencer Tracy). He'd be making $300 a week!

His performance brought him a screen test. Although sound had arrived, rendering Josephine Dillon's voice and speech coaching more valuable than ever, Jack Warner reportedly reacted to the test with a rather discouraging question, "What can you do with ears like that?" The distaff element in his life reentered in the form of two women, an agent name Ruth Collier and his second-wife-to-be, Ria Langham. Under their influence, although nothing would ever be done about his ears (that tape would soon prove an intolerable nuisance), he had his teeth capped and his wardrobe refashioned. With the help of Lionel Barrymore, who had known him on the L.A. stage, he had a second test, which brought him a short-term contract with MGM.

After half a dozen generally unremarkable performances, in 1931 he appeared opposite Norma Shearer in *A Free Soul*, in which among other things he slapped her (with her concurrence) good and hard. After the picture's release he abruptly became sensational. He bought himself a sporty Deuesenberg—second-hand, but still a Deuesenberg. That sort of behavior is called arriving.

Three years later he would appear with Claudette Colbert in their Oscar-winning performances in the Oscar-winning movie *It Happened One Night*. Even though he didn't want to.

BILL GATES

In January 1975 Bill Gates at 19 was a sophomore at Harvard, ruefully headed for a law degree—ruefully because he regretted having made a tentative promise to his parents that he'd take up law as a career. His talent, indeed his prodigious talent, was in mathematics, which they rather disdained as an interesting hobby but hardly suitable for a respectable career. Bored with the curriculum, he indulged his addiction to math with plenty of poker, although this didn't keep him from moping a great deal in his room while "being a philosophical, depressed guy, trying to figure out what I was doing with my life."

What he'd be doing would have little to do with the law and everything with mathematics. That January was the month in which *Popular Electronics* announced, with journalistic fervor, the introduction of the Altair 8800, which promised to be the first commercially marketable personal computer. Designed and built by a small Albuquerque company called MITS (formally, for Micro Instrumentation and Telemetry Systems), the new microcomputer was described fervidly enough to generate a totally unexpected avalanche of orders (on forms provided) for the basic kit of components furnished for infinitely patient assembly, all for only $397.

Ed Roberts, the founder of MITS, although elated by the stupefying response, was well aware that his microcomputer was an awkward bundle of complexities. Entering programs required operation of myriad toggle switches on the front panel—with precise accuracy, to avoid having to start all over again. Although the Altair was nevertheless selling briskly, he knew he'd have to have a simple computer language for it to appeal to a much wider market.

Enter Bill Gates with his high school friend (and fellow math addict) Paul Allen, whose reaction to seeing the magazine article was to relay to Gates the wondrous news that the age of the personal computer had surely arrived— and they'd better get in on it now or be left behind. In a trice Gates agreed. Good-by Harvard Law, hello Harvard Computer Center.

At the Center the two young men decided that the language the Altair needed was BASIC (formally, Beginner's All-purpose Symbolic Instruction Code), especially since that was the one they were familiar with from their feverish work together in, and out of, high school. They'd have to rework it for the Altair, of course, particularly for its Intel 8080 chip, which was its vital component and with which they weren't familiar. Despite these uncertainties, they phoned Roberts and asked coyly if he'd be interested. Warily, he said yes.

Indeed, in a second, friendlier phone call he invited them to Albuquerque for a demonstration of their BASIC's applicability to the Altair. Gates asked nervously how soon they'd be expected—nervously, since they were so far from completion. How about right away? Gulping, Gates replied that they could probably make it in three weeks or less—some final polishing, you know how it is. Over the next four weeks, not three, he worked an almost sleepless schedule, doing the math in his room at Harvard, checking it out in the computer lab. News that others elsewhere also were working to adapt BASIC to the Altair did nothing to ease the tension.

In February an exhausted Gates saw Allen off on a plane to Albuquerque for the critical demonstration. Despite his exhaustion, he was kept awake by needling uncertainties. Was the simulator that Allen had devised to resemble the unfamiliar Intel 8080 chip sufficiently accurate? Did he really think that he himself could design a BASIC program for a computer he'd never seen?

Whatever he really thought, he'd done just that. At the demonstration Allen methodically loaded the Altair's memory with data, his eye anxiously on the Teletype machine connected to it for readable output. Time passed with agonizing deliberation, and then, quite abruptly, the word READY appeared on the Teletype to announce that the Altair was impatiently waiting to take a program written in Gates' BASIC. The phone call announcing their success filled Gates with as much astonishment as joy. Given the overwhelming likelihood of a misreading, a miscalculation, an oversight here, there and anywhere, as a practiced poker player he could hardly believe he'd come up with this royal flush.

His exhilaration didn't prevent him from recognizing that there was still work to be done, refining the language for business applications, as in accounting and statistics. As a result of his modifications, it would be the dominant item in the market for microcomputers until the early 1980s.

In July he formed a partnership with Allen in Albuquerque for the development of microcomputer software. This was the origin of the Microsoft empire. They hadn't been left behind.

George Gershwin

In the fall of 1923 George Gershwin at 25 was doing something he liked to do. One day years earlier, in a music store where he worked, a fellow song-plugger found him assiduously practicing Bach's *Well-Tempered Clavier* during a break. He was impressed—"I see you're studying to be a concert pianist." "No," Gershwin replied,"I'm studying to be a great popular song composer."

By 1923 he was getting to be good at least, if not great. He had quite a few popular songs to his credit, as well as some scores for musical comedies. His tunes, however, had unfulfilling titles like "Do It Again" and "Tee-Ooo-dle-Um-Bum-Bo," and he was aching to do something toward lifting popular melodies to the level of "serious music." Financially he was free to do so, since his song writing gave him an income and Al Jolson's singing of his "Swanee" in 1919 had brought him a small fortune.

It hadn't, of course, also brought him a reputation as a composer of serious music. His one effort in that respect, the almost operatic score for a black-face sketch in George White's *Scandals of 1922* (with Paul Whiteman and his orchestra), had so depressed the audience that White canceled it after its first night. Its critical reception did little to relieve Gershwin's disappointment. It was, one ruffled reviewer wrote, "the most dismal, stupid and incredible blackface sketch that has ever been perpetrated."

Yet in preparing for it he had worked quite a bit with Paul Whiteman, the loosely entitled "King of Jazz" who shared Gershwin's ambition to lift popular music into the exalted domain of critical respectability. He was in a much better position to fulfill it. Then at the height of his popularity and influence, he celebrated the success of the 1922 *Scandals* by taking his orchestra, and his wife, to London for presentation to admiring British royalty—whose admiration included the Prince of Wales' briefly performing with the orchestra as a drummer. (He performed admirably.)

Whiteman had already announced his intention to offer New York audiences an "Experiment in Modern Music" designed to introduce them to "the development of our emotional resources which have led us to the character-istic American music of today"—whatever that might mean, for he was a tal-ented promoter who knew the value of imprecision in publicity campaigns. He also learned of a hazard in publicity when rumors reached him that another band leader had heard of the ambitious project and was planning to get in there ahead of him. To forestall any such competitive shenanigan, he rashly set a date for his Experiment of February 24, 1924, then just 24 days away, in New York's Aeolian Hall. (Carnegie Hall was booked solid.)

His earlier tentative, amorphous discussions with Gershwin on the sub-ject had already taken on much greater urgency and specificity. After, that is, the young composer learned of the Experimental commitment in early Jan-uary, when his brother Ira came across a newspaper announcement. He called Whiteman, who suggested that he might whip up a concerto for piano and orchestra employing modern musical themes—within the next few weeks. Not a chance, retorted Gershwin, not enough time. Whiteman persisted. Well, conceded Gershwin, there might be time enough for something less formal, less precisely constructed, like maybe a fantasia or a rhapsody. Fine, said Whiteman, go to it.

And so he did. His *American Rhapsody* was composed during the next few weeks and then retitled. Ira had visited an exhibition of Whistler's paintings, and, impressed by the provocative titles, such as *Nocturne in Black and Gold* and *Arrangement in Gray and Black* ("Whistler's Mother"), had come home with *Rhapsody in Blue*. Next came weeks of rehearsing and polishing (with a bit of polish supplied by Victor Herbert, incidentally) until the now almost dreaded afternoon arrived.

The concert, a critic remarked later, involved "a certain amount of hokum." An introductory speaker explained that the Experiment was intended to illus-trate "the tremendous strides which have been made in popular music from the day of discordant jazz, which sprang into existence about ten years ago, from nowhere in particular, to the really melodious music of today, which, for no good reason, is still called jazz." So much for imprecision in musical history.

The concert opened with an early bit of jazz, "Livery Stable Blues." It offered some lively fun, but then the concert began to drone away in all-too-familiar dance band music and even light opera entries by composers like Vic-tor Herbert and Rudolf Friml. Toward the end of the second half, the audience was doing some of its own droning. For the final piece Gershwin walked onstage, sat at the piano, motioned to Whiteman, and woke them up.

How? As Milton Cross has described it, the Rhapsody "opens with a low trill in the clarinet, the base of an ascending scale which, when reaching the uppermost note, erupts into the first theme of the work. It is a kind of head-strong, irresponsible tune; perhaps nowhere has a decade notorious for its aban-don and license found a more fitting expression." The audience, including those not addicted to abandon and license, exhibited their reinvigoration at the end with "tumultuous applause" and "wild and even frantic" appreciation during five curtain calls.

He would never write anything more popular or historically significant. Nor would he have to.

NEWT GINGRICH

At Eastertime in 1958 Newt Gingrich, then a lad of 14, was taken by his father and a friend, a fellow army officer, for a weekend visit to the Verdun battlefield. There, he was told, three quarters of a million men had been killed or wounded. A visit to the Ossuary, with its glass-enclosed basement holding the bones of perhaps a sixth of those casualties, provided a realistic testimonial to human inhumanity. On their way through the town the boy remarked on the damage to the houses from World War II only to be informed that much of it was damage from World War I.

Until that time he had expected to have a career involving animals—zoologist, perhaps, or paleontologist. "After that weekend, my ambitions changed." That summer, during a gardening job that allowed him opportunities for uninhibited cerebration, he concluded that he would have to dedicate himself to sharing in the protection of the American way against the "mortal threat from the Soviet empire." First he would have to understand what such protection entailed, and to this end he focused his reading on history and politics. One thing he learned quickly was that such a course of study would be a difficult one, but he remained undaunted. Not even Arnold Toynbee's *A Study of History* fazed him, nor did its fictional supplement, Isaac Asimov's Foundation trilogy. From Toynbee he especially drew the notion of the impermanence of civilizations, indeed their frailty—e.g., the Aztecs, the Incas, even the Romans. American civilization in our time faces lethal challenges and must remain true to its fundamental values if it is to survive for very long. Of course everyone knows what those fundamental values are.

In contrast to this academic experience, he had his first taste of the nitty-gritty of politics in the 1960 Presidential campaign, working in Georgia for the Nixon-Lodge ticket. Despite his efforts, since the Georgian electoral system was weighted heavily in favor of rural sections and was overwhelmingly Democratic, the state gave John F. Kennedy a larger margin of victory than his own Massachusetts. (Although the state was also implacably segregationist, Gingrich's experience as an army brat in a desegregated service had kept him free of that particular prejudice.)

That practical experience was enough to turn anyone from political to academic activity. After graduating from Atlanta's Emory University in 1961, he earned a master's degree and then a doctorate in modern European history in 1971. This led to his appointment as an assistant professor of history at West Georgia College in Carrollton, Georgia, where his bull sessions stimulated students and his ebullient self-confidence alienated some faculty members (those who felt, for instance, that his applying for the chair of the history department during his first year was a bit premature).

Soon his dormant ambition reasserted itself as he began talking about entering politics—indeed, running for the United States Congress and, he assured eager listeners, becoming Speaker of the House. In 1974 and again in 1976 he ran against the Democratic incumbent in Georgia's Sixth Congressional District. Although he lost both times, the losses were narrow enough to encourage persistence, and in 1978, after the incumbent announced his retirement, he ran yet again, on a platform of opposition to the Panama Canal Treaty and in favor of lower taxes (the latter putting him right in line with the Republican predilection, soon to be painfully obvious in the 1980s, for borrowing instead of taxing). This time he won, as he has done regularly ever since, narrowly on occasion but handily since 1992, when his district boundaries were changed, making it whiter and more conservative.

His boyhood turn to politics is obviously a source of great satisfaction to him. After his successful, career-terminating attack on Speaker Jim Wright in the late 1980s brought him welcome political prominence, he was narrowly elected Republican Whip in 1989. Five years later, with Republicans in control of the House, he not only was elected Speaker but soon was being compared with famous predecessors like Joe Cannon and Sam Rayburn.

And his leadership in the House, with its adroit use of the Speaker's prerogatives to maintain proper discipline among inadequately oriented members, kept that chamber so persistently aboil that a senator with experience in the House once complained that serving in the senate by contrast was like watching paint dry.

Time magazine named Gingrich their "Man of the Year" in 1995; he next served as chairman of the 1996 Republican National Convention. Political peaks often are followed by valleys. As Gingrich said: "We were to learn the hard way that there was a difference between having a Republican majority and having a conservative majority." With a poor showing for the Republicans in the 1998 midterm elections, Gingrich announced his resignation from Congress in January 1999. As Gingrich continues his personal growth, his presence will still be felt in the Republican Party.

WHOOPI GOLDBERG

In the spring of 1974 the 24-year-old Whoopi Goldberg (nee Karen Johnson—later "Whoopi" in token of chronic flatulence, "Goldberg" in honor of a twig on the putative family tree)—Whoopi Goldberg had already done a lot of living, much of it dangerously, much of it ruefully. Although her mother had brought her up conscientiously, and although she spent most of her childhood in a similarly conscientious New York community center for children where her mother worked, at 14 she began using, or abusing, alcohol and drugs because of her failure in high school. There, despite her high level of intelligence, she was tagged as "retarded." It wasn't until much later that her problem was discovered to be dyslexia.

She quit school and took to hanging out in Central Park with fellow addicts until, at 17, she entered a rehabilitation program and broke the habit, or habits. At 18 she married her counselor and at 19 she gave birth to her daughter Alexandrea. By the time she was 20 she was divorced, a single mother unable to support her child. On welfare, of course.

She lived a life largely of rueful perseverance until one day in 1974. A friend who had a couple of airline tickets, and who unexpectedly couldn't use them, offered them to her. Too excited to realize that she didn't have money enough for a return trip, she wound up with her daughter in San Diego, where, to her surprise, she found some work acting. ("I knew before I was born," she has said somewhat mystically, "that I wanted to act.") She appeared in two or three plays produced by the San Diego Repertory Theater and joined a troupe alarmingly called Spontaneous Combustion.

To support herself and her child she took on whatever work was available—laying brick, for instance, and, after graduation from a beauty college, prettifying bodies in a mortuary. (Although she was never quite sure how well she was doing as a terminal beautician, the customers didn't complain.) Yet none of the work, besides being far from career-oriented, yielded a livelihood. So she reluctantly returned to welfare and started looking, hard, for thespian roles. She found something of the sort as half of a comic duo performing in San Diego and environs. When her partner quit just before an offer arrived unexpectedly for a booking in San Francisco, she flew there alone (with Alexandrea) and learned, to her great delight, that she could vastly entertain an audience all by herself.

The success of her solo "Spook Show" in the Bay Area inspired her to take it on tour in the United States and even, briefly, across the Atlantic. She was a professional now, with an income from her gigs, although there wasn't a lot left over after expenses. It was enough, nevertheless, to take her off welfare. As she had expected, she found that it was a wonderful thing to "give a welfare check back."

In her show she dealt, comically but pointedly, with situations like her daughter's yearning to be a white television celebrity and with characters like the light-fingered drug addict with a Ph.D. in literature that qualified him to "stand in this unemployment line" and meditate on a crazy world. By 1983 the show had become well enough known that she received an invitation to include it in an off–Broadway production being planned by Manhattan's Dance Theater Workshop. Accepting with nervous alacrity, she joined the workshop for its 1983-84 season. Her audiences were captivated and so, by and large, were the show-me tribe of New York critics, welcoming her with phrases like "incredibly accurate portrayals" and lauding her ability to evoke tears of both laughter and compassion.

Some of those tears were Mike Nichols', or so he told her backstage after one of her performances early in 1984. The noted comedian of Elaine May fame and the Hollywood director-producer (*Who's Afraid of Virginia Woolf?* and *The Graduate* in the late 1960s and of *Silkwood* just the year before) was reminded of Elaine May but also of Ruth Draper, Groucho Marx and Richard Pryor, as well as of perhaps five others, unidentifiable. He'd like to set her up in a one-woman show on Broadway—would she be interested? Would she ever! This brought tears to *her* eyes.

October 1984. Broadway's Lyceum Theater. "The Spook Show," somewhat expanded and now formally and flatteringly entitled *Whoopi Goldberg*. Enthusiastic audiences, rave reviews. As usual, not unanimous praise, but even the dyspeptic John Simon tempered his *New York* diatribe with approval of her timing, her telling glances and her "real skill with accents." Not long thereafter the show was filmed for television, becoming an HBO special, *Whoopi Goldberg: Direct from Broadway*.

Once again a Hollywood producer-director, impressed with her talent, came forward with an offer. Steven Spielberg of *E.T.* fame needed someone to play Celie in his film adaptation of the Alice Walker novel, *The Color Purple*. Would she audition? She auditioned. This would be the first of more than a score of movie roles, permitting her to do what she'd always wanted to do, and profitably yet—acting.

CARY GRANT

By the fall of 1932 Archie Leach at 28 had changed his name to Cary Grant and was well along in his first year in Hollywood, a very busy year. He'd already acted in six movies and was now paired with Sylvia Sidney in *Madame Butterfly*. This marked his appearance so far in seven movies—maybe not quite turkeys or bombs or dogs, but let's say duds. Critiquewise and box-officewise, to put it in technical terms.

He'd been in show biz for 18 years, ever since he achieved expulsion from school by deliberate malingering and habitual unruliness so that, upon ejection, he could join a traveling vaudeville troupe as a clown and acrobat. Show biz, satisfying his appetite for nonacademic excitement, became his life. Excitement he had indeed, touring with the troupe not only throughout his native England but also in important cities in Europe, Russia, the Mideast and even China.

And in the United States, where he fell in love with New York, baseball, ice-cream sodas, and Sunday movies (then a no-no in England). When the troupe, having exhausted its American bookings, returned to England, he stayed in his now adopted country in a haze of wistful optimism. Optimism proved inadequate. Soon he was in advertising, arrayed in a spectacular costume with interminable trousers, perilously pacing up and down Coney Island's boardwalk on stilts while hawking the delights of an amusement park.

Any danger of this becoming a lifetime career ended when he was offered a small role in a variety show opening at the Hippodrome on Labor Day 1922—although he did do some stilt-walking in one of the skits. For the first time his name was individually listed in a program, though not mentioned in any review. After the show closed he toured America with a succession of troupes, doing vaudeville acts and taking occasional roles in a protracted series of cities, towns and hamlets. When in New York he shared digs with a friend, a talent agent with good connections who at one point urged Sam Goldwyn to get his pal's signature on a contract. Goldwyn shrugged him off.

With the thespian market on the wane, the discouraged hopeful went back into stilted advertising, this time for various stores and eateries, until he could afford a crestfallen return to England. There he toured the sticks with a theatrical group, learning his craft the hard way. By 1927 he felt professional enough to take another flyer on America.

His first year or so in New York brought him enough work for eatin' money but little else. In January 1929 he snagged a major role in a musical stereophonically entitled *Boom Boom*. Although his leading lady was the rapturously warbling Jeanette MacDonald, the show flopped. Hollywood, however, muddling through its transition from silent to talking pictures, was desperately searching for recordable voices. Both of the *Boom Boom* leads were auditioned. Before long Ernst Lubitsch signed her up to appear in *The Love Parade* with Maurice Chevalier. She took off for the West Coast. He stayed behind.

Not that he was doing so badly in the East. He was earning enough, for instance, to buy a fancy Packard motorcar and to patronize good restaurants, despite a growing feeling that he really didn't have much marketable talent. His period of relative affluence came to an end by late 1931 after the Great Depression closed almost half of the theaters on Broadway. His last role on that street was in a show with Fay Wray, who had worked in Hollywood and who would do so again, as King Kong's Dulcinea. One day, as the show was approaching its day of final reckoning, he happened to ask her if she had any job leads for him—like maybe in bricklaying? She had none but suggested that he try Hollywood. He summarily dismissed the idea, having himself been dismissed by Goldwyn because of his peculiar gait and Cockney accent.

Nevertheless, by late November of that year he and a showbiz buddy desperately decided to give Tinseltown a whirl. He still had his Packard, and they could share the costs of gas and lodging. That they did. Immediately after their arrival the two of them went to the Paramount studios, where his buddy thought he had a lead. The buddy was interviewed and rejected but was asked about his handsome companion—who was thereupon given a screen test and a contract. That at least is the most likely story.

First things first—something had to be done about that unimposing moniker. A random exploration of the phone book eventually produced the name of Cary Grant, which satisfied everyone concerned. Not only did it have a catchy ring to it, but it also juggled the initials of the current matinee idols Gary Cooper and Clark Gable. A sign from heaven if ever there was one.

He was then launched into his preliminary career of seven forgettable films. The most likely story of his turning point, somewhat embellished no doubt, is that the reigning comedy queen Mae West happened to see him glamorously arrayed in his Lieutenant Pinkerton uniform and eagerly asked who was *that*? Told that he was Cary Grant, then making *Madame Butterfly*, she murmured imperiously, "I don't care if he's making Little Nell. If he can talk, I'll take him." He could talk, so she did.

His eighth movie, *She Done Him Wrong*, was a resounding success, favorably reviewed in general and gratifyingly lucrative in particular. Whatever her role in getting his career into high gear, he later credited her with teaching him "almost everything" about working in films. After all, in that movie, after inviting him to come up and see her sometime, she'd add, "Come up. I'll tell your fortune."

KATHARINE HEPBURN

In 1938, soon after the release of *Bringing Up Baby*, a Hollywood trade paper published a gratuitous list, in the form of an ad from the disgruntled Independent Theater Owners of America, of movie stars it branded as "box-office poison." Heading the list was the name of Katharine Hepburn, who at the age of 30 had been making movies for the past six years. Fourteen of them, in fact, including *Baby*.

Things had been going quite well for her through 1935's film version of the Tarkington novel, *Alice Adams*, which had been well received by press and public. This was followed that year by *Sylvia Scarlett*, which may be presentable today in videocassette form but which then had people leaving sneak previews early, in dismay. RKO circumspectly held off releasing it until January 1936, only to lose about a quarter of a million dollars at the box office.

Although she had appeared in a money-maker in 1937, *Stage Door*, she had to share credit with highly competitive scene-stealers like Ginger Rogers, Lucille Ball and Ann Miller. *Holiday*, released in 1938 and today considered a perennial classic, met with a rather frosty welcome from Depression-era audiences, who may not have had the expected quota of sympathy for the movie's conspicuously idle rich. It barely broke even.

When RKO informed her that her next movie would be *Mother Carey's Chickens*, with a script no more promising than the title, she hastily offered to buy her way out of the rest of her contract, and the studio evidently was only too happy to accept the offer. At this low point in her career it was especially galling that the part of Scarlett O'Hara in *Gone with the Wind*, a role which she like countless others lusted after, should be given to a relative unknown.

Vacating her rented house, she headed east to rejoin her family and to think about ways to make this a turning point in her career rather than an end to it. She did some relaxing—strenuous relaxing as was her wont, sailing, swimming, playing tennis and golf, sparring romantically with Howard Hughes.

She was hoping that Broadway might offer her an opportunity for a turning point, although her most recent adventure on the stage could hardly have been very encouraging. Five years earlier, in 1933, she had learned that Jed Harris was bringing a play to Broadway from England, *The Lake*, a soap-operatic drama that had been unaccountably but unmistakenly well received abroad. He was only too happy to give her the lead, since her movie work then, especially in *Little Women*, would make her name on the Broadway bill something of a drawing card.

Trouble was—Jed Harris, whose maltreatment of actors was legendary. On one occasion he had so infuriated the reserved Ina Claire that she retaliated with a right hook that knocked him flat before she kicked him. Although Hepburn never went to such lengths, his bullying did nothing to cure her stage fright or improve her performance—with which she was thoroughly dissatisfied.

After the play's first night, on the day after Christmas 1933, the critics as thoroughly agreed. It was this performance that inspired Dorothy Parker's lamentably deathless comment, "Katharine Hepburn runs the gamut from A to B." From that point the only direction was up, and her performances, with some help from a voice coach, gradually improved. Yet when Harris, after 55 curtains by February, announced that he was taking the show on the road, she offered to buy her way out of the contract, and he readily agreed.

Now, in her bleak summer of 1938, Philip Barry arrived unexpectedly in Connecticut with news about a couple of plays he was in the throes of writing, one of which was *The Philadelphia Story*. Like Bette Davis' consolation prize in *Jezebel*, the part of Tracy Lord in the Barry play promised her considerable consolation for the loss of Scarlett O'Hara. The role was indeed tailored for her by Barry, reputedly with expert help from her at critical points.

They enthusiastically submitted the completed play to the Theater Guild only to encounter a financial roadblock. The Guild people shared their enthusiasm but at the moment were in circumstances too straitened to support a play by a playwright with four flops in six years and a star labeled box-office poison. They could, however, cough up a quarter of the production costs. She and Barry coughed up another quarter, and Howard Hughes provided the remaining half. While she was at it she acquired, with hopeful cunning, the screen rights. Just in case.

The play was a stunner, entertaining full houses for a full year. So was the movie version, which netted her an Oscar nomination and an end to the talk of box-office poison. Her next movie would be the first of the nine that she would make with Spencer Tracy over the next quarter century. Among others.

BOB HOPE

In the first week or so of 1938 Bob Hope, 34, and his wife Dolores were in Hollywood and rather wishing they weren't. (It was still winter, but what does that matter in Southern California?) She was eager to go back home to New York, and he was thinking of going back home to vaudeville. He'd appeared as a comic on Broadway, especially in 1933's *Roberta* and in *Ziegfeld Follies of 1935* and seemed to be on the verge of making a name for himself. But here in Hollywood he felt lost in Tinseltown's myriad of stars.

For his first appearance in a feature film, for instance—*The Big Broadcast of 1938*—Paramount had given him a miserable fifth billing. He was informed, however, that "they" had liked him in it and had renewed his option for another year and for a role in *College Swing*. When he discovered that the role was almost imperceptible, it was only by pressuring the producer, who owed him some money, that he got it somewhat enlarged. Not that it made much difference, since the movie furtively dropped out of sight quite speedily after release.

He nevertheless decided to stick around awhile. *The Big Broadcast* was scheduled for release in March, and he was justifiably curious about how it would be received. In addition, radio had offered a stopgap rescue in December, when he'd been offered a couple of guest spots on Lucky Strike's national variety show, *Your Hollywood Parade*. In both appearances (if that's the word for a radio show) he'd been a hit, eliciting laughs and applause from the studio audience far above and beyond the demands of studio signs. So much so, in fact, that the ad agency responsible for the show would have hired him as emcee, replacing screen star and crooner Dick Powell, except for Powell's impregnable contract.

After *The Big Broadcast* was released, on schedule, he eagerly awaited the reviews, only to wind up thoroughly crestfallen. Not even W.C. Fields' name in the credits could save it from ignominy. The kind words were few, and in between were some very nasty ones. Frank Nugent in *The New York Times*, for instance, recommended belatedly that the movie should have quit while it was ahead in rehearsals. It was a "hodge podge revue," he went on, that was "all loose ends and tatters, not too good at its best and downright bad at its worst." There was, however, a sop for Hope and his singing partner: "Mr Hope and Shirley Ross acquit themselves commendably, meanwhile, of 'Thanks for the Memory.'"

Acquitting himself commendably in a movie destined for the trash heap was hardly enough to keep Hope and Dolores off that train to the friendlier East. Yet before packing they came across a few much kinder words from Damon Runyon in *The New York Journal* about the song: "What a delivery, what a song, what an audience reception!" This declaration of rapture may have prompted others to take a second, more appreciative look, or listen, for suddenly Hope was being touted as that promising young performer by such starmakers as Ed Sullivan, Walter Winchell, Louella Parsons and Hedda Hopper. Small wonder that "Thanks for the Memory" would be his theme song for the rest of his lo-o-o-ong career.

Paramount picked up his option, scheduled him for another movie, and with the customary inducements persuaded him to stay on the West Coast. Yet this movie, *College Swing*, and its successors proved to be such reputation-gobbling turkeys that even his gradually better billing status wasn't enough to keep him from looking east again. Ironically, it was from the East Coast that deliverance would come.

A New York ad agency, Lord & Thomas, had decided that *The Amos 'n' Andy Show*, sponsored by its client Pepsodent, was for all its enormous popularity failing to sell enough toothpaste. Selling being the ultimate purpose of and only justification for radio entertainment, the agency was casting about for a likely replacement. Since Jimmy Saphier, Hope's energetically enterprising agent, was on cordial terms with the ad agency's West Coast representatives, it was only natural that New York's attention would be called to the promising young fellow who had done so well on *Your Hollywood Parade*. Within a few weeks Hope had a highly lucrative six-year contract giving him full production control and Pepsodent annual options. He and his band of quickly hired writers labored through the spring and summer getting ready for their really big broadcast scheduled for September. On a Tuesday night near the end of that month the show was aired with an enticing lead-in from Fibber McGee and Molly, a stay-tuned inducement from Red Skelton, and, incidentally, some very pleasant vocalizing from West Coast resident Dolores Hope.

The show was well received and would of course become a fixture. In its review *Variety* commented that "Hope, with the typical coloration of a true trouper, would probably swap Pepsodent, his new sponsor, for the old Palace any day."

Well, maybe. And maybe not.

EDWARD HOPPER

In July 1923 Edward Hopper celebrated his 41st birthday, but that was about all he had to celebrate. He had sold one painting in his life, ten years earlier, and not another since. Since he lived frugally, he was able to support himself with part-time illustrating for magazines, although he hated such "pot-boiling," and with his etchings, which seemed to be growing more marketable. Yet, like most visual artists, what he wanted most to do was *paint*—indeed, to earn a living by painting.

It was also in July 1923 that he met Josephine Verstille Nivison while on vacation in Gloucester, Massachusetts. About all that they had in common was their addiction to painting—and, secondarily, their fondness for French literature. At six feet five inches he was 16 inches taller than she. He was quietly reclusive, she volubly gregarious. But he respected her entertaining and often insightful discourse, and she admired his thoughtful reserve: "When he does say anything, it's apt to be very witty or wise—or both."

She was an accomplished watercolorist, and he found her talent in this respect something of a challenge. Except for some of his pot-boiling, he had done no watercolors since leaving art school. Soon the two of them were watercoloring together in Gloucester and environs, although she generally favored harbor views with ships and sailboats while he concentrated on interesting houses. Before the end of their vacation time they became aware that theirs was much more than a working relationship.

On their return to New York she was invited by the Brooklyn Museum to include half a dozen of her watercolors in its exhibition of American and European drawings and watercolors. Why not include some of Edward Hopper's watercolors? she asked the show's organizers, somewhat brashly. They were surprised: Hopper? We're acquainted with his etchings, but we didn't know he did watercolors. In that case, she replied, I'll ask him to submit some of his work.

And so it was that six of his watercolors from that Gloucester vacation were included in the show. Ironically, she received some praise while he received *the* praise from the critics. One wrote excitedly of his paintings' "vitality, force and directness." Another found them "exhilarating" and rejoiced that "he is using the medium" of watercolors. For a concrete addition to his delight, the museum bought one of his paintings, *The Mansard Roof*, for $100. It was his first sale in ten years, the second in his life so far. (As his reputation grew, *he* began recommending *her* paintings to museum directors.)

In July 1924 they were married. The marriage proved to be a happy one, although she was uncomfortable with his reclusiveness and he with her virginal inexperience and her competitive cat. (To tease her or please her, he occasionally took to competitive purring.)

After a vacation of honeymooning and watercoloring in Gloucester, they returned to New York with a new supply of paintings. Armed with a painter friend's recommendation, he took some of his to a prominent art gallery, only to be rebuffed with the comment that his pictures were "too stark." During his crestfallen retreat down Fifth Avenue on his way home, he noticed a familiar name, Rehn, on the front of an unfamiliar building. The Rehn Galley, he learned after entering, had only recently moved into these new quarters. A couple of years earlier he'd had some tenuous dealings with a dealer named Frank K. M. Rehn. Maybe, just maybe, his connection with the newly situated Rehn might be less tenuous this time.

He asked to show some of his work to Rehn, who at first declined the honor, and who was soon leaving for lunch—but on second thought Hopper, if he wished, could go to a room in the back and he'd take a look at them after lunch. Fate intervened in the form of a customer who happened to be in the back room and who, as soon as he saw one of the paintings, of a Victorian-style house, exclaimed ecstatically that it was "just like my grandmother's!" Catching Rehn before he left, he asked to buy the painting, and Rehn was only too happy to oblige. He also was happy to drop his luncheon plans, to discuss the paintings, and in the end to consider representing this promising artist.

Soon thereafter the promising artist had his first show in a commercial gallery. Amid critical praise he watched as all 16 of his paintings were sold, netting him well over $1,000. On his way home he stopped at Brooks Brothers and bought himself a long coveted, warm overcoat to protect him from New York's malicious winter weather.

Rehn continued to represent him for the rest of his long and successful career. No more pot-boiling.

LENA HORNE

In early February 1942, two months after Pearl Harbor, Lena Horne was 23 and not a little rueful. She had just recently moved from a relatively cosmopolitan New York, where she'd been enjoying an increasingly promising career largely free of racist humiliations, to a relatively provincial Hollywood, where her career was stymied and her life made uncomfortable by sporadic episodes of gross segregation. (Black actors were segregated at the MGM commissary until Louis B. Mayer interfered, and a bit later she and her family would be subjected to an effort by some color-allergic neighbors to have her and her family removed, until other neighbors, notably Humphrey Bogart and Peter Lorre, strenuously interfered.)

She had been lured to Hollywood by an offer to appear at the new Trocadero Club, still under construction, on a bill to include such black stars as Ethel Waters, Duke Ellington, and Katherine Dunham's dancers. The onset of war, however, delayed work on the Trocadero, and she had to wait, impatiently, until the "Little Troc" was opened in February 1942 as a stop-gap measure. Although this much smaller club couldn't accommodate the hoped-for extravaganza, it suited her perfectly as she emerged onto the stage simply dressed in white and simply spotlighted. She sang familiar songs, including "The Man I Love" and "Can't Help Lovin' That Man," eight of them to an audience entranced from first to last. She became quite the rage, the sensual voice to hear, the exotic face and figure to see. Her delivery gave songs new meaning, new emotional overtones. A writer of song lyrics heard her sing one of his songs and marveled that she put something into the lyrics that even he "didn't know was there." Soon she was being continually invited to parties, to celebrity bashes, although before long she gave up accepting most invitations when it became clear that she often was being used to enhance reputations for racial tolerance, or condescension.

Among her fans at the Little Troc was the movie star George Raft, who was sufficiently impressed to set up a screen test for her at Universal. Even

93

more impressed was a film musician, Roger Edens, who used his contacts with agents to arrange a test with MGM the next day. At MGM the test was extended into an audition with Louis B. Mayer. After a couple of hours of enchanted listening along with his good friend and equally enchanted Marion Davies, he offered her a contract.

Tempering her eagerness with caution, she held off signing it until she could get some professional advice. As a result her contract contained unconventional clauses protecting her from being relegated to stereotypical black roles like those, for instance, in *Gone with the Wind*. She'd be available, however, for roles in the few all-black movies being tentatively considered by the studio. One of these was the all-black *Cabin in the Sky*, a recent hit on Broadway, which included a role made to order for Lena Horne.

Her next screen test was for a role in *Thank Your Lucky Stars*, a movie of thankless memory in which she would play opposite Eddie Anderson, best known as Jack Benny's comically sensible manservant Rochester. In the test she appeared too white against his black, and a resort to dark makeup, since her features weren't typically negroid, made her seem to be in blackface. So she lost the part to Ethel Waters. Her next two movies were similarly unnoticeable, although *As Thousands Cheer* presented her in that leaning-on-pillar pose that would become her specialty.

Despite her movie contract and her success at the Little Troc, followed in July by more of same at the Macombo, she sorely missed the Big Apple, her home town. When she was told about a benefit affair planned at that town's Café Society Downtown, she found the opportunity so irresistible that she decided to fly there (she hated flying) and join her friends in the festivities. Once there, she knew she couldn't go back to Fantasy Land. "I'm never going to leave New York again."

Oh yes you are, insisted her friend Count Basie upon hearing this. "He laid the trip on me," she said later. In Hollywood she'd been given an opening habitually denied to black performers, he insisted, and she had an obligation to take full advantage of it. Return she did, in time for the filming of *Cabin in the Sky*. Hers would be a full speaking part, as the temptress Georgia Brown whom the jealous wife, Petunia, considers to be the last, succulent straw, with good reason. The movie soon was packing them in, a success due largely to her somewhat tongue-in-cheek performance. With it she achieved the stardom that Count Basie had, hopefully, in mind.

Her performance shortly thereafter in *Stormy Weather* simply burnished her star. She soon became a major morale-builder among black servicemen, as well as among many white servicemen of nonsimian mentality. Although as time passed she would occasionally feel the slings and arrows of outrageous prejudice, they would gradually become less frequent and less hurtful, partly because of her incalculable contribution to the progressive dignity and social acceptance of her fellow blacks.

JOHN HUSTON

.

In 1929 John Huston, then 23, had a speaking part in a short film entitled *Two Americans*, featuring Abraham Lincoln and Ulysses S. Grant, both of them played by his father Walter. He had all of eight lines. Before this he had done some painting, had written some short stories (and had one of them published in *The American Mercury*), and had worked as a reporter, but he liked this movie business much better than writing.

Ironically—because it was as a writer, or cowriter, that the movie business used him on two of his father's films, both forgettable, and on the Bela Lugosi *Murders in the Rue Morgue*, celebrated chiefly for spinning Edgar Allan Poe over and over in his grave. A screenplay of Oliver La Farge's *Laughing Boy* that he wrote for Universal was sold to MGM, considerably refashioned, and made into what he later described as "a wretched, vulgar picture." After his contract with Universal expired he tried writing for Darryl F. Zanuck only to be replaced by a couple of other writers of wider repute. His marriage had fallen apart, he had killed a girl in a no-fault auto accident amid a lot of unpleasant publicity, and life in general had devolved into what he later called, in his autobiography, "a series of misadventures and disappointments. Now I wanted nothing so much as to get away."

And get away he did. Off he went to London, despite his father's worried advice, in response to a scriptwriting offer from the Gaumont-British film company. One of the company's owners was, quite incidentally, a friend of his father's, and a false rumor quickly pegged him as an American with connections, overpaid (which he was) and talentless (which he wasn't). His ex-wife, a hopeless alcoholic, happened to be in London also, and his caring for her proved such a total distraction that Gaumont-British voided his contract before he had a chance to write a single line.

He put her on a ship for California, and from "then on it was steps going down for me." He and a friend, bereft of lodgings, spent nights "in the open" in whatever clothes they had left, and their days "actually walking the streets singing cowboy songs for coppers and an occasional sixpence." (He was too proud and too optimistic to ask his father for help, which "would have been immediately forthcoming.") Their luck seemed to turn when they were asked to make a movie about car racing, but the project was canceled when his friend broke a leg. They finally concluded that they should spend their last money on a trip home, and in New York he was delighted to be greeted delightedly by his father and to see that stalwart star in the splendid picture *Dodsworth*. Nonetheless, "I was twenty-eight years old now, and at loose ends." He even thought "that perhaps I should have stayed with my painting—and starved." Starvation might at least be less nerve-racking.

He moved for a while to New England, where he became involved with a new picture magazine which was abruptly and permanently eclipsed by the arrival of *Life*. Then an offer came to act in a play at a WPA theater in Chicago which had a fairly long run but nevertheless left him "flat busted." His insolvency didn't deter him from marrying his second wife, however, or from submitting an old story treatment to William Wyler, which Warner Brothers unexpectedly bought for $5,000. Offered a contract to write the full screenplay, he took off with his new wife for Hollywood, where he completed the script for *Three Strangers*, which would be released in 1946 to fairly favorable reviews. He also helped with the writing of *Jezebel*, Bette Davis' riposte to *Gone with the Wind*. He certainly seemed to be back in the movie business again.

Things were looking up financially. He built a house in the San Fernando Valley and became as much of a country gentleman as his character and outlook would permit. He also acquired an agent, his first and only agent for about the next 40 years, who among other things inserted a clause in his contract with Warners permitting him to direct a movie. *That*'s what he really wanted to do. Writing could be fun, but it was essentially a lonely occupation, and he had always wanted to work more closely, and professionally, with people.

When the time came Warners not only assigned him to direct a movie but also let him select a movie he wanted to direct. He chose one that had been filmed twice earlier but in his opinion unsuccessfully, a version of Dashiell Hammett's *The Maltese Falcon*. Although George Raft had first call to play the lead, he turned it down out of a fear that an untried director would make a hash of it. That was fine with Huston, since the alternative was Humphrey Bogart, who had recently done such fine work in *High Sierra*. He worked painstakingly on the screenplay but found that he could be more easygoing with the direction, generally allowing the actors—after all, he had Bogart, Greenstreet, Astor, Lorre and Elisha Cook, Jr.—plenty of freedom to do their own, more effective thing.

It need hardly be added that this 1941 masterpiece became an all-time classic. One critic, comparing it with the 1931 version, has written that it "shows the difference between excellence and brilliance." Nor need it be added that John Huston was finally on a roll, for the rest of his cinematic life.

JESSE JACKSON

In the summer of 1964 Jesse Jackson, 23, armed with a B.A. freshly minted in a North Carolina state college, had a career decision to make. A family decision, in fact, since he now had to include his wife Jacqueline and their young daughter in his deliberations. He thought about getting a law degree, which could provide him with a decent income and equip him to be helpful in the burgeoning movement to obtain for black Americans their elusive civil rights (as well as some measure of civility).

Nine years earlier, however, he had told his father that a dream had convinced him that he was destined to be a preacher. Again, one morning in college he told a roommate quite seriously, in a trembling voice, of a strange dream, which he interpreted as a call to the ministry. He even made an appointment to discuss it with the college president, who, in his additional role of campus minister, advised him to give the matter a lot of thought. This is what he was doing now, during the summer after graduation.

The offer of a scholarship to the Chicago Theological Seminary seemed nothing less than providential. After moving with his family to the Windy City, he enrolled at the Seminary and settled down to serious study. Not that their life was simply a bowl of academic cherries. He earned what money he could in spare time odd jobs and Jacqueline worked in the Seminary's library. Yet they were happy, and he was looking forward to being of service to his people while maintaining a reasonably tranquil domesticity. He did, however, join the local chapter of the Southern Christian Leadership Conference. The leader of the Conference, Dr. Martin Luther King, Jr., was of course a hero of his.

At the time King was acutely discommoding the Southern white establishment by shining light on the Confederacy's contrast between his nonviolent approach and the outrageously violent reactions of the nastier representatives of that establishment. Those representatives cooperated by being visibly violent enough to attract national media attention. In June 1964, for instance, seven of them in Mississippi had murdered three civil-rights workers, two white workers from up north and their black friend, punishing them in effect for their failure to recognize the victory of the South in the Civil War. A television news story.

Not to be outdone, representatives in Alabama entered the fray. First, in Selma, a group of blacks were refused their right to register to vote. Then, soon thereafter, the group's leader turned up one evening in Marion to give a speech. After the speech, although it was already menacingly dark, the audience started out on a march. The streetlights were turned off and in the gloom outraged whites, among them city police and state troopers, set about teaching them a lesson. In the ensuing melee a young black, Jimmy Lee Jackson, discovering his 82-year-old grandfather was bleeding, helped him into the nearest cafe, only to see him beaten still further by troopers with a righteous thirst for unquenchable vengeance. Unfortunately his mother also was there, so the troopers turned on her. For coming to her defense he was shot in the abdomen (and died of his wounds a week later). Another Jackson, in Chicago, was understandably horrified.

In March 1965 the indomitable King, after a march that ended in televised violence before it could really get started (on what came to be known as Bloody Sunday), called for people from all over the country to assemble in Selma for a march to Montgomery, Alabama's capital. This was a call that Jackson, whatever his scholarly responsibilities or clerical ambition, obviously couldn't ignore. Far from ignoring it, with the pregnant Jacqueline's wholehearted approval he organized half of the Seminary's students into a caravan and headed south (all craftily wearing clerical collars for what they hoped would be protection).

There in Selma he met his hero. There also, in his excitement and enthusiasm, he evidently stepped on many a toe. Some of King's aides, who had been with him for some time now, took offense at this young newcomer's brash assumption of authority in directing some of the marchers and in making a speech—a ringing speech—without being invited to do so. On the other hand, he was equally willing to take on menial tasks, like carrying messages and going out in the rain to get coffee for his fellow protesters, and he was engagingly friendly and cooperative.

He also was displaying an organizing ability that quite impressed Ralph Abernathy, a close confidante of King's who later became president of the SCLC. Although King apparently had some reservations, Abernathy convinced him to hire this promising young fellow, especially since their next project would take them north, to Chicago, to help the Chicago Freedom Movement in its program to help blacks find better jobs and better housing in that unofficially but unmistakably segregated city.

His visit proved futile chiefly because of a fraudulent mayor's failure to keep his word. However, the SCLC included a unit called Operation Breadbasket, dedicated to finding work for the poor. Before King's departure Jackson was appointed director of its Chicago branch. So much for his studies at the Seminary. Just a few months before he was slated to receive his theology degree, he now had to drop out to take up his new career.

But three years later the Seminary granted him an honorary degree, the first of many.

MICHAEL JACKSON

In the summer of 1967 Michael Jackson, approaching his ninth birthday, was disappointed because his dynamically ambitious father, Joe, was disappointed. Some three months earlier Joe, eager to get his talented sons, already known as The Jackson Five, free of their current grueling, often sordid routine of performing in seedy theaters, nightclubs and even strip joints, had mailed a demonstration tape to Berry Gordy, Jr., of Motown Records. He was utterly convinced that his kids' lively style was just the ticket for Motown. Yet after three anxious months the tape had been returned without a word. In such situations silence is not golden.

This wasn't all. Somewhat later the Five's performance at Chicago's Regal Theater as a warm-up act for the Motown singer Gladys Knight had excited her enough to induce some Motown marketability experts to catch their act. Their expert opinion was negative—who'd pay anything to see them, to hear them?

Well, one way for the Five to find out was to enter a talent contest—that notoriously tough talent contest at the Apollo Theater in Harlem. That's what they did one night in August 1967, and, to Joe's ecstatic delight, not only won first prize easily but were even treated to that rarity, a standing ovation. This brought them a contract not with Motown but with a local outfit under the Steeltown label. Their first single, "Big Boy," came out early in 1968 and was a hit. Not a big hit, but a hit.

Big enough, at any rate, to earn them an invitation to return to the Apollo Theater and this time perform *for pay*. That they did, and their act was caught by a scout for David Frost, who offered them time on his show for their first television appearance. Joe was elated—only to be forced into a dilemma by a competing offer from Motown, finally, for an audition.

The coin came up Motown. And so it was that the last week of July found them in Detroit performing for a phalanx of Motown pooh-bahs with their habitual enthusiasm and with Michael in the acrobatically energetic lead. ("You're a hell of a mover," his idol Fred Astaire once said to him.) The

100

pooh-bahs made notes almost as energetically—and quite inscrutably. "Thank you for coming. We'll get back to you." Yeah, sure. Thoroughly dispirited, Joe & Co. trudged back to their borrowed Volkswagen bus and drove home, arriving there in a midnight blue funk.

What they didn't know was that the audition tape by then had been played for Gordy and he was already having the necessary contracts drawn up. Three days later, on the 26th, the contracts were signed. The terms eventually would have to be rather bitterly adjusted, but for the moment the very word "contract" had a magical ring. Moreover, to add ecstacy to bliss, the dazzled Five were informed by Diana Ross, Motown's brightest star, that she'd been asked to help them along in whatever way she could. She was not rebuffed.

Yet what immediately followed was a long, excruciating period of frustration as the group tried again and again to create a song acceptable to the exacting Gordy. He, indeed, also found it excruciating, enough for him to urge Joe and the boys to come out to Los Angeles to enjoy his personal supervision. They arrived in early August 1969 and were promptly welcomed by Diana Ross with a magnanimous gesture in the form of an invitation sent out to hundreds of Hollywood's Important People:

> Please join me in welcoming a brilliant musical group, the Jackson Five, on Monday, August 11, 6:50 to 9:50 at the Daisy, North Rodeo Drive, Beverly Hills. The Jackson Five, featuring eight-year-old Michael Jackson, will perform live at the party. Please come and listen to this fabulous Motown group. [Michael was actually ten, but the younger the better.]

They came, they saw, and were conquered. The Daisy, a well known place to be seen, rocked with ardent applause, especially when it was announced that the Five would be making their first TV appearance in the fall, on ABC's *Hollywood Palace*. The following morning brought exuberant reviews in the press.

Another grueling period followed as the Five worked with songwriters and director to come up with a song that would meet Gordy's demands. After untold hours of rewrites and of retakes—a couple of dozen, in fact—they finally came up with "I Want to Be Free," and Gordy was satisfied. Then came weeks of training in public relations—graceful deportment at various functions, deft handling of the press, and so on—which included some very gratifying time devoted to polishing Michael while a guest of the lustrous Diana Ross.

Finally the big October night arrived when she, as guest host, introduced the Five to their first national audience on *Hollywood Palace*. For the first time that audience heard "I Want You Back" (the new title for "I Want to Be Free"), and they *liked* it. The next week saw the album in the stores, and four months later it was Number One.

And a few months after that Michael and The Other Four would be bumping the Beatles from their giddy pinnacle on the charts. For starters.

PETER JENNINGS

Christmas week in 1967 wasn't an entirely happy time for Peter Jennings. At the professionally tender age of 29 he feared he might be facing a future as a has-been. Born in Toronto, Canada, he had waited only nine years before getting into broadcasting. Indeed, at that professionally implausible age he had his own weekly show on the Canadian Broadcasting Corporation's radio network. *Peter's People* was a program for children that combined music with, yes, news. Abetting his talent were the reputation and influence of his father Charles, who was widely known as the Canadian Edward R. Murrow.

After impulsively leaving his boring prep school before graduation (a mistake that he's been correcting ever since with voracious reading), he spent the late 1950s and early 1960s broadcasting news and conducting interviews on radio and television stations here and there in Canada. In 1962 he was hired by a network to coanchor Canada's first nationwide commercial newscast. No mere desk jockey, he gladly left the studio to cover major news events, including NATO meetings in Europe, President Kennedy's fateful 1964 visit to Dallas, the 1964 Democratic National Convention in Atlantic City.

It was during his reporting of the convention that he caught the appraising eye of the president of ABC News and was offered a job as a network correspondent. He declined it at first, partly because, in the TV news business at the time, ABC was snidely called the Almost Broadcasting Company. After about three months of sober second consideration of Canadian horizons, however, he asked if the offer was still good. It was, and he accepted.

Headquartered in New York, he roamed about a great deal, covering politics and the emerging civil-rights movement, but only for a few months. Meanwhile the head of ABC News had come up with another idea. Here was this handsome, young-looking fellow who just might appeal to younger news-viewers and thereby give ABC a desperately needed answer to the painfully popular Walter Cronkite of CBS and the increasingly marketable Huntley-Brinkley combo on NBC. After getting a commitment that he'd be

102

allowed to continue doing some roaming, Jennings became, tenderly at 26, ABC's anchor for its national weekday newscasts (15 minutes in those days, later expanded to half an hour).

His youth and good looks proved to be more drawbacks than assets. Everything's relative, and compared to the competition, especially Cronkite, he seemed, for all his lack for formal education, a pretentious schoolboy. Television critics by and large sniffed at the "glamorcaster," and among unfriendly colleagues he was a "male model" and "pretty boy." He himself was uncomfortable, conscious that he really wasn't qualified to compete with nationally known veterans. Since his familiarity with U.S. history was anything but intimate, for example, he made conspicuous mistakes—mispronunciations, misidentifications—that even a young audience could find distracting. Some stations began dropping his newscasts or moving them to less valuable time slots. Despite a slight rise in his overall ratings, he was a severe disappointment. After a long, difficult trial period of almost three years, late in 1967 he agreed with the network brass that he had to go.

So he went, crestfallen yet relieved—back to reporting and, gradually, to establishing himself as one of the best correspondents in the business, especially with respect to the Middle East and the Arab-Israeli conflict. As a result of his expertise, in the early 1970s he was made head of the network's new Middle East bureau. He settled happily in Beirut, Lebanon, leaving it occasionally for such stories as the 1972 Summer Olympics in Munich (and, unexpectedly, the Black September attack on the Israeli athletes), the civil war in Bangladesh, and the continued survival of Fidel Castro. He also began collecting an impressive array of awards, not for good looks but for professional competence.

Meanwhile ABC was still casting about for ideas in its perennial battle against that stubborn competition. Early in 1975 he was brought back to Washington to serve as news reader and correspondent for the network's stab at the profitable early morning market, a program called *A.M. America*. Unable to compete with NBC's *Today*, it folded in October. Reassigned overseas, in 1978 he became the network's foreign news anchor on *World News Tonight*, with Frank Reynolds reporting political news from Washington and Max Robinson reporting general national news from Chicago, in a three-headed format that ABC hoped, irrepressibly, would be competitive.

It would be. In July 1983, after the untimely death of Frank Reynolds, he became *the* anchor of the program, as well as senior editor for more hands-on control. He had come full circle, this time to stay, fully qualified, while ABC News finally met, and more than met, the competition.

JOHN PAUL II

In the spring of 1942 Karol Wojtyla, 21, was an aspiring and patriotic actor in a conquered Poland where neither aspirations nor patriotism escaped Nazi suppression. He wasn't given to knuckling under, however. His "passion for the theater" at the time, one of his biographers has observed, "cannot be exaggerated." He had loved playing football, swimming, canoeing, and especially skiing, and poetry too. Yet one day in high school, when he was chosen to greet a visiting archbishop and when that dignitary asked the school principal (in intensely Catholic Poland) if that outstanding boy was going to be a priest, the principal replied that this seemed unlikely because "he's in love with the theater."

In 1938, after he and his father moved to Krakow from his home town of Wadowice (his mother and older brother having died years earlier), he entered the university there for an education in the liberal arts and lost no time in joining the local theatrical community. (He also elected to take elocution classes.) He trod the boards eagerly, on one occasion for instance acting in a satirical play, *Moonlight Cavalier*, a mystically symbolic work employing the signs of the zodiac. He was Sagittarius, the centaur with bow and arrow. He also joined in a popular convention of the time and place, reading aloud to audiences passages from popular works as well as his own poetry.

On the morning of September 1, 1939, while at Mass, he heard the ominous thunder of Nazi warplanes attacking the city in World War II's first air raid. Soon throughout Poland all secondary schools, colleges and universities were closed, Hitler having classified all Poles as "especially born for low labor." And so Wojtyla had to go underground to continue his education. Scholars who had evaded Nazi arrest and deportation to a concentration camp held classes most discreetly in guardedly patriotic homes, giving him and many other hardy souls an opportunity to contradict Hitler's idiotic anthropology.

He also had to do his acting underground. His theatrical troupe, having changed its name from the Theatrical Confraternity to Studio 39 to commemorate the fateful year, gave performances to *very* carefully chosen audiences in *very* carefully chosen homes throughout the war in what came to be known as the instantly movable "Rhapsodic Theater." Considering the circumstances, the record of the little group of lionhearted thespian conspirators, three actresses and two actors, was little short of miraculous—continual if irregular performances of 27 plays, five of them new, the rest Polish classics. It is hardly surprising that he is tersely described by his official biographer as having at this time "formed a sentimental attachment to a young woman." As Thomas Carlyle put it in another connection, "affection dwells with danger."

The danger was real enough for a people "born for low labor." On one day during these perilous years, for example, more than 200 actors and other artists, gathered together in a clandestine meeting, were surprised and rounded up by Nazi uniformed thugs for immediate conveyance to Auschwitz.

His life outside the theater was one of low labor indeed. For about a year he broke up rocks in a stone quarry until he was promoted to preparing explosives. In 1940 he was moved to a factory engaged in water purification, to which he contributed for some time by hauling buckets of lime on a yoke across his shoulders. The heavy work gave him an appreciation of heavy labor, and heavy laborers, that would never leave him.

In February 1941 his father died of an unexpected heart attack. Feeling terribly alone, he spent the entire night praying beside his father's body. Soon thereafter a streetcar knocked him down, fracturing his skull. During his recovery, in moments of delirium he had thoughts of becoming a priest only to remember, upon regaining his composure, that his goal was to be a fine actor. Some weeks later he was hit by a truck. He managed to survive with some spine and shoulder realignment.

His father's death, his narrow escapes, his injuries, his horror at Nazi atrocities, his recognition of his Church's desperate need for priests to replace the hundreds, even thousands, of sacerdotal victims of the Nazis' policy of discriminating extermination—all these evidently contributed to his fateful decision, in the early fall of 1942, to give up acting for the priesthood. In addition, the archbishop of Krakow, who had asked about him at that high school function and who had unobtrusively kept track of him on and off ever since, now invited him to become one of the half-dozen college-age students being secretly, and separately, prepared for the priesthood.

The new secret seminarian continued working, devoting his spare time to his covert study of theology. More and more of his spare time, in fact, until, in March 1942, he gave up his acting for good. Ruefully, but decisively.

In August 1944, reacting vengefully against a mass uprising in Warsaw, the Nazis made a homicidal sweep of the country. In Krakow they rounded up all accessible males between 15 and 50 for the customary deportation. He narrowly escaped the unfriendly dragnet, but the archbishop decided that

from then on he and his fellow seminarians would live—or, rather, camp—
in the episcopal residence, to emerge only after the war.

Now free to devote all his time to his academic work, he became an outstanding student and in November 1946 was ordained priest. He had given
up acting, yet all that intense theatrical training and experience would serve
him well in his role of Pope John Paul II.

JAMES EARL JONES

"I was nearly thirty-seven years old when we opened at the Arena Stage in Washington on December 12, 1967," James Earl Jones has reported in his autobiography. "Producer Zelda Fichandler and director Ed Sherin had given me my big chance." He was very grateful to them as well as to his lucky stars, for he "had been scraping by on my acting income for fourteen years, playing every part I could find which would help me evolve as an actor."

In this respect he had quite a respectable record, spanning more than ten years since his discharge from the army in 1955. With the invaluable help of the G.I. Bill he had toiled away in acting classes and, in 1957, received his diploma from the American Theater Wing. Soon thereafter he was given a minor part in an off-Broadway play, and from then on worked quite regularly as an actor. His roles, however, were discouragingly inconsequential, with pay to match, so that, to sustain an eating habit, he continually had to take on sideline jobs requiring such implements as brooms and mops.

His career had a preliminary turning point in the spring of 1961, when he was assigned the lead in the American premiere of Jean Genet's *The Blacks*. Despite the all-black cast (some ironically in whiteface) and the play's violence, as well as his own uneasiness with "this wall-to-wall stuff," audiences kept it alive for the next three years. Because the work was so exhausting, he, as well as others, had to bow out on several occasions, but he always returned. However exhausting, the role brought him some flattering notices, a bit of celebrity and some useful wherewithal.

It also brought him better roles over the years—Oberon in the New York Shakespeare Festival's production of *A Midsummer Night's Dream* and the lead in *Othello*. His more conventional theater work earned him the 1962 *Village Voice* Obie Award as the best off–Broadway actor of 1961-62, and the Theater World Award as the season's most promising personality.

Despite an addiction to the stage, he was happy to take roles in movies and television productions. Yes, it was he playing Lieutenant Lother Zogg, the bomber pilot in 1963's manic *Dr. Strangelove: Or, How I Learned to Stop Worrying and Love the Bomb*. He also joined Richard Burton, Elizabeth Taylor, Alec Guinness, Peter Ustinov and Lilian Gish in the 1967 movie version of Graham Greene's *The Comedians*. He could on occasion be seen in TV series such as *As the World Turns* and *Dr. Kildare*. And he continued with Shakespearean roles in Festival productions, as well as others in the New York theater. Given such feverish activity, it's hard to believe that he was merely "scraping by," but so he says. (He's also saying something about actors' salaries, of course.)

Maybe he was saying so in the sense that everything's relative, for his future would be something else again. He was in France in May 1967 helping to put the finishing touches on *The Comedians*, when he received a playscript from stage director Edwin Sherin, who had greatly admired his portrayal of Othello. Howard Sackler's play, *The Great White Hope*, traced the career of champion boxer Jack Jefferson. Based on the tumultuous history of Jack Johnson, it promised to be exciting theater, with a strong, fascinating and demanding leading role. It was a role that would fit him splendidly, wrote Sherin—would he be interested?

He was sure that it was "a role of a lifetime." It was also a role requiring arduous preparation. To slim him down to a fighting physique Sackler took him to a trainer, an ex-boxer who had reconfigured Olivier for his role of Othello and who now set up a schedule of superenergetic exercises for a similar refashioning. Besides the training ordeal Jones had to bear up under penetrating peanut-gallery observations on his unsuitability for the role. He wasn't black enough, for instance, or African-American enough (because of some Native American contamination), and he didn't have Johnson's Southern accent. Since neither blackface nor blood replacement seemed reasonable, he focused on reviving his Dixie drawl (he was born in Mississippi) as he thought a lifelong pug might modulate it. And he shaved his head for cosmetic effect.

There were also the problems of psychological interpretation, requiring long, labyrinthine discussions with author and director. Gradually he began to feel that they would find themselves "involved in a significant theatre experience." He felt even more so as the play progressed through its first night, yet he was astonished as well as gratified by the ardent reaction of the audience and by the rave reviews. "The acting is dominated by James Earl Jones," reported Clive Barnes of *The New York Times*, adding that "his presence has an almost moral force to it." Another critic maintained that his portrayal was "the most exciting by an American actor" since Brando's Kowalski.

That performance brought him a Tony and Drama Desk Award, and later a Grammy for his recording of the play. The rather eviscerated 1970 movie version was less successful than the play, although his work in it earned him an Oscar nomination. Not that it mattered greatly, given his strong preference for the stage, which he continued to indulge with enduringly gratifying results.

BARBARA JORDAN

In November 1964 Barbara Jordan, then 28, was dejected over her second failure to win a seat in the Texas House of Representatives, even though that second loss, to a white man of course, had been by a much narrower margin than the first (to the same white man). Maybe it was time, she thought, to throw in the political towel. "I considered abandoning the dream of a political career in Texas and moving to some section of the country where a black woman was less likely to be considered a novelty"—to New York, for instance, where Shirley Chisholm had won a seat in the state assembly. She was reluctant to do so, however: "To leave would be a cop-out."

With her degree from Boston University Law School, she could continue practicing law in Houston, but she had already found that the demand for black female lawyers, for various reasons, was less than overwhelming. It turned out, however, that there was an opening for a black female administrative assistant to a county judge, responsible for coordinating the work of county welfare activities. Offered the job, she was only too happy to take it and indeed found it very enjoyable, what with helping people who really needed help. And her regular salary supplemented her meager lawyering income, helping her to repay her father, now retired, for his sacrifices in support of her extraordinary education.

The white citizens of Houston seemed fairly satisfied, not unjustifiably, with the progress (precipitous or glacial, depending on one's viewpoint) being made in lessening racial injustice, specifically in desegregating restaurants, hotels, theaters and various public facilities like the municipal golf course, the public library, the bus system, and the city's public buildings. But in two areas especially, the progress still left much to be desired by those whom it directly affected. One was the school system, in which the distribution of educational resources depended largely on degrees of pigmentation, to the point where, in May 1965, more than 9,000 black students resolutely excused themselves from attending classes at their second-rate high schools and

109

marched through the city's streets, singing freedom songs in protest. Within a couple of years the schools were desegregated, at least legally.

The other problem area was political. The state's poll tax and its system of electoral districting put blacks at a severe disadvantage, contributing enormously to her two failures to win a seat in the House. But then a couple of things happened in Washington, D.C., that lightened her dark despair with a glimmer of hope. Lyndon Johnson's Civil Rights Act outlawed poll taxes, and the U.S. Supreme court ordered electoral redistricting to at least approximate a level of equal representation.

As a result of the latter, in 1966 she found herself, after redistricting, in the Eleventh State Senatorial District, with its substantial majority of blacks, Chicanos, and working-class whites. Since it included nearly three-quarters of the precincts that she had carried in her races for the House, she decided that maybe she had a chance of becoming the first black member of the Texas Senate in over 80 years.

Not that she'd be a shoo-in—a black woman running against a white man amid echoes of Confederate ultramasculinity might well have about as much chance as a Yankee snowflake on a Dixie griddle. But when State Representative J. C. Whitfield phoned her to announce that he was going to run for the Senate and to ask her if she was planning to run, she said she was.

A complication arose when she was unexpectedly offered a responsible job with a foundation that trained hard-case jobless for employment under contract to the Labor Department. Although she checked and re-checked to make sure that holding this job and running for the Senate would involve no conflict of interest, she would of course be accused of exactly that during the campaign, although she wasn't in any way concerned with allocation of funds.

In February 1966 she doggedly filed as a candidate in the Democratic primary race. At the party county committee meeting soon thereafter Whitfield accused her of being unqualified, but her stoutly delivered claim of being thoroughly representative of the district was welcomed by the audience with a standing ovation. Whitfield stomped out in a huff and shortly announced his formation of a rival faction, unsuccessfully charged her with conflict of interest, and finally stooped to a racist slogan aimed against the new districting, "Can a white man win?"—to which she answered, "No, not this time."

She was right. She won the primary and went on to win the election. Neither fanatic nor windbag, she spent the next six years in the Senate establishing a solid record of liberal legislation by working within the system so successfully that she earned the title of "Outstanding Freshman Senator" in 1967 and of president pro tem in March 1972, making her the first black woman in American history to hold this kind of political position.

Another redistricting in 1970 gave her a shot at the U.S. House of Representatives in 1972. She was solidly nominated and elected, and soon after her arrival in Washington was assigned a seat on the House Judiciary Committee.

Two years later, after she had given her speech during the Watergate hearings, the speech explaining her vote for the impeachment of Richard Nixon, she was deluged with thousands of congratulatory wires and letters. An admirer in Houston bought space on a couple of dozen billboards to express his and others' gratitude: "Thank you, Barbara Jordan, for Explaining the Constitution to Us."

GENE KELLY

In the fall of 1933 Gene Kelly at 21 wasn't singin' in the rain. More importantly, he wasn't even dancin', in or out of any rain. No, he was enrolled as a law student in the University of Pittsburgh's graduate school, headed for a legal career.

This was incredible. He was immeasurably talented as a dancer, was addictively fond of dancing, and had been dancing since shortly after learning to walk. In this he was aggressively encouraged by his energetically solicitous mother, who saw to it that he and his three siblings attended music and dancing schools at a tender age to develop any talent they might have for show-biz fun and frolic.

She even organized the children into an amateur troupe and handled their schedule of unprofitable yet quite successful bookings. In addition, Gene and his younger brother Fred (who was utterly addicted to show biz) diverted the children of their neighborhood with backyard performances of an antic disposition. Their mother, after becoming convinced that Fred was the talented one of her children, raised him from amateur to professional status as early as 1923, when he was seven, carting him about from place to whatever place would cough up the prescribed $10 per performance. Herself a would-be performer, restricted to homemaking by the conventions of the time, she obviously was vicariously enjoying her youngest son's (and later Gene's) ability to entertain.

She saw to it that every one of her children learned to play a musical instrument. Gene's was the violin, on which he took endless lessons from the age of nine until he broke an arm in a high school football game. At that point she relented, even though he had become quite a violinist. To mollify her, he took up the banjo instead. There's no record of her reaction.

Meanwhile he was dancing. In grammar school he was drafted for the school's shows, being, among other things, the only boy who could tap dance. Furthermore, he could sing, quite pleasantly. At first reluctant to perform and

112

maybe be called a sissy (instead of the good athlete that he was), he gradually found the applause and compliments gratifying, especially when so much of the adulation came from girls. At home he began doing ordinary chores in the terpsichorean manner, serving the dinner plates, for instance, while capering around the family table à la Nijinsky.

During his freshman year at college his father dejectedly joined the ranks of the unemployed, courtesy of the Great Depression. Although Gene stayed in college, he did so by working during his summer vacation and then between classes as a construction laborer, a soda jerk, a gas station attendant—until he realized that Fred, now bringing in more money with his professional dancing, could probably bring in still more if he had a partner. Moreover, the work be would at hours less likely to interfere with his class schedule. Fred agreed. Despite the Depression, the new team found it surprisingly easy to get bookings, especially for appearances in movie theaters between showings of the new "talkies." In what little spare time he had, he began taking beginner's lessons in ballet. (He considered ballet the ultimate in the art of dancing.)

Meanwhile his mother, who had been doing the books for a Pittsburgh dance studio, decided to open a studio of her own in a suburb of Johnstown, some 60 miles away. After she did so with capital inveigled from her current employer, it became clear that this would have to be a family enterprise, and soon all the children were involved. Since lessons were given only on Saturdays, he was relatively free to cooperate. After an alarmingly slow start, the school became profitable. As for him, he found the role of teacher so stimulating that, with his mother as financial adviser and bookkeeper, he opened a school of his own in Pittsburgh. He was a superlative teacher, and both schools flourished. A major reason for their success was the annual summer show. These revues, with attractive costumes and scenery and a full orchestra, earned the schools rave reviews and a glowing reputation.

During their summers he and Fred continued performing, in 1932 even traveling to Chicago for the World's Fair, where they played as many as 10 shows a day. In Chicago he also spent a couple of weeks taking lessons from fellow members of the National Association of Dancing Masters, seeking perfection, always perfection. And, on request, he also did some teaching. The summers of 1932 and 1933 sped by all too quickly.

And so here he was, in the autumn of 1933, sweating it out in his law classes. Curiously, he was there at his mother's insistence. For all her fascination with show biz, she didn't want her children (with the probable exception of Fred) to make a *career* out of the arts and entertainment. (She had almost induced her oldest son, a fine painter and splendid commercial illustrator, to go into engineering.) As for the incipient lawyer, as he was half-listening one day to a droning law lecture, he heard the professor mention a book on torts, which the students "would be using for the rest of their lives."

That promise, that threat, ended his law career abruptly and permanently. Despite his mother's temporary disappointment, he returned to dancing. In the years ahead were Broadway, the scintillating success of *Pal Joey*, and an invitation from Metro-Goldwyn-Mayer.

JOHN F. KENNEDY

In late 1945 Jack Kennedy, 28, had good reason to expect a career as a writer. Six years earlier, in his senior year at Harvard, he had written a thesis on the problem of a democracy's inherent, and disturbing, tendency to be unprepared for war. It was so warmly praised by its reviewers that his proud father, the Croesus-rich and politically influential Joseph P. Kennedy, nudged it into publication under the title *Why England Slept* and then, with a further gentle nudge, onto the best-seller lists. As a journalist for the Hearst newspaper chain the son reported, with much unsolicited yet appreciated political commentary, on the San Francisco conference that launched the United Nations, on the German surrender at Potsdam, and on the British elections that summarily dismissed his fellow war hero Winston Churchill.

About a year and a half earlier, however, his older brother Joe Jr., a navy pilot, having completed his quota of 50 missions over Europe, volunteered for one more, flying an experimental bomber packed with explosives for neutralizing the launch sites of the new German V-1 buzz bombs. On its way over the Channel the plane suddenly and inexplicably disintegrated in an enormous explosion. The large Kennedy family was grief-stricken, but Joseph Sr., who had been fondly expecting a spectacular political career for his eldest son, was utterly devastated. It took many months for him to recover fully enough to begin thinking about his second son in similar terms.

That son, although manifestly interested in the political and social issues of the day, admitted later that he would never have run for political office if Joe Jr. had lived, and would "have kept on being a writer." (As he did to some extent anyway, as evidenced by his popular mid-fifties book, *Profiles in Courage*.) His father, also later, declared that it was he who "got Jack into politics," explaining that Joe's death had made it mandatory that his next son run for Congress. The son, now the eldest, knew how desperately his father wanted his eldest son in politics. Indeed, "'wanted' isn't the right word. He *demanded* it. You know my father." Not that the son was reluctant initially.

115

He decided that doing something in politics (a.k.a. "public service") probably could be more satisfying than reporting on things from the sidelines. Although he had doubts about his aptitude for it, he accepted his part in the game.

The game wouldn't be all pleasure—he was sure he'd detest campaigning. Years earlier his mother's father had represented the chiefly Irish-Italian blue-collar Eleventh District in Congress. Joe Sr. fixed his ferociously ambitious stare on that district (where he'd been born and where his father-in-law had been mayor of Boston) as soon as he heard that the current Representative, James Michael Curley, a famously predatory pol, had *his* ferociously ambitious stare fixed on the Boston mayoralty. Just to be ready, he had his son rent a hotel room in Boston to establish residency. The son was technically prepared, therefore, when Mayor Curley vacated that seat in Congress.

But not so well prepared practically. His health was rather precarious, his wartime heroism having left him with a permanently painful back. Thin and rather reedy, he looked even younger than he was. His voice was too high and scratchy to project much weighty conviction, although his unreliable delivery did provide opportunities, when he made a mistake, for a very appealing grin. His good looks and attractive personality soon had many older women in the district wanting to mother him and many younger women wanting him otherwise. (He had quite a penchant for the otherwise.)

He worked on his speechifying, assiduously but not very fruitfully. The pace of the campaign quickly grew strenuous. By February 1946 he was working the district sedulously, giving a brief speech here, glad-handing constituents here, there and everywhere, refueling with only four or five hours of sleep each night. He tried to make time each day for a brief nap, a hot bath and a rubdown to ease his back pain, which was severe—one campaign worker remarked that "the guy was in agony." To most of his associates he often seemed ill—if indefatigable. One day a newspaperman discovered him in a back room of his campaign headquarters virtually in tears over the grueling routine and his frustrating predicament. "I'm just filling Joe's shoes. If he were alive, I'd never be in this." Nevertheless "sometimes we all have to do things we don't want to do." Especially when a fellow has Attila the Hun for a doting father.

Attila reportedly was spending enough money to get his chauffeur elected to Congress. He also was cashing in countless political chits to influence the outcome of the Democratic primary. His son, although rather diffuse in his voiced opinions, was running as a Democrat, opportunistically. Democratic guru Tip O'Neill later observed that JFK "was only nominally a Democrat. He was a Kennedy."

That Kennedy's sweeping victory in the primary in his district meant that he would win the fall election without further travail. His election to Congress, after all, was only the beginning. During the campaign Attila, responding to charges that his son was too young for Congress, had predicted that his son would be elected President in 1960.

LARRY KING

In November 1952 Larry King, just turned 19, was at loose ends. His father's untimely death eight years earlier had been a severely traumatic experience for him. It had made him feel utterly deserted and had turned him in grade school from a top-flight, grade-skipping young scholar into a listless goof-off. His behavior in high school earned him the title of troublemaker, and his scholarship earned him a grade average just one point above the minimum for graduation.

During the next four and a half years he wandered aimlessly from job to lowly job—delivery boy, mail clerk, etc.—in his home town of Brooklyn while devoting his spare time to listening, also rather aimlessly, to radio broadcasts of Dodgers games and of various dramas and comedy shows such as that of his idol Arthur Godfrey. Under their influence he grew ever more aware of what he wanted to do for a living. Broadcasting, that was it—but how does a fellow get a start in the business?

Go to Miami, he was told, that's where a beginner can get his start in radio. And so he went there, early in 1957. What's more, he got a start, sweeping floors at a tiny AM station—until one day in May the station's disk jockey for its three-hour morning show unexpectedly quit. How about it—would he like to replace him? Would he ever! Trouble was, on his first time at the mike he froze, fading the music out and then, in his terror, simply turning it up again instead of speaking. Eventually the station manager rushed into the studio and reminded him that they were in the communications business.

That was his first and only experience with mike fright. Before long his entertaining patter was attracting not only new listeners but also the attention of rival station managers, ever on the lookout for undiscovered, employable talent. Within a year he was offered a DJ job by a larger station. Not only was the pay better, but he would have an enviable early-morning time slot with a more or less captive audience of car-encased commuters desperate for distraction.

117

In addition, the station encouraged him to be imaginative. He seized the opportunity, populating his show with various imaginary characters. There was a fellow named Wainwright, for instance, a whimsical captain in the Miami State Police. He was a treasure-house of unconventional ideas, among them the suggestion that Miami cops should accept and place bets in order to save people all that travel time to and from the race track. Gridlocked listeners loved it.

At the time the proprietors of Miami's Pumpernik Restaurant were casting about for a gimmick that might revive their waning early-morning business. It occurred to someone to invite him to do his four-hour show at the restaurant during its breakfast hours. Since the invitation had all the outward signs of opportunity, he accepted it with alacrity.

The gimmick proved to be a word-of-mouth success, with people telling other people about those entertaining breakfasts, especially after he began interviewing patrons at random—tourists, visiting firemen, the waitresses, whoever might look interesting and vulnerable. Sometimes an interview would take a comic turn, as on the occasions when he picked on Don Rickles and Lenny Bruce. At the time these two were noncelebrities, but one day early in the game Bobby Darin of stage and screen came in for breakfast. King's inevitable interview of Darin entertained not only the patrons but Bobby as well, and before long the restaurant became *the* place for a visit from celebrities when they were in Miami.

His experience at Pumpernik proved to him that he was adept at interviewing people, chiefly because he was sincerely interested in them and their viewpoints. This was, he wrote later, the turning point in his career. Soon he was doing his interviewing for a still larger station and then on television, in addition to contributing a column to Miami papers.

However, *the* turning point proved to be *a* turning point. Turned giddy by his success and exhilarating income, he developed an uninhibited taste for fancy consumer goods and for the races, so that his income was no match for his outgo. His burden of debt not only bankrupted him, and even precipitated a brush with the law, but also gave rise to a flood of excruciating publicity. This led, unsurprisingly, to sudden and unmitigated unemployment.

Over the next three years (1971–74) he freelanced as best he could in Miami, and then did some broadcasting in Shreveport, Louisiana, before taking a job as a sports commentator in San Francisco. On a pre-season visit to his mother in Miami, however, he was, surprisingly, rehired into his former TV and journalistic jobs. Yet once again debt burgeoned, and this time he formally declared bankruptcy, turning over the handling of his financial affairs to others.

That was the saving of him from himself. By the end of January 1978 he was doing a late-night talk show, this time nationally, on 28 stations throughout the country. Within a few years the show would be carried by ten times that many outlets, and he'd be on his way.

MARTIN LUTHER KING, JR.

In the fall of 1955 Martin Luther King, Jr., at 26 had been the new pastor at the Dexter Avenue Baptist Church in Montgomery, Alabama, for about a year. He was there as a result of a fateful decision, or perhaps two fateful decisions. In an earlier one he had chosen the ministry over the law for a career. It would, he felt, offer greater opportunity to be of service to others. In the more recent decision, in the fall of 1954, he had chosen the Dexter church over a number of others—the Ebenezer Baptist Church in Atlanta, Georgia (his father's church), as well as churches in Tennessee, New York, Massachusetts and Michigan.

It wasn't an easy decision. His new wife was Coretta Scott, whom he'd met in Boston when he was working toward his Ph.D. in systematic theology. She was a student at the New England Conservatory of Music, and hoped he would choose a Northern church (or maybe a teaching job in a Northern college) over one in the repellently segregated South. He was determined, however, "to live in the South because that's where I'm needed," and she understood. For all his delight in the pleasures of life (obviously more readily accessible to them north of Mason-Dixon), he knew a call when he heard one.

By the fall of 1955 he had received his doctorate and was earning a local reputation for being quite a preacher. The young couple, comfortably ensconced in the Dexter parsonage, became a family in November when the first of their four children was born. This would be their last month of domestic tranquility, but not because of children.

It was in December that the black citizens of Montgomery began their celebrated boycott of city buses to protest against the treatment of Rosa Parks, who had been arrested and jailed for wearily refusing to yield her bus seat to a white man, her superior according to redneck exegesis of God's Holy Word.

Boycotting blacks demanded the introduction of some civility, if not complete integration.

Knowing that a boycott can be effective only as it approaches 100%, leaders of the black community held a meeting to infuse it with some organization (carpools, for instance). To that end they formed an alliance, significantly called the Montgomery Improvement Association. It would need a president, and someone nominated King. For all his focusing on home, church and dissertation-writing, he had earlier joined the local chapter of the National Association for the Advancement of Colored People and had even, rather reluctantly, accepted appointment to its executive committee. That summer, however, when the chapter's presidency had become vacant and he was asked to take it on, he had declined.

This time, however, the call seemed more urgent, the responsibility entailed more specific. "Well," he responded, "if you think I can be of service, I will." He was elected unanimously. As one observer remarked drily at the time, it was just a matter of getting someone to bell the cat. This aspect of it was somewhat confirmed when a few of those present urged that the activities of the MIA be kept secret—until they were persuaded that a secret mass boycott was an oxymoron, like timid defiance. The white establishment would have to realize what they were up to, and what *they* were up against.

Yet he was now faced with something of an oxymoron, a dilemma, of his own. In his undergraduate work at the seminary his deep hostility toward contemptuous whites in general had abated under the influence of the Gandhian other-cheek philosophy, and particularly the dedication to nonviolence in the achievement of goals. The boycott in a way involved a kind of negative, passive economic violence threatening the financial survival of the bus service and of many a white merchant. As such (or in any case), it would surely invite unmistakably physical violence from those genetically so inclined. Could nonviolence be relied on as a reaction to violence? In the end he decided it could. At least there was a way to find out.

Shortly after New Year's Day 1956, the city bus company, after pitiably announcing that its losses were becoming unbearable, asked the city commission for a doubling of its fares. The commission agreed to half that, 150 percent, generously making life harder for poor whites who relied on bus transportation. Meanwhile a whispering campaign against King became so viciously slanderous that he almost tearfully offered to resign from the MIA presidency—an offer that was immediately and solidly rejected. At about the same time, at a mass rally of the local White Citizens Council, the police chief pledged his solidarity with that sodality's anti-boycott activities. These included continual harassment, obscene threats, property damage, bombing, sly efforts to divide the black community, heated denunciations of "outside agitators," and the jailing of King for driving on a city street at five miles an hour over the speed limit. And jeremiads against godless Communism, of course.

Through it all, despite occasional and unavoidable misgivings, he stayed calm. "Our demands are simple," he insisted to newshounds. "Until they are met we will continue to protest." And protest they did, nonviolently, for 382 days. In mid–December the U.S. Supreme Court, in response to a city appeal, unexpectedly nullified the state's laws requiring segregated bus seating. The MIA distributed "Integrated Bus Suggestions" leaflets to the black community recommending, for instance, against sitting next to a white "unless there is no other seat." It was now time, King declared, to "move from protest to reconciliation."

A couple of days later, at 1:30 in the morning on the following Sunday, the Lord's Day, a blast from a shotgun tore through his front door. Since the family was asleep in the rear, no one was hurt. He decided that calling the police would be an exercise in utter futility.

The next morning at church he conceded to the congregation, "It may be that some of us may have to die."

SPIKE LEE

His great-grandfather graduated from the Tuskegee Institute in Alabama. His grandfather and father both earned degrees from Morehouse College in Atlanta, while his grandmother and mother attended Spelman College. His three brothers and sisters are all college graduates. In such an overpoweringly educational milieu it was virtually inevitable that Spike Lee would choose an academic way of making a career out of his early, more than casual interest in movies. In the fall of 1979, having graduated from Morehouse, the 22-year-old hopeful entered the acclaimed Institute of Film and Television at New York University and began working toward a master's degree in filmmaking.

He early demonstrated his conviction that a black filmmaker should make movies about the black experience. In his first year he made a 10-minute movie excoriating the racism in the film classic *The Birth of a Nation*. It proved colorfully controversial and earned severe criticism from the faculty of a school in which D. W. Griffith was something of a divinity. Although he was nearly expelled, his subsequent films earned friendlier receptions and his last one, in his final year, was not only generally praised but even received a student award from the Academy of Motion Picture Arts and Sciences, a kind of junior Oscar, and was shown at several national and international film festivals. In 1982 he received his master's degree quite uncontroversially.

When some talent agencies, after showing interest in him, failed to bring him any work, he decided that he "would have to go out and do it alone, not relying on anyone else." To this end he got a $200-a-week job with a distribution company cleaning and shipping film while he devoted his free time to writing a script. He quickly found that he couldn't "do it alone" if the "it" required money. He was able to afford a camera, collect a crew, select a cast, and start shooting—but no more than start. He needed money to continue, and it would have to come from family members, friends, actors and crewmembers, anyone with a little scratch. It was embarrassing enough to have

122

to do this sort of soliciting, but the ultimate humiliation came in disappoint-ing all his faithful, trusting—and poorer—investors when the project had to be abandoned.

Yet it proved to be a learning experience. After his abject discourage-ment had abated, he recognized that his ambition had needlessly exceeded his resources, or so it seemed. Next time—he was sure that there would be a next time, and soon—next time he would exercise more restraint, keeping the scenario simple, more spare, making the production practically producible.

The next summer, 1985, he began work on his first feature-length movie. For all his determination to keep costs down, and indeed his success in doing so, bills payable accumulated into backbreaking, mind-boggling piles. They were "killing" him, he confided to his diary, yet he wouldn't give up because he "was born to be a filmmaker." With that in mind he devised some more imaginative methods of financing, including periodic showings of rough-cut portions of the new film, *She's Gotta Have It*, to potential investors. He also persuaded crew and cast members to await payment until the movie made enough money for both owners and workers.

In addition, he tried to make the movie marketable, as the intriguingly ambiguous title may suggest. He chose a theme practically guaranteed to attract audiences of young women, especially blacks, though by no means exclusively. Convinced that they resented the possessiveness of young men who collected girlfriends in a kind of competitive numbers game, he found support for this opinion in an ad-hoc survey of some 30 neighborhood belles. And so the "She" in *She's Gotta Have It* became a girl openly juggling three boyfriends simultaneously. At the film's conclusion she looks into the cam-era and explains to the audience, "It's about control. *My* body. *My* mind. Who's gonna own it, them or me?"

Somehow the filming was completed—in a preposterous 12 days. Lee did the editing himself in his apartment between battles with creditors. For a total of $175,000, about the cost of a television ad, he had brought a full-length movie to life which, after its release early in 1986, would be so warmly welcomed at the San Francisco Film Festival that it would quickly become the object of competitive bidding from film distributors who knew a hot prop-erty when they saw one. Soon thereafter it won the prize for best new film at Cannes. After its official opening that August at the Cinema Studio in New York, it began receiving satisfying critical notices. *The New Yorker's* Pauline Kael wrote a sentence that must have touched Lee's heart where he could feel it most deeply: "When a director has it, it's as if nature intended him to make movies."

The movie eventually grossed more than ten times what it cost. His next pictures, *School Daze* and the celebrated *Do the Right Thing*, would be bud-geted at $4 million and $6.5 million respectively. Spike Lee was well on his way to *Clockers*, and beyond.

Maya Lin

In the fall of 1980 Maya Lin, just turned 21, was a senior at Yale University majoring in architecture and currently enrolled in a course in funerary architecture. In selecting this course she had been at least partly influenced by a course she had completed earlier in existentialism and its surrender to the solace of death. She wasn't sure where this might be leading her when the architecture professor announced a special assignment for his students, to design a memorial for the dead and missing veterans of the war in Vietnam.

Meanwhile a surviving veteran, Jan Scruggs, who had seen half of the men in his infantry company killed in that dreadful, perilous, hopeless conflict, had decided to counter the widespread aversion to the war with a memorial bearing the names of the dead and missing. To this end he and some others of the same mind founded the Vietnam Veterans Memorial Fund, to which, in a surprisingly short time, some 275,000 Americans gave seven million dollars, enough to justify announcing an architectural competition. After strenuously extracting permission from Congress to site it on an appropriate two-acre tract on Washington's Mall, they announced the competition in the fall of 1980, giving entrants four months to submit their plans.

She had her assignment, her interest in funerary architecture, those four months—and nothing to lose. She also had no idea of what the memorial should look like. To have a look at its location, she and some of her classmates traveled to Washington and found the site beautifully appropriate, located between the Washington Monument and the Lincoln Memorial. As she took photographs here and there, an idea began to form of a memorial that would seem to emerge from the ground with its thousands of engraved names, symbolizing remembrance of the war's forgotten victims.

After returning to Yale she began sketching and modeling in clay. As she did so she found herself tending toward unconventional simplicity. There was that rigid requirement, after all, of almost 60,000 names, which she felt should be an integral part of the memorial, not merely an accompaniment to some

124

traditional statuary. With considerable misgivings she turned in her final design for the course and class discussion. Her sketch showed two black walls rising out of the earth, surrounded by grass and trees. Black rather than white, she explained when asked, not only to symbolize death but also to make the names more legible against a black background—more legible to the viewers reflected in the polished surface. At the professor's suggestion she changed the design to bring the walls together at an angle and to list the names chronologically by date of death rather than alphabetically. (There were more than 600 Smiths and 16 James Joneses. Furthermore, a chronological order would do more toward keeping the names of comrades together.)

Such an unconventional proposal, she felt sure, wouldn't be given any serious consideration in a competition. Her professor agreed, considering it "too strong" and awarding it only a grade of B. But, he suggested, send it in anyway. One never knows about artistic taste and, again, she had nothing to lose. And so she entered it.

Each entry was to be accompanied by an explanatory statement for the judges' enlightenment. In hers she described entering and leaving the memorial "gradually," making it in a sense "a moving composition," both physically and emotionally. "As we turn to leave, we see these walls stretching into the distance, directing us to the Washington Monument, to the left, and the Lincoln Memorial, to the right, thus bringing the Vietnam Memorial into historical context." The statement may have been as persuasive as the design.

The phone call came to her at school from a Fund staff member, informing her, "We're coming up to talk to you." She was astonished. Could she have won, say, some sort of honorable mention? Even when "they" arrived and told her that she'd won first prize, she still refused to believe it. Of more than 1,400 entries—*hers*?! Skeptically she agreed to come to Washington as soon as possible for a press conference. When she arrived, presenting her slender five-foot-three and looking much younger than even her 21 years, she wasn't a very impressive figure. But her entrance was greeted with more than polite applause, and then she believed she'd won. In the final announcement of the verdict were the words, "superbly harmonious."

The verdict was a bold one. One of the judges warned of hostile reactions, remarking with considerable foresight that "many people would not understand the design until they experienced it." By those addicted to ancient sculpture the memorial was described as bizarre, degrading, shameful. Some of the attacks on its creator included the word "gook," a clear indication of the attackers' artistic credentials. The prescient judge was right, however. As more than two million visitors a year (including Ronald Reagan) came to "experience it," they indeed came to understand.

It hardly need be added that from then on Maya Lin received more commissions than any architecture or sculptor in her twenties had any reason to expect.

MADONNA

In the fall of 1982 Madonna Louise Veronica Ciccone was 24 years old and rather at loose ends amid an aimless, pillar-to-post career of song and dance that seemed to be getting nowhere. Although her earlier hard times, when for instance she had subsisted for a while in an abandoned synagogue, seemed to be over, she was in a rut—until her visit one night to the club Danceteria in Lower Manhattan. It was one of many such clubs that she kept visiting not so much casually as desperately, carrying with her a demonstration tape of songs she had written and fervently hoping that somebody would give it a listen.

Somebody finally did. Mark Kamin, Danceteria's sophisticated, flamboyant and very popular young deejay, after listening to it to please his newfound inamorata, was so impressed that he played it for the dancers. They loved it, wildly, passionately, and very expressively. So much so that he decided to take it, and Madonna, to a friend, Michael Rosenblatt, of Warner's Sire Records. After listening to the demo a couple of times (the first song was "Everybody"), he agreed that it was good, though no better than good, but what interested him more immediately was this radiantly sexy, "incredibly wild-looking" woman. He asked her why she'd come, what she wanted to do. When she replied that she wanted to make records, he promptly drew up a contract stipulating an advance of $5,000 plus $1,000 for each song she turned in. Evidently her demo was better than good, or at least better than he had said it was.

Sire president Seymour Stein thought it so good that he demanded to meet its author at once, even though he was in a hospital recovering from heart surgery. He and Rosenblatt weren't so carried away, however, as to release a Madonna album without first introducing her on a single to test the reaction. It would have "Ain't No Big Deal," Stein's favorite, on the A side and "Everybody" on the B, and would be scheduled for release in a couple of weeks.

After it was cut it was reviewed, and Side A proved disappointing, not up to public-release standards. Rather than bolix up release schedules with the delay involved in setting up another song for Side A, Rosenblatt decided to put the frolicsome "Everybody" on both sides. That's the way it was issued, and that's the way it soon rose to the top of the dance charts.

This inspired the Warner people into cranking up the flackery for her debut, including a high-temperature act for stage performances in connection with the customary tour. Those performances turned out to be so volcanically visual that soon the idea of getting her on television became fiscally irresistible.

And so the next step was an "Everybody" video, for which she worked very hard and very professionally. It proved popular enough to keep the record high on the dance charts and even on *Billboard*'s pop Hot 100 listing. Yet there still was some hesitancy at Warner over producing an album. Maybe a 12-inch "mini-LP" would furnish a fairly reliable test.

It did. "Physical Attraction" climbed so quickly to the heights on the dance charts that the Warner light finally flashed green for an album. She greeted the news with the it's-about-time impatience of unwavering ambition. In this mood she shed her manager in favor of Freddy DeMann, Michael Jackson's former manager, as someone who had experience in handling skyrockets.

That's what he had to handle, although not right away. Her 1983 debut album, overconfidently entitled *Madonna*, took some time to generate the preposterous enthusiasm that eventually carried its sales to nine million copies, plus six smash singles. Her second album, released in 1984 and more provocatively entitled *Like a Virgin*, proved to be more in the instant-hit tradition and launched her into the spectacular recording and MTV video career that we know today and that led to her outstanding performance in the movie *Desperately Seeking Susan* in 1985.

By the 1990s her show-biz acumen and in-your-face persona had brought her untold wealth, vast popular infatuation, reverberating censure, and even academic scrutiny in a large number of university courses. Art Buchwald has told his readers of a visitor from Tanzania who asked to be taken to a Madonna concert. After it the visitor, wildly excited, exclaimed, "Wait until my people back home hear that I went to see Madonna!"

Public reaction to her behavior hasn't been unmitigated adulation. On David Letterman's show her remarks were bleeped 13 times. As Norman Mailer has observed, she has been "called sick, sordid, depraved, unbalanced, out of control, offensive, outrageous, and stupid." But then it was Mailer to whom she confessed that when performing she was "detached from myself," another person—and "I have no control over that person." She didn't seem unhappy about it.

NELSON MANDELA

In the late summer of 1988 Nelson Mandela, just turned 70, was in the hospital of the Pollsmoor Maximum Security Prison suffering from what the attending doctor diagnosed as an acute attack of tuberculosis. He had been living, if that's the word, in South African prisons for more than a quarter of a century, and the generally harsh treatment had finally conquered his body if not his spirit. His wife, Winnie, and the few friends allowed to visit him, were shocked at his appearance and by his inability to recognize them right away.

Yet his spirit remained indomitable, and by October, although still in the hospital, he had regained his normal weight and strength and was even back to doing his morning push-ups. Meanwhile the South African government (President P. W. Botha & Co.) was riven with uncertainty over how best to respond to the increasingly insistent demand for his release, both national and international. If he weren't released, the government would be increasingly subject to contempt, both national and international. Yet if he were, he'd once again (by his own account) be spurring that irrepressible African National Congress into all that intolerable trouble again.

The compromise was to remove him in December 1988 from maximum security to minimum. The Victor Verster Prison, some 30 miles from his family in Cape Town, provided him with a separate cottage. The cottage and the prison's swimming pool were accorded much flattering publicity in newspaper accounts and photographs. The cottage was large enough for his family to live there with him, with the government's magnanimous permission, whatever their opinion of participatory imprisonment. None of these amenities would he accept, however. He refused to live any better than the multitude of his fellow political prisoners throughout the country.

Meanwhile the government was finding the trouble quite intolerable even without him. Indeed, it was with him in the sense that his endless confinement simply added to the ferocious resentment of the violently repressed majority. That resentment was growing ever more alarmingly aggressive, as in June 1988, when some two million black workers went on strike to protest antiunion and antiapartheid legislation. In August 1989, after government officials' discussions with Mandela had convinced them that apartheid was not the wave of the future in South Africa, President Botha resigned in resignation and was replaced by Frederik W. de Klerk.

Although de Klerk was certainly no firebrand integrationist, he was a welcome improvement over the uneasily rigid Botha in that he was willing, however reluctantly, to accommodate the inexorable. In December he persuaded his cabinet to authorize him to restore the outlawed African National Congress to full legality and to release Mandela by the following February. Before the release the two men met in the presidential residence to discuss the inexorable. The meeting was quite amicable, much more so than their relationship over the next few years, during which they discovered their sharply differing views of inexorability and accommodation.

After a world tour in the spring of 1990, in acknowledgment of the persistent international support largely responsible for his freedom (including surprisingly discomfiting international sanctions), he returned to the formidable task of bringing democratic order out of South Africa's political chaos. Violence was on the increase. Indeed, as he put it in his autobiography, the "country was bleeding to death, and we had to move ahead faster."

They tried. In August the ANC and the government formally agreed to call a halt to the violence and give negotiation a chance. On both sides, however, among black partisans and government police, were addicts of intractable hostility. Some black dissidents needed the paraphernalia and opportunities for violent expression of their dissatisfaction, and some of the police were only too happy to oblige. Mandela's protests to the government proved futile, as did his incessant attempts to moderate intertribal belligerence. By May 1991 the general turbulence was so epidemic, and seemed so endemic and hopeless, that all negotiations were indefinitely suspended.

In July the ANC held a democratically elected conference, its first in the country in 30 years, at which he was elected ANC president. He continued to argue for negotiation, and in December the ANC and other dissident groups entered into what he has called "the real talks" at the Convention for a Democratic South Africa. Bitter controversies, over matters both petty and significant, failed to extinguish the determined optimism on both sides, although they did cause frustration and occasional breaks in the talks. It wasn't until September 1992 that he and de Klerk arrived at their Record of Understanding specifying that, among other things, a constitutional assembly, freely elected, would draft a new constitution for the country. Under this constitution, in April 1994 (after he and de Klerk had received the 1993 Nobel Peace Prize), elections open to all South African citizens were held. Citizens, including blacks, after waiting in endless lines at the polls, incredibly gave the ANC nearly two-thirds of their votes. As South Africa's head, he became the country's first elected black President.

Many serious problems lay ahead for him, both political and personal, but surely they wouldn't daunt someone who had changed his role from prisoner to President in only four years, and against such odds.

THURGOOD MARSHALL

In the fall of 1961 Thurgood Marshall at 53 had earned an enviable reputation as a civil-rights lawyer, surely the best known and probably the best in the country. As counsel for the National Association for the Advancement of Colored People he had led a team of attorneys in arguing 32 civil-rights cases before the U.S. Supreme Court and had won 29 of them. One of these was the momentous 1954 case of *Brown vs. Board of Education* outlawing (if not abruptly eliminating) racial segregation in public schools. For all his success, however, he was frustrated by the slow pace of integration, or even acceptance of black competence. Shortly after the Brown decision he complained to the reporter Carl Rowan, in a rather awkward metaphor, about how it troubled him "to go from one courtroom after another in one state after another, north or south, east or west, and never see anything but white faces on the bench."

In the White House in September 1961 the brothers Kennedy, among others, had come to recognize that the country's court system, especially the Federal judiciary, was proving unexpectedly effective in the desegregation of society. The Administration could maintain, even increase, that effectiveness by appointing judges known for their awareness of the Constitution's "equal protection" clause. And so they recommended, for Senate approval, the appointment of Marshall to the Second Circuit Court of Appeals.

Marshall received the news with considerable misgivings. His entire legal experience had been one of advocacy, of arguing cases, not judging them. This would require a fundamental turnabout in attitude, in temperament, in perspective. Would he prove to be *judicious* enough for the bench? In civic-rights cases, could he be fair? After much thought, he decided he could—it was certainly worth a try. His NAACP work could be carried on by his highly competent litigious team, and he would have a chance to make the court system not only a little more colorful, but more color-blind.

Anyway, his throes of decision might well prove utterly academic, since

131

his nomination required the approval of the Senate Judiciary Committee, chaired by Mississippi's James Eastland, for whom "black" was simply a dirty word. By many or most political reporters he was considered "one of the southernmost points in the country." His home was in Sunflower County, noted for a black voter registration of 3 percent and a devotion to the noose as an instrument of breakneck correction. During his chairing of the Subcommittee on Civil Rights he had contentedly prevented 127 proposed civil-rights bills from finding their way to the full Committee. What faced Marshall's nomination was at least a solid wall of political white cement.

Fortunately political, for it was politics that provided the solvent. Eastland had a friend, Harold Cox, a former college roommate whom he wanted nominated to fill a vacancy on the Fifth Circuit Court, which handled many if not most of the South's civil-rights appeals. So when Attorney General Robert Kennedy approached him concerning the Marshall nomination, he was astonished to find the senator not at all intransigent but rather cordially open to making a deal. If the administration nominated Cox, the Marshall nomination would be permitted a full committee vote. As the senator tastefully phrased it, "Tell your brother that if he'll give me Harold Cox, I'll give him the nigger."

As a result, Harold Cox became, easily and speedily, the President's first appointee to the federal judiciary. Marshall would become his second, but by no means easily or speedily. With Eastland promoting Senatorial lethargy at every opportunity, the hearings were fended off until the following May and then were held on six days scattered through the next three months. Marshall was variously accused of being a racist, a communist, and an advocate of political vengeance "when the colored folks take over," but also was praised by Northern senators who pointed out that he had been formally rated as "well qualified" by the American Bar Association. As a result, the Committee as a whole, evidently concluding that he was at least a well qualified racist and communist, sent his nomination on to the full Senate without recommendation. In September the nomination was approved by the Senate, 54 to 16.

Consequently, he now had an opportunity to exhibit his judicial temperament. How well he fulfilled it may best be shown in a comparison with his opposite number in the political bartering. Harold Cox, an Eastland mind-alike, was overruled on appeal of civil-rights cases more often than any appeals court judge. Marshall, in his four years on the appellate court, wrote 98 majority opinions, eight concurrences, and only twelve dissents. Of the 98 majority opinions, none was reversed.

After leaving the court in 1965 to serve as U.S. Solicitor General, he had another opportunity to exhibit his judicial temperament (a long-lasting one) after being named by Lyndon Johnson in 1967 to the Supreme Court, a body known for its not infrequent outbursts of judicially intemperate opinion.

GRANDMA MOSES

By the fall of 1935 Grandma Moses, a.k.a. Anna Mary Robertson Moses, at 77 had been doing a little painting now and then, as time permitted, for about 17 years. At least she had produced her first "large" painting in 1918, to decorate the fireboard in the family parlor. Most of her time was taken up with the care and feeding of her husband and their five surviving children (out of ten), leaving her only occasional opportunities to create paintings and artistic embroideries for friends and relatives.

Painting was really secondary as a hobby to what she called her "fancy work," her picturesque (and quite representational) embroidery. After her husband died in 1927, her time was still mostly devoted to her children and *their* children. She continued painting, "but I thought no more of it than doing my fancy work." After several years of this spasmodic yet relentless creative activity, she had accumulated "quite a few" paintings. A friend urged her to put them on display at "old Thomas' drug store in Hoosick Falls." Old Thomas apparently was agreeable, and so she had her first informal exhibition. She won a prize for her canned fruits and raspberry jam, but not for the paintings.

They had caught the eye, however, of Mrs. Thomas, who in 1938 decided to set up a sort of trade mart at the drugstore, affording the local ladies a market for selling, buying, bartering the products of their incidental domestic activity. Some Moses paintings, she realized, should be just the thing for a window display. And that's how they came to be in the drugstore window during Easter week in 1938, when they caught another, more appraising, eye.

Louis Caldor was a civil engineer who lived in New York City, about 100 miles to the south. He and his wife and daughter were vacationing in the Hoosick River area. Civil engineering was his occupation, but art was his preoccupation, as was his art collection. That appraising eye was ever on the lookout for something new and reasonably collectible as well as something new and profitably promotable. Those four paintings in that drugstore

window, he decided at first sight, were certainly collectible and probably promotable.

Neither Thomas was at the store, but the manager informed him that,
yes, there were more paintings like that in the back storeroom. The store had
had them back there, as well as those on display, for more than a year now.
All told, maybe about a dozen. At Caldor's perfervid request he brought the
back-room items out for inspection, after which he decided to reap some har-
vest out of this curious tourist's enthusiasm. The tourist asked if there had
been any sales. Not a one, came the answer, but if you're interested I can let
you have the lot with ten percent off the price. Since the price was already
ridiculously low, Caldor emerged from the story fully encumbered and tri-
umphantly jubilant.

After preparing the paintings for transportation, he returned and asked
where he could find the artist. The answer was "down on Cambridge Road,"
where she lived with her family in a farmhouse. On his arrival, after a warily courteous welcome, he explained to her that he not only liked her paintings but also felt sure that he could find a market for them. A rather intense
man, he apparently got carried away with his own eloquence, promising her
that any financial worries she might have were about to be a thing of the past,
while the rest of the family sat and listened in amazement, pop-eyed and
agape.

Reality set in with a vengeance. For more than a year, although he continued to buy her paintings and steadfastly encouraged her to keep up the
good work, he was also ever more desperately trying to interest New York
galleries in her pictures. Occasionally exhibitors would concede at least that
her homespun paintings were "nice," yet none felt compelled to invest in an
unknown lady artist in her late seventies.

It wasn't until late 1939 that he was able to write her, "I have finally made
good my promise to you and your folks." Having heard of plans for a show
at the Museum of Modern Art, to be entitled "Contemporary Unknown
American Painters," he persuaded the advisory board that he knew of a painter
who fit the bill only too exactly. Three of her paintings were selected for the
exhibition.

Unfortunately, it could hardly be called an exhibition, since it was enig-
matically closed to the public. It yielded nothing more than the return of the
paintings and a conventional letter of thanks. Although another year of persistent rejection followed, Caldor was even more persistent. Meanwhile one
Otto Kallir, a dealer in modern art who had recently fled to New York from
Nazi Austria, was in search of distinctively American paintings. Before long
he and Caldor and Grandma Moses' paintings were getting along famously.

And so, in October 1940, about three dozen of her pictures, mostly small
ones, were shown in an exhibit provocatively entitled "What a Farm Wife
Painted," and three were sold. Only three, but then the Gimbel's Department

Store repeated the exhibition, advertising it with frenzied hype (e.g., Grandma was "the white-haired girl of the U.S.A."). After that she gradually began receiving invitations to show her work, which, also gradually, became marketable, profitable, even lucrative. It had taken him considerable time and effort, but Louis Caldor had finally fulfilled his promise.

She was no longer an "unknown." Governor Rockefeller declared her birthday "Grandma Moses Day" in New York, and President Eisenhower commissioned her to paint his farm.

RUPERT MURDOCH

As the year 1990 drew to a close Rupert Murdoch was an emperor. His commercial empire was his News Corporation, a vast, multifaceted, world-encircling "information" enterprise. Rumors abounded of an imminent auto-biography revealing the secret of his unique, astounding business success.

Trouble was, the chief secret was going into hock. The business was so deep in debt that it faced imminent liquidation. Murdoch, ever anxious to keep the business under family control, had always preferred debt to equity in financing its expansion, or proliferation. Through the years debt had piled on debt until now it totaled almost $8 billion. Further, credit generally had grown frustratingly tight, largely because of a recession and problems in the troubled banking and S&L industries, and as of December 1990 the continued survival of News Corporation depended on creditors' willingness to renew their loans. The willingness of *all* its creditors, that is, since a single refusal could start an avalanche. The situation was just that desperate.

And so, when early that month a small bank in Pittsburgh refused to renew its ostensibly insignificant loan of $10 million, David DeVoe, Murdoch's chief financial executive, phoned Pittsburgh and asked how come. The answer was simple: the payment was due, the bank needed it, so pay up. DeVoe protested that he simply couldn't, not without starting a house-of-cards collapse that would mean liquidating News Corp. The bank officer was undisturbed: that's okay, we'll have to be satisfied with our share of the debris—how about immediate receivership?

DeVoe was painfully shocked, and his report to headquarters soon had Murdoch in a state that might be expected from staring financial catastrophe in the face. But one thing about being heavily in debt to someone is that the someone has to take intense interest in your financial survival and so can be called on for help. In this case that someone was Citibank, the empire's biggest creditor, which was already engaged in the risky job of rescue. Any reluctance was irrelevant.

To handle the job the bank board had assigned a vice-president in whom they had a great deal of well-earned confidence, although the image involved was hardly what would conventionally be expected of a bank V.P. or loan officer. Ann Lane was a slim, handsome women of 34, her bright expression enhanced by a lovely smile, her direct gaze enhanced by bright blue eyes. In addition to her educational credentials from the University of California, she had had experience in handling this sort of problem, enough for her to realize that this one was really a corker. (News Corp.'s various companies were in debt to 146 creditors.) Fortunately, she quickly came to like Murdoch and wish him well. He would be trustfully relying on her for his business survival over the coming months. Liking him would make restraining him much easier, and some fiscal restraint, she felt sure, would be unavoidable.

Investment, and therefore persuasion, in the financial marketplace rest on two emotions, hope of profit and fear of loss. Under the circumstances, Lane, with vital help from DeVoe, chose the latter route, the route of "we're all in this together, sink or swim." Although she wasn't able to persuade News Corp.'s major creditors (nine large banks) to increase their loan amounts for a resource operation, she did get some new loans from some middle-sized lenders eager to avoid that sinking feeling. She also insisted on bringing some order out of the News Corp. chaos, introducing a plan for reorganization that might cool down the hot breath of consternated creditors. A plan it was indeed, its description filling a folder several inches thick. When asked for a backup plan, she said there wasn't any.

She demanded, for instance, that one of the companies, Sky Television, was simply too expensive and unpromising for News Corp. to afford, and it was sold off. This helped greatly to appease the major lenders, who agreed to control their impatience, and this agreement facilitated the sales job with the middle-sized institutions. Murdoch also helped at the incessant meetings by promising to make his management techniques more consultative, less autocratic.

Things were looking up by December, and then came the news of Pittsburgh's adamancy. Everything seemed to hang on that bank's willingness to renew the loan. A refusal probably meant that another loan, an Australian billion-dollar loan, would be called, and that would surely lead to the collapse of the fiscal house of cards. Murdoch was as close to despair as his personality would allow, but Lane, refusing to give up hope, decided that the time had come for exerting some pressure. She phoned Citibank and asked that its chairman call the Pittsburgh bank and explain the disastrous implications of its adamancy. Fully aware of the implications for Citibank, he was glad to oblige.

That done, Lane convinced Murdoch that he now had to call the Pittsburgh bank himself and ask for that renewal, *beg* for that renewal. Murdoch, who was used to having heads of governments take his calls, was hardly encouraged when the bank chairman refused to talk to him and had the call shunted to the chief loan officer, the source of the adamancy who earlier had told DeVoe of his preference for receivership.

The pressure had been effective, however. Before Murdoch could start begging, the loan officer greeted him most cordially, assuring him that the bank would be accommodating.

Over the succeeding years Murdoch has brought the corporation debt down to about $5 billion while his profitable acquisitions, notably his hundred-plus newspapers and his eight Fox TV stations, have provided reassuring cash accumulations. In May 1995, indeed, *Business Week* pictured him as a man with "a few billion burning a hole in his pocket."

RALPH NADER

In the spring of 1964 Ralph Nader at 30 was already a crusader, even a single-minded zealot, but a frustrated one. After receiving his Harvard law degree he had spent some of the early 1960s touring Europe, Africa and South America and had been appalled by what he saw as the gross indifference of major American corporations to the social and environmental damage resulting from their devotion to unrestrained profitability. By now, as a staff consultant in the U.S. Department of Labor, he had narrowed his general exasperation to a specific subject, highway safety, on which he was writing a formal report.

To date in the twentieth century more than 1.5 million Americans had been killed in automobiles. Traveling in them safely was becoming a major concern among voters and therefore a matter of interest to politicians. It also was of interest to Nader, who as early as 1959 had published an article in *The Harvard Law Review* ominously entitled "American Cars: Designed for Death." The conventional approach to the auto-safety problems at the time was to find ways to improve *driver* safety. His approach, as his title suggests, was to focus on *car* safety. This was a major feature of his Labor Department report, which of course began to gather dust almost before its release.

Thus his frustration. And thus his decision to go public with his carefully documented study, incorporating its major argument in a manuscript entitled *Unsafe at Any Speed*. In September 1964 a small New York publisher accepted it, but it wouldn't be published until November 1965. In the meantime he emerged only slightly from his obscurity with some articles in *The Christian Science Monitor*, including one revealing that speedometers in some American cars gave perilously unreliable readings of miles per hour.

Meanwhile also the U.S. senator representing his native Connecticut, Abraham Ribicoff, had managed to get himself appointed chairman of a senate subcommittee on executive reorganization, a topic broad enough to justify hearings on almost anything. Since "Hearings on Almost Anything" might suggest a rather indiscriminate curiosity to a skeptical press, he instructed

139

the committee's chief counsel to dig up a hot topic. As governor he'd been interested in highway safety, conducting campaigns against speeding and drunk driving. After some research the counsel revived his interest by suggesting that he shift it from drivers to cars. This seemed to be a new idea in the literature on highway safety, he explained, an exploitable idea that offered an opportunity to launch a newsworthy investigation into the irresponsibility of big business, thereby appealing to electorate prejudices.

His suggestion proved quite timely. In Detroit at the General Motors Corporation concern was growing over the dubious performance of the flashy Chevrolet Corvair, which had inspired more than 100 potentially very expensive lawsuits for personal injury due to accidents resulting from its instability. Now, in November 1965, someone directed the GM lawyers' attention to this newly published, unpleasant little book called *Unsafe at Any Speed*. No only did it indict the auto industry generally for its emphasis on styling at the expense of safety, but it particularly zeroed in on the Corvair as "one of the nastiest-handling cars ever built." And there also were those rumors that Ribicoff was planning to hold hearings on safety in auto design.

The book was pretty convincing, the lawyers concluded, which meant that its buttinsky author would probably be called as an expert witness at some or all of the trials and at the hearings. The first thing needed was information on him, preferably discrediting, especially on his motivation but also generally on the way he lived, his associations, his drinking, his sex life, all that sort of thing.

He soon became aware that he was being investigated, even tailed. When *they* became aware that he was on to them, they resorted to harassment, perhaps out of frustration over his clean living, abstemious frugality and impregnable integrity—for investigative purposes, a dry hole.

The investigative efforts, despite their futility, continued into March 1966. On the twelfth of that month, with his cooperation, they were brought to light by *The New Republic* and then by a number of newspapers, including *The Washington Post*. As a result, when Ribicoff opened his subcommittee hearings on the twenty-second, the subject was no longer so much auto safety as the investigative shenanigans.

A week or so earlier James Roche, president of GM, had received an urgent and rather unsettling invitation from Ribicoff to attend the hearings "as a witness." The hearings would be nationally televised.

Witness Roche, particularly under some relentless questioning by Senator Robert Kennedy, conceded that the probers' activities had gone far beyond any justifiable investigation. Although of course he personally hadn't known what was going on, as president he was ultimately responsible, and he apologized.

The hearings gave Nader a David-vs.-Goliath public character as well as a public platform. Safety in auto design, of course, would be only the beginning.

In 1969, after three years of precipitously declining sales, the Corvair was taken off the market.

LAURENCE OLIVIER

In the summer of 1938 Laurence Olivier at 31 was an actor of wide acclaim in the British theater, in friendly competition with John Gielgud for the title of Very Best. He'd had his share of failures and of unwelcome criticism, however, and the acclaim was limited to his work on the stage. His British movies had earned him no plaudits, and his brief work in Hollywood in the early thirties making three pictures, although moderately lucrative, he considered simply "an appalling waste of time." He might be splendid on stage, he'd been advised there, but on the screen he just didn't have it, certainly not enough of it, for instance, to compete with Ronald Colman.

Yet in 1938 he made a British film, Alexander Korda's *The Divorce of Lady X*, with Merle Oberon. Korda soon thereafter was asked to lend Merle Oberon to United Artists for a movie version of Emily Brontë's *Wuthering Heights*. On being told that the director, William Wyler, was having some difficulty finding an actor for the part of the erotically smoldering Heathcliff, he dispatched a print of *Lady X* to him. Olivier's performance in the movie wasn't very persuasive, but fortunately Wyler had seen enough of his acting, and especially now of his face and physique, to feel that he could be readily molded into a powerful Heathcliff. He invited him to come at once to the land of cinematic milk and honey.

The invitee was reluctant, chiefly because he had dreams of a Lunt-Fontanne partnership with his temperamental truelove Vivien Leigh, dreams that could be shattered by a separate movie career (as indeed they were). Wyler's persistence and her reluctant consent finally swayed him, and by early November 1938 he was in Hollywood, however ruefully.

His next two years in Hollywood were anything but an appalling waste of time. During them he made only three movies, yet all three were of superlative quality and enduring popularity. Two of them earned him Oscar nominations. In the early days of the production of *Wuthering Heights*, however, he displayed his stage actor's disdain for, and ignorance of, movie acting technique and thereby created, in Wyler's tactful account of it, "some difficulties." His relationship with Merle Oberon, whom he considered far inferior to his Vivien as a choice for the role of Cathy, was taut at best, especially after she demanded that he stop "spitting" at her during his ardent speeches in passionate close-ups. Yet long before the final reel Wyler had grown enthusiastic over the stage actor's transformation into a movie star, judging his performance to be "the most important single contribution" to the movie's success, and Oberon, on sober second thought, had grown delighted with "witnessing a great actor adapting his art from stage to screen."

Meanwhile Vivien, unable to put up with their separation any longer, arrived in Hollywood from England just as David O. Selznick & Co. were desperately searching for someone to fill the bill as Scarlett O'Hara in *Gone with the Wind.*

In the filming of *Rebecca* it was Joan Fontaine's turn, since of course he felt that his beloved Vivien would have been a far better choice, and in his less than benign treatment of her he was abetted this time by the director, Alfred Hitchcock of keep-the-ladies-under-control fame. The splendid result, a movie of enduring distinction, can only be a tribute to the professionalism of all concerned. (Despite Selznick's anxiety over his star's "throwing lines away," it won 1940's Oscar for Best Picture.)

Greer Garson, fortunately a favorite of his, was treated much more chivalrously during the making of *Pride and Prejudice*, although he had tried to induce L.B. Mayer into giving Vivien her role of Elizabeth Bennett—so chivalrously indeed that Vivien became acutely and quite conspicuously jealous. Her shiny new Oscar and her scintillating celebrity (with apologies, she was now the Scarlett woman) were only consolation prizes.

His addiction matched hers, of course, and in early 1940, after completing his part in *Pride and Prejudice*, he defiantly decided to join her in a stage production of *Romeo and Juliet,* which he produced and directed and into which they sank all their savings. After opening in San Francisco they took it on trial tour across the country to New York, behind flamboyant advance publicity trumpeting the approach of the passionate pair. (The nadir, perhaps: "See real lovers make love in public!") Despite some mild critical acclaim and full houses on tour, in New York it was an unqualified disaster with critics and theatergoers alike, with people standing in lines at the box office demanding their money back. (One reviewer complained that Romeo's speeches sounded "as though he were brushing his teeth," and historians of the theater are still scratching their heads.) In May the passionate pair, having lost their savings to togetherness, returned to England to join in the war effort, and, three months later, to get married.

As for their careers, Hollywood had provided a turning point for each of them. Like her, he was a *film* star now, and this new celebrity brought him prestige and influence—and cinematic opportunities. Two years earlier, when he was considering the *Wuthering Heights* offer, he'd consulted his old friend Ralph Richardson. As he has reported it in his autobiography, "Ralph obligingly thought for a moment and then said, 'Yes. Bit of fame. Good.'"

Exactly. That fame ultimately enabled him to earn a knighthood and a peerage, and to create an artistic legacy nonpareil.

ROSA PARKS

It was a little before six in the evening of Thursday, December 1, 1955, when Rosa Parks, 42, boarded a city bus. She was worn out from a long workday as a seamstress at a downtown department store. Her shoulders and neck ached, and all she wanted was a quiet ride home.

Her problem was, or would turn out to be, that this was in Montgomery, Alabama.

She was too tired to be apprehensive, but she had reason to be. A hundred years earlier in this state a "colored" could demand human treatment only through a display of suicidal spunk. Since the abolition of chattel slavery in the mid–1860s, a hallowed tradition of residual abuse called segregation had kept blacks in the grip of fear through means ranging from murder to legal harassment. Examples of the former could often be found hanging in trees within living memory. An example of the latter was provided by the laws of Alabama that governed segregated seating in public conveyances.

On Montgomery's streetcars in 1900, for instance, a black was required to yield his or her seat to a white under all circumstances—until a boycott that year compelled the city council to modify the law so that no one would have to yield a seat if another seat was available. As streetcars were replaced by buses the relevant laws were adjusted so that blacks were assigned the rear five rows of seats and whites the front five, with the middle eight rows to be apportioned at the discretion of the driver, a white male carrying a revolver for emergency enforcement of his discretion. Another aspect of that discretion was his legal right to decide whether or not to let a black stay in the bus after entering and paying the fare, or, instead, to order the newcomer to get out and enter again through the rear door.

It was under such a considerate arrangement that Parks had her first confrontation on a bus. One winter day in 1943 her bus arrived crammed with black riders in the back, some even hanging on at the rear door. When she got on and paid her fare she was struck by the sight of the vacant seats in the

144

front section. After she had joined the tightly assembled blacks and turned around, she saw the driver looking back and glaring at her. Come up front, he ordered her, get off "my bus" and get back on through the rear door. Although she knew that sometimes drivers would leave blacks standing in the street while they drove away, she had gotten a transfer that would be good on the next bus, and so she decided to obey. She'd had her fill of the paragon of Southern courtesy.

She was already a member of the National Association for the Advancement of Colored People. Her husband belonged to the local chapter but had warned her against joining as being "too dangerous." Deciding to take her chances, she immediately ran up against another kind of discrimination. It so happened that at the first meeting she attended there was an election of officers, including a secretary to take minutes. As the only woman there, she naturally was elected. With her husband's support she hung in there and came to enjoy the responsibility—and the feeling of belonging to an organization which, when the U.S. Supreme Court in 1954 declared for the desegregation of schools, had been working to achieve exactly that for the preceding 30 years.

She continued to work for a living, of course, as that fateful day in December 1955 approached. Ten years earlier Alabama's legislature had passed a law requiring all bus companies to enforce seating segregation, the law to be interpreted at the discretion of each driver. The law that no seat would be yielded while another was available had come to be generally ignored by assertive white drivers and passengers and by cowed blacks.

As she boarded the bus that evening and paid her fare, she was dismayed at the sight of the driver—the very one she had encountered 12 years earlier and luckily had managed to avoid ever since. Perhaps because the bus was crowded and he was busy, he didn't bother demanding that she go through the front-door/rear-door routine. Of the rows available to blacks, only one had a vacant seat, the eleventh row, the first behind the white section—the aisle seat, next to a black man and across from two black women.

The bus began filling up until finally the front section was fully occupied, with one white man left illicitly standing. Since divine law and city ordinance decreed that no black might sit in a row occupied by a white, she and her three fellow passengers of the wrong pigmentation would have to get up and stand in the rear. At the menacing demand of the driver ("Y'all better make it light on yourselves and let me have those seats"), the other three did so while she moved to the now vacant window seat. And there she stayed.

After futilely threatening arrest, the driver went to a phone and called the police, who naturally arrived very quickly in response to his momentous report of uppity criminality. She was indeed arrested and confined in a nearby pokey until her husband, with a leader of the black community and an enlightened white couple, a lawyer and his wife, arrived to post bail. After her trial the lawyer won a lawsuit against the city, which promptly appealed.

The Monday after her Thursday arrest was the first day of the celebrated black boycott of city buses. Led by Martin Luther King, Jr., it would last for 382 days until the U.S. Supreme Court, responding to the city's appeal, outlawed segregation in the Camellia State of Alabama.

LUCIANO PAVAROTTI

In the latter part of 1960 Luciano Pavarotti at 25 was thoroughly disheartened by his lack of progress. "I had been studying voice for almost seven years and had not even started professionally." He watched enviously as his friends, his contemporaries, got married and settled into careers. He and his girl Adua "wanted to get married too, but financially it was out of the question."

He had always liked singing, despite some discouraging reactions that it could evoke. Twenty years earlier, he reports in his autobiography, he'd go to his room, close the door, and sing "*La donna è mobile*" so loudly that, "of the sixteen families in the building, fourteen would yell at me to shut up." Although the neighbors came to enjoy his courtyard serenades with a mandolin, "when I tried singing opera a few years later, they all went crazy and wanted to kill me."

He was now in the singing business as a result of a deal made with his parents. Much as he liked to sing, he'd never thought of making a career of singing until, when he was about 12, he heard, and was "enraptured" by, Beniamino Gigli. (He admits that if Gigli had been a soccer player, he'd probably have taken up soccer.) The deal, made after his graduation from high school, promised him room and board with the family until he was 30, by which time it should be clear whether or not a singing career was in the cards. He'd have to work to pay for his singing lessons and for odds and ends—which he did, first as a teacher and then as a surprisingly if not exceedingly prosperous insurance salesman, although he had to stop selling insurance when the incessant sales pitching began to damage his voice.

"There are many things a nineteen-year-old Italian would rather do than stand endlessly singing scales and mouthing over and over A, E, I, O, U." In the process his teacher discovered that he had perfect pitch, without which "many incredible voices are lost." One amateur singer who evidently didn't have it was a young donna, Adua Veroni, whom he met at a party and with whom he fell quite durably, if not permanently, in love.

147

For some time his singing dates were strictly amateur. For a friend who was courting a girl who loved singing, for instance, he agreed "to stand out of sight under her window while he pretended to serenade her. Just like Don Giovanni or Cyrano." He even agreed to his friend's request for "*Di quella pira*" from *Il Trovatore*, which is "about as romantic as *The William Tell Overture*." Since it is an immensely popular operatic showpiece, it worked, although she was not so much touched as overwhelmed.

Even after three more years of arduous study, his only dates were a very few recitals in small towns, embarrassingly unpaid. Seven years of studying voice, yet those splendid tonsils and their perfect pitch had yet to bring in a cent. "My morale started to go down and down." Especially because of the uncertainties about his future—if you study law or medicine, at least you can be fairly sure of earning enough money within a few years at least to get married and start thinking about raising a family. But with singing, who knows?

"Probably because of my discouragement," a nodule developed on his vocal chords that had him sounding "like a baritone who was being strangled." This did nothing to further his career, which he decided to give up on, completely. After this one last concert.

Somehow that decision "seemed to release a strange energy in me." Perhaps, he ruminated later, it relieved him from the tension of striving to do better than his best, and as a result he did his best. The nodule disappeared, but not the audience. The prematurely last concert was a scintillating, exhilarating success. He continued singing at every opportunity.

This experience seemed to teach him to overcome any nervousness in performing. A test of this came a few concerts later when Ferruccio Tagliavina, a great tenor and longtime idol of his, turned up in the audience. Despite his intimidating presence, Pavarotti was able, after a preliminary case of nerves, to relax as soon as he began singing. The audience, including his idol, were most appreciative.

As with most performers, that preliminary nervousness stayed with him, even when he won first place in a singing competition early in 1961. His earlier concert, after his reconsidered decision, had been "the psychological turning point in my singing career." Now "the other kind of turning point" was his operatic debut, as Rodolfo in *La Bohème*, the first prize in the competition. After about a month of his rehearsing the role, the conductor during the dress rehearsal stopped the music after his first aria and told him, "Young man, if you sing like that at the performance tomorrow night, you'll have a triumph."

With that kind of encouragement, how could he miss? His performance brought him more than enthusiastic applause. By almost hackneyed coincidence, a noted talent agent happened to be in the audience. Backstage, he made the young tenor an offer to represent him. Except for a lifelong effort to achieve perfection, that's really all he needed.

I. M. PEI

In October 1963 I. M. Pei at 46 could point to a couple of dozen architectural projects he'd completed, including the notable National Center for Atmospheric Research in Boulder, Colorado, as well as to another half dozen in various stages of progress. Lately, however, he had become more of an executive and accountant than he cared to be, what with the satisfying yet burdensome growth of his firm, I. M. Pei & Associates. His career was moseying along tolerably, but it really needed a boost.

One day in that same month President John F. Kennedy was visiting Harvard University, which had just recently offered a two-acre site on the Charles River for a library to house, among other things, his presidential papers. Since the idea of a library at or near Harvard had been close to Kennedy's heart ever since a few months after his inauguration, he was delighted. As he was leaving the campus that day with some aides he pointed out the site with evident pleasure. A few weeks later he was dead.

And a few months later his widow and the Kennedys launched a sporadic yet determined effort to make his dream a reality. The first step was to choose an architect, with Jackie as final arbiter. To find one the Kennedys asked for help from a family friend, William Walton, who had proved not only politically adept but also knowledgeable about architecture. With the advice of a panel of architectural experts assembled for the purpose, he invited a number of noted architects, not merely from the United States but also from Finland, Italy, Brazil, Sweden, England and Japan, to a meeting in Boston in April 1964, to make their recommendations.

There would be no competition, since it could result in acute embarrassment if the winner didn't meet with Jackie's approval. Instead, after much animated discussion, the architects agreed that each of them would submit a list of three other candidates capable of handling the project—to Walton, in a sealed envelope. The architects at the gathering (including panel members) offered possible choices, of course, and a reason for assembling them had been to give

149

Jackie & Co. a chance to meet them, somewhat appraisingly. She was greatly attracted to Louis Kahn ("He had that light.") until he waxed too mistily poetic. ("Bobby would look at me and just roll his eyes.") A promising candidate was Mies van der Rohe, then 78 and dean of the group, but he gave her the impression "that he really didn't want the job."

Pei was part of the group, although not very noticeably. His name cropped up repeatedly, however, in the lists of recommendations, along with half a dozen others. After reviewing the work of these seven individuals, the Kennedy appraisal team interviewed each of them. Because his list of achievements was perhaps the shortest, Pei wasn't uppermost in their minds.

Indeed, on their arrival at his headquarters (which had been subjected to much spit and polish for the occasion), he greeted them with an apology that what he had to show was modest and largely irrelevant, since he rarely handled "big commissions of the monumental sort." Yet in showing and explaining slides of his work he managed to convey a ready adaptability, a talent for creating designs appropriate to the location and context, to the purpose of a structure. In this connection, for instance, at one point he grew expansive in referring to the late President's attachment to the sea.

Maybe that's what did it. In any case, Jackie evidently was quite convinced. In the elevator afterwards she confided to her sister-in-law, "I don't care if he hasn't done much. I just knew he was the one." Her feeling was strengthened by a visit to his Kips Bay Plaza in New York "on a wonderful misty evening" that seemed to emphasize the emotional over the intellectual element in the decision. Whatever the technical reasons for the selection of Pei, it "was really an emotional decision. He was so full of promise, like Jack. They were born in the same year. I decided it would be fun to take a great leap with him." No mention of Bobby's eyes.

Assuming that the commission would go to someone with a more impressive résumé, Pei was on vacation in Italy when he received a wire asking him to call William Walton posthaste. And that's how he got the news.

What he didn't get was a premonition of the difficulties ahead. Because this was now to be a memorial as well as a library, the site had to be changed to another, also in Cambridge but more commodious. His first design was centered on a glass pyramid, foreshadowing his celebrated entrance to the Louvre. Although approved by Jackie, it had to be radically changed during the years required for preparing the new site. And so a second, less ambitious and nonpyramidal design in June was submitted in July 1974, only to be succeeded by a third, more expansive design in March 1976—for a new site about eight miles from the first, since the people of Cambridge couldn't abide the thought of the crowds that the library and memorial would attract.

The library didn't open until October 1979, to less than ecstatic initial reactions. But that also was the year in which he was honored with the Gold Medal of the American Institute of Architects, its highest award.

ROSS PEROT

In May 1962 Ross Perot, 31, was frustrated—again. His four years in the Navy, from 1953 to 1957, had ended in frustration over the glacial pace of promotion, governed as it was chiefly by seniority. Although his academic ranking at Annapolis had been only middling, his service at sea had been better than respectable. Yet his goal of Admiral Perot seemed not only very distant but quite problematical. This really was no career for anyone of his driving ambition and restless energy. Much as he loved the Navy, when a reserve officer, an executive with the International Business Machines Corporation, suggested that he apply for a job at IBM, he did so without serious misgivings. After passing the company's aptitude tests and surviving the customary interview, he was offered a job in Dallas as computer salesman. And so with his new wife Margot he quit the Navy to see the real world.

The real world has its quota of frustration, of course, depending largely on the character of one's bosses. His last year or so in the Navy was one of confrontation with a new unsympathetic captain, and he was destined to experience a similar situation at IBM. His first four years were pleasant enough, productive and highly lucrative, but after his boss, who appreciated energetic and profitable noncomformity, was transferred to Washington, D.C., in 1961, he felt stymied once again. In addition, the company about this time changed the rules, imposing a ceiling on salesmen's commission incomes (lest they impertinently make more than their immediate superiors). To someone like Perot this was intolerable. After earning his full commission quota for 1962 before the end of January, in effect he found 11 months of unproductive idleness staring him woodenly in the face.

While waiting for a haircut in a barbershop on Saturday and thumbing through a copy of a recent *Reader's Digest,* he happened across Henry David Thoreau's famous observation, "The mass of men lead lives of quiet desperation." Too close for comfort. And so he decided to get out from under and do his own thing.

151

After quitting IBM he got a job as data-processing consultant with Blue Cross–Blue Shield of Texas to supplement the family income while contemplating his next move. The fact that firms needed consultants like him to help them get the most out of their mysteriously intricate data-processing equipment suggested a promising market. Why not sell such expert help as a business service? And so in June 1962, on his thirty-second birthday, he founded the Electronic Data Systems Corporation.

He started off with great caution, renting an office from Blue Cross and employing only a secretary for EDS operation. Each day after his consulting work he made phone calls. He'd made arrangements with a local insurance firm for his use, in off hours, of its IBM 7070, in processing any data he might receive from his customers, and what he needed now was a customer. More than 100 companies in the country owned IBM 7070s. If any of them had more data than they could process, he could take care of their overload.

The telephoning turned out to be a disheartening operation—no, thank you, we don't need any such service. So it went until the seventy-ninth call, to a radio company in Cedar Rapids, Iowa. Yes indeed, a new project is producing more data than we can handle on our computer. We can send the excess tapes, along with a few of our programmers, to process the data on weekends. Four months later the job was done and EDS was richer to the tune of $100,000.

Such opportunities weren't all that plentiful, however, and it wasn't until the following February that he landed a big one, Frito Lay, which needed help in developing an accounting system for its multifarious sales routes. Because this was a major, long-term job, he preceded it with a feasibility study to estimate the cost of doing the processing in off hours on rented computers. The study completed, he quoted Frito-Lay a price of $5,128 a month for EDS services, which was acceptable. Although he hadn't actually figured it that closely, in those early times he was given to quoting "odd numbers," as he later explained, because "it made it look like I knew exactly what I was doing and had figured everything down to the last penny."

Within a few months he had hired seven employees, former colleagues who could appreciate his frustration with industrial bureaucracy, all carefully selected and then severely overworked. Aware of the demanding schedule, he took time off one afternoon to visit their families. When they finally got home that night they learned that he had apologetically given each family 100 shares of EDS stock, a paltry gift, which some 20 years later would be worth $200,000.

After the introduction of Medicare/Medicaid in 1965, EDS was swamped by insurance companies' sudden, pressing need for its services. By 1968 it had grown to 300 employees, still barely enough to keep up with the demand. Its happy situation was well enough known by this time to justify selling shares on the New York Stock Exchange, and before the year was out Ross Perot was, to the last penny, worth nearly $2,000,000,006.27.

PABLO PICASSO

One day in mid–1907 Pablo Picasso, 25, was roaming about the Trocadéro Museum in Paris. Among its exhibits was a collection of primitive art from Africa and several Pacific islands. Like other avant-garde artists of this time, he was acquainted with primitive art, yet on this occasion he seems to have been almost bowled over by the items on display, by their imaginative distortion of reality, their unreal representation of things familiar. He was especially impressed by some of the faces resembling the famous monoliths of Easter Island.

By this time he had achieved a soupçon of fame and fortune. Six years earlier, despite the admiration of the dealer Ambroise Vollard for his work, his paintings—influenced by, and thus generally indistinguishable from, voguish impressionism—had been greeted mostly with disdainful reviews and by shrugs instead of sales. Moved perhaps by such indifference, he entered his Blue Period, painting almost exclusively in various shades of blue, a melancholy color for the melancholy subjects he chose—destitution, hardship, disability, destitution.

It was emblematic of his life at the time. For quite a while he lived in a single room with the poet Max Jacob. Since there was only one bed, Jacob worked during the day while Picasso slept, and Picasso worked or roamed the boulevards at night while Jacob slept. During the cold winter nights they often stayed together for mutual shivering, their misery alleviated only when Picasso had accumulated enough drawings to be burned in the stove for a little warmth. Small wonder that in January 1903, when Jacob lost his job, Picasso headed south for Barcelona.

The relative warmth of Barcelona did little or nothing to brighten his painting. He continued depicting, in blue, such subjects as *The Old Guitarist* and *The Blind Man's Meal*. Even after returning to his addictive Paris in April 1904 he persisted with blue, which he managed to convey even in his famous colorless etched illustration of involuntary anorexia, *The Frugal Meal*.

In Paris he was lucky enough to find a decrepit studio and some living room in a dilapidated apartment building. There, for the next five years, he would work and live with his beautiful and romantically accommodating friend Fernande Olivier (who at first had found him unappealing except for those piercing black eyes). They had little more than their love to keep them warm—or, indeed, fed, to the extent that sometimes, when a delivery boy knocked on the door with groceries, she would call out that she couldn't come now because she was naked. The boy would leave the food, and they'd pay for it when they could.

Their attachment marked the beginning of his Rose Period, sometimes called his Circus Period because, instead of blue pictures of the miserable, he now offered rose-colored views of jollier acrobats, clowns and other figures from the circus life that he had come to admire. His spirits doubtless were lifted also by his rosier prospects. His Blue Period paintings were beginning to sell, a change due in part to the interest and acquisitiveness of a couple of American art collectors and expatriate Parisians named Leo and Gertrude Stein.

It was not long thereafter that he started his celebrated portrait of Gertrude Stein. This evidently required many long sittings during which her conversational style, like her poetry, could readily influence a somewhat younger artist into some distortion of reality. In addition, his slowly improving finances brought him into contact with a community of rebellious artists, including the unconventional poet Guillaume Apollinaire.

He was now emotionally and artistically prepared for his stimulating encounter with primitive art. For some time he had been engaged in preliminary work on a large painting of nudes, apparently inspired by memories, fond or otherwise, of a brothel on Avignon Street in Barcelona. Although his early, preparatory sketches were fairly representational, the finished work, *Les Desmoiselles d'Avignon*, presented the ladies as geometrically ambiguous, curvaceously seductive yet angularly repellent, with faces out of Easter Island and darkest Africa. What he was up to only he could know, although of course there has been no dearth of cocksure attempts at enlightenment. Was he, for instance, suggesting the mixed emotions some women can evoke?

Among the mixed emotions that the picture did evoke were those of Braque, who likened it to a bad taste, and Matisse, who considered it a hoax. Barely escaping oblivion, it was shown publicly only twice over the next 30 years. Defiantly, Picasso followed it immediately with his very similar *Three Women*.

Braque changed his mind almost immediately, as of course did many others eventually. It was Braque who then teamed up with Picasso to introduce the world to cubism, turning art sideways if not on its head. And art collectors, somersaulting, began to buy.

In the fall of 1909 Picasso and Fernande moved into a large, handsome apartment next to an enormous studio.

And hired a maid.

COLIN POWELL

In February 1954 Colin Powell graduated from high school in New York's South Bronx. Although he was only 16 going on 17, his early graduation, he has reported, was due to an accelerated school program "rather than any brilliance on my part."

His problem may have been not so much lack of brilliance as lack of perseverance, an "inability to stick to anything." He realized that this characteristic bothered his parents, but he really didn't know what to do about it. One thing he did especially enjoy was his dutiful church work as acolyte and subdeacon, in an atmosphere of "organization, tradition, hierarchy, pageantry, purpose," although it was too early for him to associate such atmospherics with a military environment. Despite his attraction and his mother's unspoken yet unmistakable preference for a career ecclesiastical, he didn't persevere.

In high school he was an uninspired C student with a sporadic interest in sports. He quit cross-country track out of boredom and switched to the 440-yard dash because it was over more quickly, but not quickly enough for him to stick with it. He tried basketball but soon tired of bench-warming. For all this record of adolescent ennui, however, his parents expected him to go to college, since attending college was something of a tradition in his extended family.

After applying to New York University and the City College of New York, he was delightfully surprised and somewhat encouraged by acceptance from both. Since the private university charged a tuition of $750 a year and the public college charged $10, there was little debating about his choice. Nor was there any family indecision over his next option, concerning curriculum. Engineering was *the* thing those days, so, whatever his distaste for mathematics and the hard sciences, engineering it would be.

During his first day on campus he happened to walk by "an undistinguished old building" that barely caught his eye. It was the drill hall for the

155

Reserve Officers' Training Corps, which during the next four years would catch a great deal more than his eye.

What didn't catch his eye at all was engineering. His first semester, he has reported, "went surprisingly well, mainly because I had not yet taken any engineering courses." In a mechanical drawing course that summer, when asked to draw "a cone intersecting a plane in space," he drew a complete blank and concluded that he was meant for something besides engineering. That something, academically, turned out to be geology. Although virtually his entire extended family protested with shocked vigor ("What possible use…?"), he felt comfortable with it and later even recommended it to other strugglers as an escape hatch.

During that first semester he'd noticed uniforms of the military persuasion on campus. That autumn of 1954, after a little investigation, he joined the campus ROTC. He still doesn't quite know why. He had grown up during World War II and into the Korean stand-off and currently was eligible for the draft, and, like many others, preferred volunteer gold bars to enlistee work fatigues. After being issued a uniform and trying it on, he discovered that, besides being even more comfortable than geology, it relieved his loneliness (none of his old buddies being in college)—it gave him "a sense of belonging." Beyond that, it gave him a feeling of individual worth: "I felt distinctive."

Indeed, to his great delight a bit later, three of the campus military fraternities tried to pledge him. He chose the one he deemed best, The Pershing Rifles, and was thereupon subjected to the ritual of beer-guzzling smokers laced with thigh-slappin' porno movies, and of course the requisite military hazing—Yes, *sir*! No, *sir*! Very good, *sir*! (to put it mildly). Yet when pledge time was over he found himself wearing spirit-lifting symbols like "distinctive blue-and-white shoulder cords and enamel crests on our uniforms." And loving it.

Of greater importance was the feeling of comradeship. Without color or class prejudices, the Rifles were buddies, doing their drills together, having parties together, chasing skirts together (well, at least in spirit), all in an emotional milieu of all for one and one for all. It was enough to make a fellow want to be a soldier—especially this fellow.

In his third year he enlisted in advanced ROTC. He soon rose to the rank of cadet sergeant and then, giddily, to battalion commander. He had discovered that he was a natural leader, and so had some others. He exhibited this ability as drillmaster, at least in a limited sense, but more importantly after he became the Rifles' pledge officer, when he persuaded his fellow guffawers to replace those enticing porno movies for pledges with films showing the Rifles' training activities. He needn't have been as anxious as he was about the results of the change, for it brought the largest number of pledges in several years. He now not only felt distinctive, he felt influential.

After a summer during which he had an unfamiliar taste, though only a taste, of civilian racial segregation while in North Carolina for training at Fort Bragg, he returned for his senior year to CCNY or, more significantly, to the ROTC. Not only was he elected company commander of the Rifles, but he also was appointed colonel of the entire ROTC regiment. In those responsible positions he learned something worth remembering, and remembered, "that being in charge means making decisions, no matter how unpleasant"—to others as well as oneself.

In June 1958 he left college as a "Distinguished Military Graduate" and accepted a regular commission in the U.S. Army. In his autobiography the chapter after this point is entitled "A Soldier's Life for Me." The die was firmly cast. He had only 31 years to go before becoming Chairman of the Joint Chiefs of Staff. And then another six before becoming a best-selling author.

ELVIS PRESLEY

In mid–July 1954 Elvis Presley at 19 was thoroughly frustrated. Ever since his graduation from high school the year before, he'd wanted to be a gospel singer. He hated that assembly-line job, inserting rods and screws into an insatiable succession of shell casings. Driving a truck for Crown Electric, as he was now, was more interesting and more lucrative, yet it could hardly make up for the failure of his singing to be accepted by the Songfellows. Or by anyone else, for that matter.

The Songfellows was a gospel quartet to which he'd become addicted late in his high-school days. He'd tag along when they went out on gigs and sometimes would be invited to sing with them, for they admired his extraordinary talent for imitating popular singers like Crosby, Sinatra, and his idol Dean Martin. They wouldn't go further than that, however, since they had four singers and felt that was enough for a quartet.

What made it tough for him was that they were pretty successful, enough to buy their own plane, a two-engine Beechcraft, for their increasingly popular gigs. But on June 30, 1954, it all ended in a blazing tragedy when three of the singers, during a test flight, were killed in a crash. The fourth, devastated, insisted at first that he'd never sing again. Yet, after soon discovering that this would do nothing to ease his pain, he decided to form another group and go on with his gospel-singing life.

And so it was that in mid–July Presley was offered a chance to fulfill his dream of becoming a gospel singer. But when he was approached with the offer, he shook his head in frustration, as though fate had dealt him a deuce when he desperately needed an ace. Dejectedly, he answered, "I can't do it." Pressed for an explanation, he answered, "I done signed a contract to sing the blues."

Not simply the blues, but specifically rhythm and blues, the music of the black rural slums that was beginning to be heard elsewhere—out of a small Memphis radio station, for instance, aimed at a black audience but clearly audible to others, a station to which an impressionable Presley had been lis-

158

tening avidly since its inauguration in 1948. And so, on a Saturday in June 1953, he'd stopped off at the Memphis Recording Service to make a record, for whatever reason. One story is that he wanted to make it for his mother, who liked his singing—genuinely, not merely loyally, having given him at eleven the very guitar he was now carrying. He may (also?) have wanted to hear what he could do.

He sang and played two songs, one borrowed from the Pied Pipers and another from the Ink Spots. Then he took his experimental record, paid the tab of four bucks, and left. But the woman in charge of the operation, an employee of impresario Sam Phillips' Sun Records, was impressed by the Presley sound and by his offhand boast, "I don' soun' like nobody," meaning nobody *else*. She particularly recalled Sam's saying that he could make a billion dollars if he could find a white man able to sing black music. This fellow with the sideburns and the varicolored clothes, she felt, had "this Negro sound." And so during the recording, she also made a tape for Sam's appraisal.

Sam was not impressed. Nor was he impressed during the fellow's second visit, when Sam himself handled the recording. During the third, however, in the summer of 1954, he tried him out with a recording of some R&B, enhanced by a good deal of electronic ornamentation, and found that he had virtually invented a one-man band. And a very sexy one-man band at that. "That's All Right Mama" had never sounded so irresistible.

The next step was to get the record played by a radio station. After the disc jockey aired it one evening a little after nine, the switchboard was engulfed in calls. It was the only record played for the rest of the night—"That's All Right Mama" and, on the other side, "Blue Moon Over Kentucky." Presley had to be called out of hiding at a movie (he hadn't dared to listen) to be interviewed on the air. "I don't know nuthin' 'bout bein' interviewed," he protested fearfully. It's okay, he was told, "Jus' don' say nuthin' dirty." The DJ interviewed him only briefly, but long enough to ask where he'd gone to high school so that the Southern audience would have to believe the unbelievable, that the singer was white.

Five thousand copies of the record were sold in its first week, and before the end of its second it was No. 3 on the local charts. Meanwhile arrangements were made for the erotic newcomer to do a little singin' at a July 30th show to be put on in an open-air theater, the Overton Park Shell. As the current New Sensation, he was scheduled to open the show.

He started right off with "That's All Right Mama," giving it his all. Almost immediately he was distracted by a surge of sound, or noise, from the audience, but he kept right on singin' and gyratin'. During his second, "Blue Moon" number, the same thing happened. At the end, amid the applause and calls for an encore, he asked a couple of the band members what was goin' on.

"It was your leg, man, your leg!" they explained with appreciative grins. "It was the way you were shakin' your left leg. That's what got 'em screamin'!"

LEONTYNE PRICE

In June 1948 Mississippi's Leontyne Price at 21 graduated from a college in Ohio with a degree qualifying her as a music teacher. The degree would give her something respectable and enjoyable to fall back on, if what she later called her "frou-frou idea of becoming an opera singer" failed to pan out.

Two years later, although by then she was on a full scholarship at the Juilliard School of Music, she was finding living in New York intolerably expensive. She even was growing afraid that she'd have to quit and resort to the backup, or perhaps find work as a nightclub singer. Only some timely financial assistant from a generous, well-heeled family friend kept her frou-frou idea alive. Timely indeed, for at about the same time she wangled standing room at the back of the house for a City Center production of *Turandot*, and then a Metropolitan Opera House production of *Salome*. After these, her first experiences with grand opera, hope gave way to determination: "I've *got* to be an opera singer."

And so she took aim at Juilliard's Opera Workshop. With the aid of a remarkable voice she managed to gain admission in only her second year at the school. Soon she was taking every role she could get, however small, in the Workshop's operas, in a practice-makes-perfect plan of operations. The director cooperated, yet assigned her only minor parts. Although he told his wife privately that this young woman had "the voice of the century," his experience with experience assured him that she needed the experience.

By autumn in 1951, however, he had grown confident enough in her talent to assign her the role of Mistress Ford in Verdi's *Falstaff*, presented in the school's Recital Hall in February 1952. In spite of being a black, indeed the only black on the stage, she played the part without makeup and, to judge by the applause, was accepted whole-heartedly—especially by two members of the audience, Virgil Thompson and Robert Breen.

Breen was then in the planning stage for a Broadway production of *Porgy* and Bess and had yet to find someone to play the part of Bess. Until now, that is—he was sure that here was a gal who could do it. Yet it was too early to make the selection. But Thompson was much further along in the process of staging a revival of *Four Saints in Three Acts* with black singers for the upcoming International Arts Festival. Although the part of St. Cecilia was a tough one, he was sure she could handle it. (For one thing, he felt that African American singers are blessed with very good diction and with a special ability to portray religious faith.) He offered her the part, and she accepted with alacrity.

He was right about her—she handled the role superbly. Since she was committed to it for the New York run, then expected to continue indefinitely, a conflicting offer from Breen to audition for the role of Bess was at least as frustrating as it was flattering. Yet a benign fate interfered quite unexpectedly when a glitch developed that closed *Saints* after only two weeks. Since the company would be leaving soon for a Paris run, she took the opportunity to resign. Before long, after being auditioned and selected, she was busily rehearsing the part of Bess.

Her rehearsing mightily impressed William Warfield, the production's Porgy and her future husband—so mightily that he invited friends to the rehearsals to hear this "most wonderful voice." It wasn't merely the voice, it turned out, for she also had the dramatic spark, the vibrancy, that the role demanded. The show opened in June 1952 in Dallas, where the exhilaration caused by its enthusiastic reception was a bit dampened by the city's segregationist disdain in such things as restaurant and hotel accommodations. After unrestricted enthusiasm in northern climes had burnished the show's reputation, its widespread popularity earned it an invitation to the National Theater in Washington, with President Harry Truman as guest of honor. Since the theater management had lately abandoned its treasured policy of whites only in the audience and on the stage, color was now officially endurable.

After Washington came a tour of Europe, partly supported by the State Department. Although the black cast was provided with less than adequate transportation (the bus broke down, the plane had to turn back in mid–Atlantic), its reception in Europe was downright rhapsodic, and unalloyed by chromatic snobbery. In the applause of both audiences and critics during the show's run of two full years, here and abroad, she was regularly singled out.

Nevertheless, although *Porgy and Bess* may reasonably be considered opera, it's not considered *grand* opera, for which she was now fully qualified. That at least was the conclusion of Peter Herman Adler, the musical director of NBC-TV Opera, after he heard her Bess. That was enough for him to ask her to audition for his upcoming television production of Puccini's *Tosca*. Despite misgivings about Southern attitudes, after a couple of arias at the audition she was delightedly selected for the role. Although 11 Southern NBC affiliates, unable to stomach the color scheme, dropped out, her performance earned her rave reviews and star casting in several more television grand operas.

It took some time, but she clearly was on her way. In September 1957 she made her operatic stage debut in San Francisco, and in January 1961 gloriously sang the role of Leonora in Verdi's *Il Trovatore*, receiving an ovation that lasted 42 minutes, the longest in the Met's tradition of long ovations.

The rest is musicological history.

YITZHAK RABIN

In the spring of 1941 Yitzhak Rabin was unexpectedly filled with a 19-year-old's exultation. As a volunteer in the Hagana, the underground military group in the Jewish agency in Palestine, he'd been selected for the Palmach, a section of the Hagana consisting of special assault companies. After this flattering selection, however, he had waited and waited for an assignment while World War II approached ever closer to home. Finally the Hagana, in response to a British request, ordered the assault units to the Lebanon border. "At last," he wrote in his autobiography years later, "I was about to take part in a battle on a global scale."

It wasn't all that glorious, of course. The orders were simply to cut some telephone lines in advance of an oncoming Australian force. Yet it was the beginning of an outstanding military career, for he became convinced that after the war, and after exhausted Britain's likely decline, Jews might well be left to shift for themselves and "we would have to fight for our lives in Palestine."

He would become a leader in that fight, in those fights. His early intention to study engineering gave way before the urgent demand for soldiering. After the war, when the British retreated from the Middle East and the United Nations voted for a partition of Palestine with the creation of a Jewish state, he welcomed the political victory with a note of skepticism, predicting that it would have to be sustained "by force of arms."

And so it did very soon thereafter, in 1948, after Israel formally declared itself a sovereign state. Six surrounding Arab nations responded to this intolerable impudence by invading the new state, only to discover that every Goliath may encounter a David. As a brigade commander in the Palmach, Rabin was only too happy to help David greatly in sending the assailants packing. (However, although Israel wound up with more territory, Egypt still held the Gaza Strip and Jordan the West Bank.)

During the next 15 years, despite his being sidetracked during the

163

abortive campaign against Egypt in 1956, he continued his inexorable rise in the Israel Defense Forces. In December 1963 Major General Rabin was appointed Chief of Staff. As such he improved IDF management and modernized operations so manifestly that, when his three-year term came to an end, he was asked to continue for an unprecedented fourth year.

As such, also, he warned that the current arms buildup in Egypt under a bellicose Gamal Abdel Nasser was a serious threat, while at the same time inveighing against a rising pessimistic view that a Jewish population of millions had no chance against the surrounding tens of millions of Arabs. On the contrary, he insisted, Israel could hold its own against Palestinian guerrilla attacks, Syrian artillery harassment, and Arab hostility in general even in an all-out war—the IDF would prove to be one tough customer. In his fourth year, on the eve of what would become known as the Six-Day War, the pessimistic view was on the wane.

In mid–May of 1967 he inadvertently suggested in a newspaper interview that Syria, because of its support of terrorists, might well be the target of some Israeli military precautions. The statement may have tossed a match into the tinder, giving Egypt's combative Nasser an excuse for launching a war across the Sinai Peninsula. (That at least was Nasser's subsequent explanation.)

As Nasser made obvious military preparations in the Sinai during the latter part of May, Rabin (along with the more colorful but probably less effective Moshe Dayan) decided not to await his pleasure. On June 5 Israel launched preemptive attacks not only against Egypt but also against Iraq, Jordan and Syria. They all reacted with such aplomb as they could summon up, but within a week the war was over, with Israel in control of the Sinai, the land west of the Jordan River, the Gaza Strip and the troublesome Golan Heights, all amounting to a 250 percent increase in territory. The pessimistic view was extinguished.

Over the next 20 years the soldier gave way to the diplomat and politician in him—five years as ambassador in Washington followed by a dozen or so in Israel's parliament, the Knesset, and three years as prime minister (1973–76). Amid the uncertainties after the annoyingly close election results of 1984, he alternated with Shimon Peres as prime minister but was continuously minister of defense. It was in the latter role, in December 1987, that he encountered the beginning of the unprecedented, sustained, widespread uprising among Palestinian Arabs that came to be called the *intifada*.

The uprising, fueled by bitter resentment over years of disdainful neglect, stayed uprisen, offering the world's television news broadcasts daily pictures of unarmed, civilian rock- and bottle-throwers being felled by gunfire from Israeli soldiers. His first reaction was to "enforce order," whatever the risk to Arab lives. Then, as the ballistic hostility continued, with widespread support from the Arab population, he switched to a policy of controlling it "by force, not by fire"—leading to television pictures of Israeli soldiers mercilessly beating unarmed civilians.

It took him about 100 days of this to conclude, as he explained to the Knesset in late February, "you can't rule by force over one and a half million Palestinians." Thus began the process that slowly, hesitantly led to the accord-signing ceremony in Washington in September 1993. Although he showed some reluctance in shaking hands with Yasir Arafat, whose career he felt had not been noted for unalloyed trustworthiness, he nonetheless had reason to do so with this man who had said, "Wars are an impossibility for everybody." He himself had ended his autobiography, as early as 1979, with the guarded assertion that "the risks of peace are preferable by far to the grim certainties that await every nation in war."

DAN RATHER

In early September 1961 Dan Rather, about six weeks shy of his thirtieth birthday, was doing all right in his home state of Texas. In his early twenties, armed with a B.A. in journalism, he had paid his journalistic dues as a reporter for *The Houston Chronicle* and United Press International before taking a job with KTRH, a Houston radio station affiliated with CBS. There he stayed for about the next four years, writing news and reporting and eventually being promoted to news director. His competence in all three jobs brought him three annual awards from the Texas Associated Press Broadcasters in the late 1950s.

It also brought him a job offer from the local CBS television station as director of news and public affairs as well as anchor for the two evening news shows at six and ten. He was in his element, tirelessly reporting on cops and criminals, cars and crashes, and other ingredients in the standard fare of local television news, including of course the weather, which in hurricane country could at times be quite engrossing.

It was indeed a hurricane that released him from the confines of local reporting, that made him, as he has put it, "a child of the storm." On September 5, a Tuesday, he began expressing some anxiety over Weather Bureau reports of a low-pressure system meandering its way across Mexico in the direction of the Gulf and the roofs of Texas. He knew of course that if it reached those roofs after traveling over the Gulf, it would have picked up enormous, roof-raising power. He began pestering the station managers to send him with a small team to the coast, where the storm would hit first and where, in Galveston, the Weather Bureau had radar facilities for tracking its approach. They hesitated, a bit skeptical and occupationally concerned about the expense. As the storm continued its approach they became less so, however, and before the end of the week he and the team were in windy Galveston.

On Saturday evening his Channel 11 had its scoop, offering live coverage of Hurricane Carla, then somewhat over 200 miles from the Texas coast. He had persuaded the Weather Bureau people in Galveston that their menacing radar pictures should be televised as a public service. The pictures revealed that Carla was a biggie, covering much of the Gulf with its 400-mile diameter and its 50-mile-wide eye, surely enough to cause some consternation under those Texas roofs, as well as some precautionary measures. A public service indeed. The next day the evacuation began—a third of a million people, largest in America's peacetime history. Although Carla proved to be an extravagant exercise in demolition, causing millions in damage, only 12 lives were lost. An additional life saved was that of a terrified horse which Rather, during his live reporting, imperturbably freed from a rapidly flooding pen.

His 36 hours of almost uninterrupted broadcasting, as well as his waterlogged interviewing of resolute survivors after Carla's departure, didn't go unnoticed by CBS management. Good man in a pinch, they decided, a fellow we could rely on. And so they invited him to New York, where he was offered a job as head of the network's new southwestern bureau.

At first he politely declined the honor. Channel 11 had risen to Number One in local news coverage, and he enjoyed the reflected glory, especially since so much of it was his own. Furthermore, acceptance meant moving his family to Dallas. But with sober afterthoughts came an appreciation of the offer as an opportunity for painting on a much larger canvas. And so he changed his mind and accepted.

Characteristically, as bureau chief he plunged right into the major news story of the early 1960s, the emerging civil-rights movement. It was a risky business, dodging bullets often and on one occasion having a sawed-off shotgun poked into his ribs in a very unfriendly fashion. He became so thoroughly involved that he was generally reluctant to take on anything else, but one day late in November 1963 he agreed to interview the 98-year-old former Vice President John Nance Garner, whom President John F. Kennedy was scheduled to visit during his brief stay in Dallas.

After the interview he returned to the newsroom and was told that they were short a cameraman and reporter for coverage of Kennedy's motorcade, at a spot just beyond the Texas School Book Depository building. He agreed to fill in. Not long thereafter, although he hadn't heard any shots, he saw the motorcade speeding by his position in what seemed a state of utter confusion. Rushing back to the station after hearing something about Parkland Hospital, he phoned there, desperately seeking information. ("I'm a reporter—Dan Rather, CBS—don't hang up on me!") The president had been shot. He got the story, and CBS was on the air with it first. (Fortunately for him, it didn't have to be double-checked.)

Two months later, with a bow to his "unusual reportorial energy and enterprise," he was named the network's White House correspondent. And he was on his wide-ranging, often boisterous and controversial way.

RONALD REAGAN

In the summer of 1962 Ronald Reagan at 61 had a turning-point decision to make.

He had always been interested in politics, at least since the first inauguration of his political idol Franklin Roosevelt. And he had always been a Democrat, a supporter of Roosevelt's New Deal and Harry Truman's Fair Deal, an advocate of government help for the victims of the economic raw deal—of whom to some extent he was one during the Great Depression.

He believed therefore in the ethic that expects the talented and lucky to take on some responsibility for the welfare of the less talented and lucky. A major reason for his union activity in the Screen Actors Guild (he was president from 1947 to 1952 and again in 1959) was that, when he became a member of the board of directors, he was impressed, emotionally as was his wont, to find so many major stars as fellow board members—people "who could call their own tunes on screen salaries" yet who "were willing to use their personal power to better the lot of their fellow actors." He may have been quite mistaken about their motivation (for they've been accused of wanting to protect their power to "call their own tunes" from government interference), yet the mistake all the more clearly reveals his basic philosophy at the time, or at least his emotional predilection. Indeed, he has described himself in those days as "a near-hopeless hemophiliac liberal."

Meanwhile he continued appearing in movies more than 50 in all. Yet his movie work was anything but giddily lucrative. After his marriage to Nancy Davis in 1952, and after the couple had invested in a modest home in Pacific Palisades and in a mountain ranch—and although as a couple they were almost addictive homebodies—their lack of cash motivated him into joining a nightclub act in Las Vegas. In it he introduced talented performers, explaining to the audiences with characteristic self-deprecating charm that he was given this job because he had so little talent of his own. The act was fairly short-lived, for the nightlife routine was no life for a homebody.

168

To their rescue, at least financially, came an offer from the Music Corporation of America. The General Electric Company, he was told, was planning a new dramatic television series and needed someone to introduce it each week as host and occasionally take a role in one of the plays. The president of GE, Ralph Cordiner, admired him not so much for his acting ability as for his disarming amiability and his talents as a public speaker. (He had often exhibited that talent in promoting the movie industry on what he called "the mashed-potato circuit.")

Reagan found the GE offer, with its six-figure salary, downright irresistible. He also admired what he'd heard about Cordiner and his policy of decentralized management and employee communications. It was the latter aspect of this policy that resulted in his being asked, early on, to tour the GE empire frequently, giving pep talks and meeting with workers and managers. The company's PR man had hesitated to broach the idea to Reagan because he was reluctant to take on the additional duty of writing his speeches. When Reagan assured him that no one would have to write *his* speeches, the deal was done.

After his first couple of visits and speeches proved resoundingly successful, requests for such a visit arrived at GE headquarters by the carload. He cooperated arduously until his homebody instinct inspired a protest, which moved the company to lighten his burden. Yet the burden proved a boon. His promotional touring over the next eight or nine years proved highly profitable not only financially but also politically. It was after all very like the routine that a campaigning politician must endure, and he learned to endure it without losing his voice, his sobriety, or his temper. Publicly, at least.

The experience also, as biographer Lou Cannon has put it, was what changed him "from an adversary of big business into one of its most ardent spokesmen." Although he would write his own speeches, he wouldn't reject recommended topics, as the titles of some of his speeches indicate—"Encroaching Controls," for instance, and "Our Eroding Freedoms." Further, it brought him into incessant contact with the just-folks character of Americans outside of Tinseltown. He "was seeing the same people that I grew up with in Dixon, Illinois," people who worked hard for a living and who were payin' too much in taxes. This was another result of his GE employment, which, by raising his income into the high-bracket tax percentages, quite changed his views on progressive taxation and thus on the ethic of taking at least political responsibility for the welfare of the less talented and lucky.

Never given to deliberate hypocrisy, he decided in 1962 "to reregister and become a Republican." Eighteen years later this now self-styled conservative would introduce the country to a dozen years or more of ravenous credit-card consumerism led by a governmental replacement of taxation with a Federal debt in the trillions of dollars.

JANET RENO

In the fall of 1977 Janet Reno, 39, was earning a gratifying salary and doing satisfying work as a partner in a law firm in Miami, Florida. Fourteen years earlier the same firm, responding to her application from Harvard Law, had rejected it on the grounds that this was an all-male firm and intended to stay so. In May 1976, when she applied again, it was still an all-male firm but had doubled its number of lawyers and had thereby become somewhat younger in outlook and more tolerant of inappropriate gender. And by then her work experience may have made her imposing stature (at six foot two inches) seem more intimidating.

She had been with the firm somewhat less than 18 months, having been hired after spending three and a half years on the staff of Richard Gerstein, State Attorney for Dade County, and assigned chiefly to introducing administrative reforms. She switched to the private law firm partly because her income would be almost doubled but mainly because she wanted "to practice law." And she hoped to have more time to indulge her addiction to weekend hiking, canoeing and scuba diving, putting the Keys to good use.

Late in 1977 her old boss Gerstein announced that 21 years as State Attorney were enough. It was his turn to take up private practice. His resignation would be effective January 20, 1978. This left Governor Reubin Askew the task of finding someone to replace him until the November elections. He had about 50 names to choose from, but one to which his attention was continually called by various advisers was that of Janet Reno. After about a month of hesitant deliberation, he offered her the job, and she accepted, becoming the first State Attorney of inappropriate gender in Florida's history.

She was the only one asked, Askew later explained. "I did not appoint her because she was a woman, but because she stacked up better than the others." A rather proper man, he was promptly embarrassed by the unintentional double entendre, but she was delighted enough to use it for enlivening audiences.

170

She now headed up Florida's largest law office, employing some 250 lawyers and 650 other workers handling more than 100,000 cases a year. It took some time to get settled, of course, although her experience in the office made the transition much easier. (She had been Gerstein's chief assistant.) Inevitably she made changes, one of which was to list her home number in the phone book so that people could call her with complaints—which they did.

She was a rather stern administrator, intolerant of alibis, negligence and misinformation. She also expected her lawyers to obey the law, quite scrupulously. When one of them accumulated 116 parking tickets, or $580 worth at $5 each, she demanded that the account be settled and the practice stopped (although he persuaded a sympathetic judge to reduce the payment to $75, and then quit to join the office of the public defender). As for herself, she became celebrated for punctiliously paying the full amount for her purchases, however tempting the opportunities to do otherwise. (Her favor was considered worth the currying.)

Her first nine months in office, though unspectacular, were noticeably successful enough for her to garner 76 percent of the vote in the November election.

The first months of her first full term proved nearly painful enough to make her regret that pivotal decision to leave private practice. Dade County's blacks were, unsurprisingly, victims of racial oppression and neglect, so that their lack of educational and job opportunities invited many of them into compensatory crime. Early in 1979, after Reno's office successfully prosecuted some prominent Miami blacks, the black community began to resonate with some resentful rumbling. Then in May several cops were charged with giving a black traffic violator the kind of on-site punishment later televised in California's Rodney King incident, and, despite a vigorous prosecution, were acquitted by an all-white male jury. The rioting that followed the verdict caused 18 deaths and $200 million in damage to property.

Subjected to savage criticism, she insisted that her office was doing its job conscientiously with inadequate resources and against heavy odds. She did her insisting at as many black social gatherings as she could attend, explaining the difficulties her office faced in a biased judicial system, noting her hiring of black attorneys, citing her longtime membership in the National Association for the Advancement of Colored People. She made a point of marching in the Martin Luther King, Jr., annual parades. By November 1980 she had repaired the damage enough to win by a two-to-one margin, including three-quarters of the black vote. Despite controversies continually erupting over her no-nonsense method of operation, she would win reelection six more times.

In June 1988 she gave a memorable performance as witness before Senator Joseph Biden's Senate Judiciary Committee. In mid–1993, after President

Bill Clinton's failure to get two "AG" nominations approved, Biden remembered her and recommended her. Clinton, who knew something of her public service through his father-in-law, was much relieved to find such an
impregnable candidate. And so in March, after proving herself impregnable
in the confirmation hearings, she became the first Attorney General of the
United States of inappropriate gender.

Pat Robertson

In late March 1956 Pat Robertson, just turned 26, was casting about for something worthwhile to do with his life. He'd done a great variety of things with it already, but that seemed to be the problem. He'd done some farm work, some boxing, some wrestling and soccer-playing during his years at Washington and Lee University, from which in 1950 he'd graduated *magna cum laude* and Phi Beta Kappa. After that he had done some boxing in Golden Gloves competition and had served a two-year hitch in the Marine Corps.

Since his father was a lawyer and professional politician (who eventually served 34 years in the U.S. Congress), he decided to follow the paternal suit, pursuing the law at Yale University Law School, doing work in the summer on the staff of the Senate Appropriations Committee, and joining his father in attending the 1952 Democratic National Convention. By the time he received his degree in 1955, however, he'd become thoroughly disenchanted with the law, especially as a career, and especially after failing the New York bar exam. The law, he concluded, was bereft of ideals, was grubbily realistic, and was certainly unworthy of a lifelong dedication. (This was, after all, case law.)

By this time he was married to his wife Adelia ("Dede") and was a father with responsibilities for family support. And so he turned to business—"If I couldn't get fulfillment through the law, perhaps having a lot of money would satisfy me." A job as troubleshooter for the W. R. Grace Company proved quite fascinating, what with excursions to evaluate the operation of textile plants in Peru and cement plants in Bolivia. Yet the poverty of the people, especially in rural areas, troubled him, with American companies complacently draining families' meager resources, urging them to buy things they thought they wanted with what little money they had for things they needed.

Thus disenchantment set in again, although he continued working arduously and avidly in the hope of accumulating enough business experience to strike out on his own, to abandon the corporate rat race to others more suited to it. He wanted now to make "some real money" and "be successful," but "I'd rather do it my way than take a salary." Although his salary at Grace was gratifying, affording the family a good home and car and good-life amenities, wife Dede found him "restless," even unnervingly so.

And so he and a couple of fellow Yale Law graduates went into business for themselves, the business of making loudspeakers as the Curry Sound Company. The electrostatic speakers offered unusual reliability at high frequencies and enough flexibility for use in various applications. There was a drawback, however, in the impractically high voltage needed to drive them, a severe restriction on sales. And so it was that, having lately done some Bible reading on the side, he came home one day and told Dede that he was thinking of taking up the ministry. As soon as her astonishment was under control, she offered a suggestion: if he was serious, "perhaps we'd better start going to church to see what it's all about."

They tried but were put off by such aspects of church attendance as cacophonous music and aggressively hearty fellowship, and by one pastor's dismayingly evident discomfort, during a home visit, amid such amenities as their Modogliani nude and expensive liquor. Robertson found Dede less and less supportive, for, as a former Catholic with a casual attitude toward religion, she was beginning to detect intimations of fanaticism. Even his mother, a fundamentalist of firmly embedded religious beliefs, failed to encourage him, on the grounds that to be Christian one had to "know" Christ, and he clearly didn't.

To correct this oversight she recommended that he get in touch with one Cornelius Vanderbreggen, an evangelist who ran the Bible Truth Depot. Her perspicacity was immediately rewarded. He invited the man to dinner at a fancy restaurant and was there subjected to the explanation that Jesus Christ is not merely the world's Savior, but Pat Robertson's. By his own account, that revelation saved him from that worrisome restlessness.

After returning home and discussing with Dede his new intimacy with the personal Jesus, he found that she preferred a more conventional, remote relationship, wanting "my children to grow up in a normal home." His business partners, in responding to his announcement that he was forsaking business for the seminary, uneasily reminded him of his share in the company's debt, a reminder that inspired a spell of prayerful supplication.

Sure enough, a man who happened on the word "organ" in his wife's Bible recalled seeing an ad for a high-frequency loudspeaker, visited the Curry Sound Company, and was so impressed with the speaker's quality that he bought Robertson out, relieving him of his share of the debt.

Somehow the family survived (Dede, a graduate nurse, was highly employable and was finding his intensity infectious) while he earned his divinity doctorate and his ordination, in 1961, as a Baptist preacher. Even before his ordination fate gave him a chance to go on the air. In 1960, having gone into debt again to acquire a rather dilapidated television station in Portsmouth, Virginia, he founded the Christian Broadcasting Company and began broadcasting the next year. Needing $7,000 a month to continue, he appealed on the air, in a telethon, for $10 a month from 700 listeners (at least). The response was overwhelming.

And thus was born *The 700 Club*, among other things.

PAUL ROBESON

In the fall of 1923 Paul Robeson at 25 had *had* it. No law career for him. After only a few weeks with the law firm of Stotesbury and Miner he quit in frustration.

He had more than enough reason to be frustrated, bitterly disappointed, and angry. His parents were prominent, respected residents of Princeton, New Jersey, and through his mother he was descended from American Revolutionary War patriots. At Rutgers University, which he attended on an academic scholarship, he proved himself (at six-foot-two) a splendid and astonishingly versatile athlete, earning an unprecedented dozen major letters in football, baseball, basketball and track, despite the initial hostility from some teammates that resulted in various injuries, including a broken nose. He ended each year with the highest average in the class, entered and invariably won oratory competitions, and graduated Phi Beta Kappa in 1919. *But* he was black.

His record at Columbia University Law School was much less spectacular, surely because his interest in the law was less than all-consuming, and perhaps partly because he met an attractive graduate student in chemistry named Eslanda Goode and married her in August 1921. After he received his law degree in February 1923 he seemed uncertain as to what to do with it. What he found to do with it did little to diminish his uncertainty, for the job he took in the Stotesbury and Miner law office consisted of writing briefs and other work well below his qualifications. He encountered daily racial slights, which one day culminated in a secretary's refusal to "take dictation from a nigger." At that point he quit.

Or to put it another way, he cast himself adrift. He'd abandoned the law (or vice versa), but what was the alternative? Seemingly at loose ends, he worried his wife with his casual, Micawber-like optimism in simply waiting because "something will turn up." After a surprisingly short wait (she soon decided that he was wiser than she'd thought), something did.

Shortly after their marriage she had induced him to put his magnificent

176

speaking voice to what she considered good use. The YMCA in Harlem, she pointed out most pointedly, was putting on a play, *Simon the Cyrenian*, and the title role was made for him. He protested—too much interference with his law studies. Dismissing this objection, she pressed him to audition. He did so reluctantly, was chosen for the part, and performed it with distinction. Although the play attracted little notice during its brief run, she invited a couple of impresarios from the Provincetown Playhouse in Greenwich Village to come see the play and be impressed. They were, yet that seemed to be the end of it. He knew nothing of this and considered the experience as nothing more than a brief, inconsequential interruption of his Columbia routine.

It proved otherwise, bringing him an invitation to spend the summer of 1922 touring England and Scotland with a company putting on a play mystically entitled *Voodoo* and starring the famous Mrs. Patrick Campbell. The tour was successful and he enjoyed the experience, which gave him an opportunity to do some singing—and of course he appreciated the racially indifferent environment of Britain. As for Mrs. Campbell, she was so enthusiastic about his talent that she wanted him to play Othello. He turned her down—the law, you know.

Yet now, in the fall of 1923, having given up the law as a dead end and having decided to cock an ear for the knock of opportunity, he had to wait only a couple of months for the welcome rapping. It came in the form of a marginal note penciled in a printed thank-you letter from a playhouse acknowledging the Robesons' subscription. The note, from one of those Provincetown impresarios who'd seen his Simon the Cyrenian, announced that the Playhouse was planning to stage Eugene O'Neill's new play, *All God's Chillun Got Wings*, early in 1924. Would he like to talk about appearing in it?

Why not? What did he have to lose? Maybe the stage was something more than a momentary distraction. Could he even make a career out of it? When he read for the part, an assistant director later wrote, he was "flabbergastingly impressive" with his beautiful build, his grace in movement, and that "marvelous, incredible voice." The part was his.

Not so fast. Rumors soon abounded that the play involved miscegenation, setting a spark to the emotional tinder of dullards who feared it whether or not they could spell it. The resulting furor, plus a spell of sickness in the female lead, brought about a delay in the opening, and to fill the gap the Provincetown managers opted to revive O'Neill's *The Emperor Jones* for a week or so before opening *All God's Chillun*. Would he take on the double duty? Although doing so would entail a prodigious feat of accelerated memorization, he agreed.

The reviews of his performances were downright rapturous. He was, wrote the critic George Jean Nathan, for instance, "one of the most thoroughly eloquent, impressive, and convincing actors that I have looked at and listened to in almost twenty years of professional theatergoing." And Mrs. Patrick Campbell would have her wish. Not only did he act Othello five years later, but eight years after that his second Othello, in London, would run for 296 performances.

His notorious harassment during the McCarthy era would prove but a temporary, dimly lit interruption of a spectacular career.

JACKIE ROBINSON

In the summer of 1945 Jackie Robinson at 26 was giving serious thought to quitting. Having been a star athlete in college (UCLA) and having received a premature discharge from the army in November 1944 (reluctantly honorable because he had been disgracefully insubordinate, refusing to move obsequiously to the back of a bus), he was now playing baseball for the Kansas City Monarchs of the Negro American League. Although the Monarchs were probably the best team in the league, he was seethingly impatient with their second-class salaries, cheap equipment, Jim Crow tour accommodations, and general ill treatment. On tour in Alabama that summer a gas-station attendant had raised such a furious row over his using the whites-only restroom that Robinson had decked the canonical cracker into insensibility—in Alabama! His terrified teammates hauled him back into the bus and departed posthaste.

Meanwhile agitation for an end to racial discrimination in baseball had been growing more widespread and more intense, sparked by the Communist Party on the left through Commissioner Kennesaw M. Landis to Westbrook Pegler on the right. Before the war the Washington Senators had wedged open a crack by hiring Cubans in a tentative not-*that*-black experiment, without serious redneck repercussions. And during the war...

In 1943 Branch Rickey, manager of the Brooklyn Dodgers, wanted to expand the team's farm system. To gather up enough talent, he decided, he might have to use some unconventional means. In a meeting with a Brooklyn banker and major financial backer of the team, George McLaughlin, he warned that he was really going to beat the bushes and might flush out a black player, maybe a couple. Okay, McLaughlin answered, no objection.

Beating the bushes took a much longer time than he'd expected. He wasn't sure what he'd be getting into, but he was sure that a black player would need a great deal of talent and even more self-restraint. As his scouts reported on prospect after prospect, a standout began to emerge. This fellow Robinson seemed downright ideal—a talented ballplayer, quick on his feet and quick-witted, energetic, a non-drinker and non-smoker, college-educated, used to competing in sports with whites (during his years at UCLA) yet experienced in putting up with the slings and arrows of outrageous bigotry. (Rickey's research may not have included that gas-station attendant.)

The two men met in the Dodger offices in late August 1945. Rickey put on a prodigious bit of grilling, acting out confrontations that Robinson would be likely to encounter—with a disdainful hotel room clerk, an insolent waiter in a restaurant, an imperious railroad conductor, a resentful fellow Dodger, a sharp-tongued, even ham-fisted opponent. Suppose you're playing shortstop and an opponent stealing base spikes you with a grin and asks, "How'd you like that, nigger boy?"—what would you do, or not do? And so on.

Finally Robinson asked in frustration, "You mean you want someone afraid to fight back?" Rickey stiffened. "No, no," he answered, "I want someone with the guts *not* to fight back." Whereupon he handed Robinson a copy of Papini's *Life of Christ* and urged him to read the passages on turning the other cheek. Robinson also was handed a contract, a good one, which he signed.

His first assignment was with the Montreal Royals. That October the president of the Royals called a press conference and introduced him as a fine ballplayer who nonetheless would "have to fight for his place at training camp like every other rookie." Robinson, referring to himself amiably as a guinea pig, said he was happy to be the first to try to break through the color bar. The hard-bitten reporters generally were charmed. "He talked with that easy fluency of an educated man," wrote one, answering questions "with easy confidence, but no cocksureness, no braggadocio." In April 1946, in his formal debut with the Royals, he hit three singles in five at-bats, hit a three-run homer, stole bases twice, and scored four runs, two of them by causing the pitcher to balk. Good enough for a rookie beginning to work his way up.

He was promoted to the Dodgers the next year. Although during home games racial scurrility was more exception than rule, on tour he and his wife Rachel found that Rickey's warning fell short of the reality, especially in the South, still struggling out of its addiction to chattel slavery. Nevertheless, the color line was no longer what it used to be. Over the next several years it would very gradually fade away not only in baseball but in other sports as well—from professional football to bowling—while society in general looked on and even more gradually followed suit.

In 1949 he was named the league's Most Valuable Player and in 1962 was elected to baseball's Hall of Fame.

GINGER ROGERS

By 1940 Ginger Rogers was already a veteran Hollywood star, having appeared in more than 30 movies. These included eight of her ten major films cavorting with Fred Astaire, which in turn included the immortal *Top Hat*. Her ever appreciating, and appreciated, six-figure income kept her and her beloved mother on the quite respectable side of Easy Street. She was a valued fixture in the industry, and had been for quite a while—1933's *Flying Down to Rio*, for instance, in which she and Astaire first danced together, was his second movie and her twentieth.

Many a girl would have given her virginity as well as her eyeteeth to be in those gorgeous gowns, those magic shoes, and the arms of the world's most renowned male dancer. But that dancer's partner was growing weary of being that dancer's partner. Not of the partner, despite his demanding routines, nor of the dancing, despite those sore and sometimes bleeding feet, but of the type-casting: "I had been making movies for almost ten years and the head men at RKO thought of me only in terms of musicals."

And so RKO, aware of a lull at the time in the popular demand for musicals, gave her comic leads in a few films, roles about as weighty as the feathers in that famously plumose gown she wore in the "Cheek to Cheek" dance with Astaire. A producer, David Hempstead, knowing of her frustration with froth and having heard that RKO had bought the film rights to Christopher Morley's best-seller *Kitty Foyle*, sent her a copy of the book.

Her immediate reaction was thoroughly negative. For all her long exposure to Hollywood's moral flexibility, she was a properly brought-up girl who was deeply disturbed by the book's "explicit love scenes." At her earliest opportunity she phoned Hempstead to ask for an explanation—why would he think she'd be willing to appear in a movie with scandalous episodes like these? But she had called him at the studio, and he was on his way home.

While waiting for her next opportunity she showed the book to her mother, knowing that she'd sympathize with her reluctance to appear in any such scenes. She was told not to worry. Not a chance of a snowball in southern Arizona that they'll make a movie with scenes like that in it. With a meaty role like that, you'll probably want to do it. And sure enough, she had a phone call from Hempstead the next morning. After hearing her reaction to the book, he begged her to be patient until he could send her the screenplay. He knew she'd like it.

She liked it, to put it very mildly. Reading it gave her a couple of hours of emotional roller-coasting, laughing, crying, and lusting after that leading role. When he called back later, she reminded him that she was in the middle of *Lucky Partners* (a forgettable film but one that she didn't forget because she played opposite the magnetically romantic Ronald Colman). After doing this movie she was due a vacation, but she eagerly promised to forego any vacation to play Kitty Foyle. And although the completion of *Lucky Partners* was delayed by someone else's illness, that's what she did.

She respected and worked well with the director Sam Wood, although she long remembered thereafter a nervous habit of his that caused considerable difficulty in one intensely emotional scene in which Kitty is in a hospital, having just borne a child. To help her get in the mood for this demanding scene, she asked for a few minutes in her dressing room to listen to a recording of music from Tchaikovsky's overture to *Romeo and Juliet*. Being emotionally impressionable, she had tears in her eyes when she emerged, ready for the scene. At the critical moment, director Wood indulged his nervous habit of jingling coins in his pocket. She couldn't suppress some highly inappropriate giggles.

The scene was reshot, of course, sans jingling. And the movie brought an Oscar to Ginger Rogers, dramatic actress, who still had 30 movies to go.

JOHN STEINBECK

In the summer of 1925 one John Ernst Steinbeck, Jr., 23, arrived in Greenwich Village after a long trip through the Panama Canal (and a riotous stopover in Havana) from his home state of California, where he had led a piebald worklife as common laborer, ditch-digger, ranch worker, store clerk, maintenance man, limousine driver, whatever. These jobs had been money-earning interludes to pay for his intermittent intrusions into academe at Stanford University. He had chosen his courses carefully, not to earn a degree but to help him realize his ambition to be a writer, an ambition that had been gnawing at him since high school.

In New York he got a job pushing cement in wheelbarrows until he decided that it might kill him simply by breaking his back. Maybe a newspaper writing job would be less strenuous, and that's the route he took in spite of his fear that such a writing job could kill his urge for spare-time, consequential writing. As a general-assignment legman he found little opportunity for honing his literary skills but plenty for learning about the seedy side of the opulent twenties' miserable poverty and its contrasting scenes of conspicuous wealth. And of Prohibition times awash in alcohol.

After a few months of this journalistic routine he and his editor decided that this wasn't his bag, and he returned to day labor. He kept right on doggedly writing in his off hours, short story after short story, followed by rejection after rejection from magazines until finally, after he had written enough stories for a book, they were all summarily rejected by a book publisher. Well, *that* for New York!

And so he took a job as deckhand on a freighter to carry him back through the Canal to California. There he settled down in the northern mountains. His job as caretaker at a private Lake Tahoe estate ended after a violent windstorm blew a tree down on the house, severely damaging it (but he saved the library). His next job, supervising trout at a fish hatchery—where, he said, he played "midwife to lady trout"—gave him much more leisure time for writing,

183

fulfilling his prime requirement. In view of his New York experience, he decided that maybe he should give up short stories and try his luck with novels.

His first, *A Cup of Gold*, was a fictional account of Sir Henry Morgan's rise to dull respectability by means of colorful piracy. It was an attractive, floridly yet quite well written story (a judgment reached by critics later rather than sooner), good enough to be published (after seven rejections) in the late summer of 1929 but not enough to overcome the effects of the historic stock market crash or to sell more than about 1,500 copies.

But at least he'd been published and had earned all of $250 (about $2,500 today), enough to give him some encouragement. He even started work on two novels simultaneously, both set in the central California that he knew so well and both about the sort of people he knew rather than piratical swashbucklers. *And* he was accepted as a client by a New York literary agent, Elizabeth Otis, who indeed would represent him until death did them part.

Concentrating on one of his two novels, *The Pastures of Heaven*, he managed with her help to get it published—in 1932, with the book market plummeting deep into the general pit of economic woe. The book earned him all of $400 and a deafening critical silence. Meanwhile, with his new wife Carol Henning he had visited his parents and from his father had received a promise to send him $25 a month until he found out whether he could support himself and Carol with his writing, or couldn't.

The couple moved to the coast, near Monterey, where he met a marine biologist named Ed Ricketts, a popular resident of Cannery Row. They became bosom buddies, especially as they became mutually engrossed in endless conversations and arguments over whatever might occur to their active minds. He also returned to the other of his two novels, *To a God Unknown*, a rather mystical treatment of life during a drought in a north central California valley. It was published, bringing him a grand total of $250. Financially, his writing career was in reverse.

At Stanford he had rather carelessly taken a few science courses, and now the course in chemistry got him a job as a chemist in a sugar mill where the workers were mostly Mexican *paisanos* for whom the term "worker" was a rather serious mislabeling. He found them an irresistibly likeable lot, to the point of comparing them to the knights of Camelot. (Actually they were a good deal more likeable than those devotees of noble violence.) At least, as he saw it, they weren't pillars of stifling middle class propriety, and surely these bibulous eccentrics were colorful and intriguing enough for him to write a book about them, a series of picaresque stories about their adventures, their good-natured machinations, their appealing characters, their happy-go-lucky lives.

Tortilla Flat was accepted by the twelfth publisher to whom it was submitted. It was a best-seller for several months after its publication in 1935 and brought him a California Commonwealth Club award as the year's best novel by a Golden State author. It also earned him a respectable amount of money, including $4,000 from a Hollywood studio (which later sold it to MGM for $90,000 for the 1942 production of the movie with Spencer Tracy, Hedy Lamarr and John Garfield).

He was on his way now, through other novels including *Of Mice and Men*, to his 1939-40 masterwork as book and movie, *The Grapes of Wrath*.

MOTHER TERESA

One day in 1946 Mother Teresa, born Agnes Gonxha Bojaxhiu 36 years earlier, had that nagging feeling once again. She was taking a train in India from Calcutta to Darjeeling, a town in the Himalayas, to make a spiritual retreat, and again she had what she would later describe as "a call within a call, something like a second vocation."

She had already spent 18 years in her first vocation as a Sister of Loreto teaching at St. Mary's High School in eastern Calcutta. As she has reported it, she had felt a vocation to become a nun in childhood. It disappeared between the ages of 12 and 18, and then reappeared quite urgently. She had read letters from hardy Jesuit missionaries in India that "used to give us the most beautiful descriptions about the experiences they had with the people and especially with the children," and she was hooked. Referred by a visiting Jesuit to the Sisters of Loreto, she joined the order in the fall of 1928, arriving in India the next year.

For the next two decades of her life she couldn't have been happier. She loved teaching, loved the children, loved the order, loved the Lord from Whom she had heard the call. Her first call—and now this second call. It would be hard to leave her first vocation for a second, but this second call seemed gradually to become quite specific: "to renounce everything and to follow Christ into the slums, to serve the poorest of the poor."

Two years passed, doubtless because her unconventional impulse had to pass muster with the church bureaucracy. Her Loreto superiors proved most sympathetic, and eventually permission was received from the office of the presiding bishop. Meanwhile some of her more starry-eyed pupils, after learning of her ambitious plans through the grapevine, volunteered to become nuns and join her in her new apostolate. She had to explain that first she'd have to get started, and as to details of even that she was at a loss. For the moment, that is—she was awaiting further instructions.

She was already sure of the place—right there in Calcutta, with its teeming masses of the poorest poor. Soon after her departure from the convent, as she was walking along a street, a priest approached her and asked for a contribution to the Catholic press. She had already given four of her five rupees to various beggars, so that even she hesitated before giving him her fifth. Yet she did of course—soft touch was now her middle name. A few hours later he came looking for her. Some fellow who'd heard about her plans had come to him with this envelope, he said, to give to her. It contained 50 rupees. A good start for a woman destined to become one of the world's most effective money-raisers. (One who never had to directly ask for money, incidentally.)

A dozen of her former students proved as good as their word. The first one joined her in March 1949, and after some months her little congregation, including her, numbered a baker's dozen. Gradually other young women of all economic classes began arriving from all over the world, formally attesting in their written applications, "I want a life of poverty, prayer and sacrifice that will lead me to the service of the poor." Before the end of 1950 a new religious order was formed with the approval of the Vatican, the Missionaries of Charity. (A girl's final commitment is made only after more than eight years of working in the congregation. By then she's thought ready to make up her mind.)

The very poor of Calcutta subsist on a diet consisting almost exclusively of rice and salt, and the new missionary sisters' first impulse was to live on nothing more than that, in Christian sympathy. When word of this reached some more experienced missionary authorities, their leader was admonished most severely. Downright sinful, they advised, almost an insolent challenge to divine providence. With such a diet the sisters will simply grow ill and die young like the poor they're committed to help. They must eat well to resist the diseases they'll encounter and continue to do the work to which they're dedicated. The diet thereafter was greatly improved. No doubt the advice was providential.

What kind of experiences did they have to be prepared for? She has described an illustrative incident in Bombay when "our sisters picked up a man from the street. In lifting him up, the whole of his back remained on the street. They brought him home, cleaned him, washed him, but the man never said a word." In that experience, said one of the sisters, never had the presence of Christ seemed so real. What was that about dedication?

In succeeding years the congregation would grow into more than 150 communities of more than 1,800 nuns in 25 countries serving the destitute in schools, clinics, leprosariums, and food distribution centers. As she traveled tirelessly about the world overseeing such efforts, Mother Teresa received many awards, including the 1979 Nobel Prize for Peace.

MARGARET THATCHER

In early 1981 Margaret Thatcher at 55 had for 21 months been England's first woman prime minister. The British people had never seen anything quite like her public personality since Boadicea, the warrior-queen of the first century. Her introduction of aggressively conservative monetarism (shrinkage of government into a money-supply regulator) to the British economy had shown her to be fully worthy of the sobriquet "Iron Lady." Now, however, what with the curtailment of public spending and the withdrawal of government measures to maintain economic stability, the country's unemployment rate had risen to 10 percent, the highest since the Great Depression of the 1930s. In the House of Commons, one day when she wore a black suit, she was greeted by a member of the opposition with the question, "Is my Right Honorable Friend dressed in black because of the unemployment figures?"

Her second budget revealed her anxiety over inflation, which of course is threatening to haves as well as disastrous to have-nots. The budget raised sales taxes on everyday commodities—on cigarettes, on gasoline, even on Scotch whisky, her favorite drink. The haves were displeased, but their displeasure was insignificant compared to that of the have-nots. In south London West Indian blacks rioted for three days and nights, damaging and destroying property, trading injuries with police. Before long the rioting had spread to other parts of London and to cities like Manchester, Birmingham, Liverpool (where one resident compared the devastation to that of World War II).

In addition, the economy in general was performing as dismally as ever. Debate in the House grew even stormier than usual, and more personal— "You *stupid* woman!" Opposition to her policies came not only from Labour but also from Tory Members of Parliament and even from members of her cabinet. Her response was to fumigate the Cabinet with dismissals and reassignments. She was adamant: "The lady's not for turning." A Labour MP remarked that she had "replaced the Cabinet with an echo chamber."

Meanwhile her Conservative Party was suffering a precipitous drop in popularity as measured by the pollsters, led by an even sharper decline in her own. The polls also revealed that fewer than half of her fellow Tories wanted her to continue as party leader, and only a third believed that she could be reelected. By the fall of 1981 her political esteem was being compared to that of Neville Chamberlain.

Meanwhile in distant Argentina, President General Leopoldo Fortunato Galtieri, suffering from somewhat similar political adversity, decided to revive his political esteem by ordering an invasion of Britain's Falkland Islands off his country's southern coast. In March 1982 forty of his soldiers, disguised as civilian workers, landed uninvited, sang their national anthem, and raised their national flag to a position of assertive prominence. London, informed by island authorities of the puzzling newcomers, asked Buenos Aires for their removal or an explanation, and met with a curt refusal. Galtieri & Co. were girded for battle. After all, their adversary was merely a woman.

The mere woman asked the First Sea Lord what the navy could do about this unpleasantry. When he replied that he could have a full-scale task force ready to go in three days, she ordered him to get it ready. Whatever the problems in dealing with an aggressor 8,500 miles away, Britain would have to fight. A fellow Tory predicted that "soon we will learn what metal the Iron Lady is made of."

The few British marines were no match for the thousands of Argentine infantrymen hastily pouring onto the islands, supported by a very respectable air force. The governor ordered them to surrender and unceremoniously departed. The Argentine general in charge of the invasion considered the lack of ceremony most discourteous.

Even more discourteous was the subsequent visit of a Vulcan delta-winged bomber from Ascension Island and its calling card of 20 half-ton bombs, followed by similar deposits from carrier-based jets. Such measures weren't enough for retaking the islands, of course, a task that would have to be completed before the Antarctic's brutal winter weather could bring all operations to a frozen halt by about mid–June. And so the Iron Lady, brushing aside suggestions for negotiations coming at her from all sides, ordered a full-scale invasion. In mid–May, well ahead of any Antarctic interference, British troops captured the Falklands capital, Port Stanley, in a brief though bloody battle, and accepted the Argentine surrender.

In the House her announcement of the surrender brought her an uproarious, unanimous ovation, and on her return to Downing Street she was greeted by crowds singing "Rule Britannia." In the polls her popularity had risen to downright giddy heights.

So what if the unemployment rate was still stymied at Depression levels?

SPENCER TRACY

In March 1935 Spencer Tracy, a month short of his thirty-fifth birthday, was once again trying to ease his discouragement with resort to the bottle. (That's why he drank—in good times he could be a virtual teetotaler.) After seven years in the theater, some of them on Broadway, his lack of notable success had driven him to Hollywood in 1930, only to spend another five years making mediocre movies for Fox—20 of them, in fact. He had recently been warned by George M. Cohan that he was "a good actor—*almost* as good as you were five years ago." His relationship with the studio brass was generally one of seething resentment punctuated by open turmoil. He had even put out some feelers to MGM in the hope that, if he received a positive response, Fox would be disgusted enough to release him from his contract.

He had yet to receive a response. In mid–March he wound up at least three sheets to the desert wind in Yuma, Arizona, arrested on a charge of drunkenness, resisting arrest (with unbridled profanity), and destroying property (mostly dishes and the targeted wall). On his return to Hollywood he sought out the advice of his friend Will Rogers, who counseled patience until he learned what was in store for him in Fox's new big picture, *The Farmer Takes a Wife*. He did wait patiently, only to learn that the lead was to be given to a young newcomer, Henry Fonda, and that he'd be assigned a secondary role. At the risk of being fired, he refused to do it. And so he was fired.

Over at MGM his work was much admired by producer Irving Thalberg, who felt that he was a fine actor whom Fox had assigned to a succession of miserable movies. Hearing that he was available, Thalberg wanted to pick up his option without delay, but Louis B. Mayer objected. We've already got one drunken galoot with the studio, he protested (with Wallace Beery ruefully in mind), and we certainly don't need another. Thalberg, aware that Mayer didn't know just how drunken-galooty Tracy could be when on a tear, won him over by proposing a contract replete with restrictive loopholes. The actor accepted the restrictions, especially since the contract would pay him

190

more than Fox had paid him, and thus began a wary association that would last for 20 years.

His first movie for his new employer was a fill-in to keep him soberly occupied during a delay in the start-up of his first scheduled movie, *Riffraff*, with Jean Harlow. Entitled *The Murder Man*, it was thoroughly forgettable except for his introduction to a new young actor just arrived from Broadway, James Stewart. He preferred working with actors with stage experience and advised Stewart to "just forget the camera's there." The two of them got along just fine throughout the shooting of the picture.

One change at MGM concerned the daily rushes, the raw-film showings of the day's work. At Fox the actors didn't attend the showing at the end of the day, but at MGM they did. At the end of a day early in the shooting of *Riffraff* ("It ain't art," later intoned *Variety*, "but it's box office"), Harlow, having noticed that he wasn't attending the showings, invited him to join her. After suffering through it, he asked her never to do that again. She didn't, and he never again saw any rushes. Seeing the finished product was bad enough. He never did share the opinion of so many others about the superlative quality of his acting.

When Thalberg asked director Sam Wood about that quality, Wood replied that "the red-headed bastard is the best actor on the lot!" The pejorative term was appropriate—not long thereafter Tracy made headlines by emerging from a fight at the Trocadero with a shiner glorious enough to test the limits of makeup artistry.

After *Riffraff* came *Fury*, with Sylvia Sidney, directed by Fritz Lang. To his astonishment, Tracy found himself in a *good* picture! No more "It ain't art." On the contrary, one of the many enthusiastic critics hailed the film as showing "what this new art can do." The celebrated novelist and screenwriter Graham Greene greeted it with similar elation, praising it as "astonishing" and as "the only film I know to which I have wanted to attach the epithet of *great*."

One great thing often leads to another. His next movie, in 1936, was the classic *San Francisco*, the first of his three movies with Clark Gable, which the critic Frank S. Nugent welcomed as "prodigally generous and completely satisfying." His fan mail burgeoned from 300 letters a week to 3,000, and MGM doubled his salary to $5,000 a week in a single jump. The next year his performance in *Captains Courageous* earned him the first of his two Oscars and the first of his nine nominations.

That performance won him something else. After seeing it Katharine Hepburn told her good friend, the writer and director Garson Kanin, "I don't know this man, but he has enormous power, versatility and masculinity as an actor. I'd like to do a picture with him some day."

HARRY TRUMAN

In the summer of 1944 Harry Truman at 60 was right where he wanted to be, representing Missouri in the United States Senate. He was sociable and enjoyed the fellowship in that exclusive club, of which he'd been a member for ten years. He was accumulating a goodly amount of seniority. He belonged to three important standing committees, and his special committee on military affairs had earned a great deal of respect in ferreting out and publicizing, and thereby discouraging, costly corruption in military purchasing. He had a consequential, fulfilling job, and he wasn't looking for another.

President Roosevelt, however, had an irritating political problem. He'd decided to run for a fourth term. It was a risky decision, since he'd already broken hallowed precedent with his third term, and a fourth might be too much for the voters to swallow. He needed a reasonably safe bet as candidate for vice president. His current VP, Henry Wallace, was too pinkish liberal, and of the other principal aspirants Alben Barkley was too old, Jimmy Byrnes was too Southern for blacks, William O. Douglas was too unexciting, and so on. Harry Truman seemed a good choice, tentatively.

He was sounded out. He had no interest in leaving a satisfying, productive job, he explained drily to FDR's messengers, to become vice president, who "simply presides over the Senate and sits around hoping for a funeral." Byrnes, who was then director of war mobilization and who had reason to know for sure that he'd been chosen by the ever Machiavellian Roosevelt, asked Truman to nominate him at the convention for the vice presidency. Truman agreed.

He was happy to make the commitment if only to discourage any further speculation about that unobjectionable fellow Truman. Although to most hopefuls Roosevelt's failing health was all the more reason to lust after the vice presidency, it wasn't so for him. Pennsylvania Avenue, he wrote in a letter to his daughter Margaret, "is a nice address but I'd rather not move in through the back door—or any other door at sixty."

As the urgings continued, especially from variously motivated politicians and union leaders, he reported them faithfully to Byrnes, who insisted that all that talk from the White House about Wallace and Douglas was merely Roosevelt playing his brand of politics and that the name of Byrnes would soon be undeniably at the top of the list. Thus reassured, Truman was hardly prepared for the news brought to him soon thereafter by Bob Hannegan, chairman of the Democratic National Committee. He was shown a handwritten, apodictic note from the White House reading, "Bob, it's Truman."

Although that was clear and direct enough, he protested that he was committed to Byrnes, who was still insisting that he had FDR's unwavering support. Of course, FDR also had written a letter expressing satisfaction with either Douglas or Wallace and his personal preference for the latter. For all Truman knew, he could have been making promises to just about everyone but Tom Dewey, his Republican opponent. When he told Byrnes about the laconic note, he was again assured that it nonetheless would be Byrnes all the way. Byrnes just *knew* he had the go sign.

This was the situation on the day before the vice president was scheduled to be nominated at the convention in Chicago. On that day, responding to a phone invitation from Hannegan, he reported to a roomful of Democratic leaders at Chicago's Blackstone Hotel—governors, mayors, pooh-bahs all. You've got to let your name be presented at the convention, they demanded. You've seen The Note. FDR.

"I said no and kept saying it." Hannegan, thoroughly nonplussed, resorted to phoning Roosevelt, then in San Diego, with Truman sitting on the twin bed opposite him. FDR characteristically spoke quite loudly on the phone, in this instance so loudly that Truman could clearly hear both ends of the conversation. After some preliminary political chitchat the Happy Warrior asked, "Bob, have you got that fellow lined up yet?" (At least he didn't refer to that fellow as What's His Name.) "No," Hannegan replied rather testily. "He's the contrariest Missouri mule I've ever dealt with." Silence ensued during a moment of almost audible frustration. "Well," the Warrior replied not so happily, "you tell him if he wants to break up the Democratic Party in the middle of a war, that's his responsibility!" And the line went abruptly, and rather noisily, dead.

Truman was thunderstruck. He paced about the room for a minute or two, the cynosure of huddled expectancy. At last he exploded, "Well, if that's the situation I'll have to say yes, but why the hell didn't he tell me in the first place?" Those in the room who knew FDR far better than he did doubtless could have answered that question, but no one did.

The country could hardly expect that a "great" president would be immediately followed by another "great" president, but that's what happened, as historians are increasingly asserting.

As for his tenure as vice president, his persistent opinion of it can be found in a brief paragraph in his autobiography: "Some time after I became President one of the radio shows asked a sixty-four-dollar question, which was to name the living Vice Presidents. The person asked named all of them but me!"

LECH WALESA

In early August 1980 Lech Walesa at 37 was an electrician with a grow-ing family to support but without anything like a steady job, despite his bosses' testimony as to his competence and excellent work habits. Over the past four years, during and between jobs, he had been arrested and jailed on several hundred occasions—though never for more than day or two because he was never formally charged, as was legally required for an imprisonment of more than 48 hours. What brought him all this unwelcome attention was his irre-pressible effort to organize workers, hardly grounds for formal charges in a Communist Poland ostensibly dedicated to workers' comfort and joy.

Fourteen years earlier, after completing high school and a hitch in the army, he had moved north from his small home town to the very cosmopolitan city of Gdansk (formerly Danzig), where he found a job as electrician in the Lenin shipyard. In December 1970 his fairly perfunctory participation in labor activities intensified when the shipyard and some other factories erupted in what came to be known as "the bread riots"—strikes against the people's government's increases in the people's food prices. When some of the strik-ers at the shipyard, frustrated by management's refusal to discuss their prob-lem, took to the streets to broaden their protest, they were accosted by the people's police and were murdered by the dozens. (The people's police bash-fully avoided an exact count.)

Walesa also was frustrated. Workers couldn't win a battle against armed police, he maintained. It would be safer and more effective to use the sit-down tactic, simply occupying the workplace, idly, until a flummoxed management agreed to talk. (Not that this was a completely new, untested stratagem—it had proved useful for Polish communists in the 1920s.) But in the current battle of wills a sudden turnover in the uneasy government brought the work-ers enough relief to quiet things down.

In this quieter atmosphere he took a much more active interest in work-ers' problems, participating ever more vigorously in the growing trade union

195

movement. By 1976 his vigor was becoming an irritant not only for management but also for the trade union's manageable officialdom. In March of that
year his lack of manageability during a union meeting brought charges of "dis-
orderly conduct," resulting in punitive unemployment. He had quite openly
been writing up a petition, for presentation to management, listing workers'
grievances concerning pay and working conditions. Since this was insufferable
behavior amid all that comfort and joy, he was summarily fired.

No more company unions for him. During the next four years, in and
out of employment, in and out of jail, he worked ceaselessly for the idea of
independent unions, free of management control. He cajoled, buttonholed,
coaxed, wheedled at every opportunity. Before long his ideas began to spread,
along with his reputation as a zealous advocate of free trade unions. In April
1977 he and other malcontents in Gdansk organized a "Baltic Committee of
the Free Independent Trade Union" and began publishing, every other week,
a provocative broadside for distribution to fellow workers.

In September 1979 it carried a declaration of workers' rights—a 40-hour
workweek, indexing of pay to prices, more attention to workplace safety, elim-
ination of prerogatives for Party hacks, an end to censorship, and recognized
rights to strike and to elect genuine representatives. In addition to what workers deserved, it proposed what they should *do*—remain unified. That was the
key to success, worker *solidarity*.

In July 1980 the government sought to ease its burden of foreign debt
by raising the people's meat prices and thus provoking brief, indignant strikes
across the country. In mid–August the Lenin shipyard was taken over by
grimly sitting strikers demanding the rehiring of three workers, including
Walesa, who wasted no time in climbing a factory wall to join in the protest.
Soon he was leading it, exhilarated by the news that strike fever was proving
contagious, spreading through Polish factories and involving more than a
quarter of a million workers. In a minor government quake, hopelessly conservative officials were replaced by ostensibly liberal ministers.

By the end of the month Walesa & Co. extracted an agreement from
the latter recognizing union independence and the right to strike, as well as
yielding to demands for higher pay, better benefits—essentially the whole
package. Two months later he called a brief strike that motivated the government to stop dragging its feet in carrying out the agreement. Meanwhile
he pursued a legal effort to have union independence formally recognized,
and in November Poland's Supreme Court ruled that the country's unions
could legitimately be consolidated into one free national union. With Walesa
as its chairman, it would be called Solidarity.

The country's labor unrest was by no means over, but in Solidarity there
indeed was strength—as well as in the passive resistance which he advocated,
as opposed to violent confrontation. For that advocacy, in 1983 he would be
awarded a Nobel Peace Prize, six years before his election as president.

BARBARA WALTERS

In the fall of 1957 the 26-year-old Barbara Walters entered what she later described as her "dark ages" period. After three years of frustrating work for NBC-TV and then for the CBS-TV *Morning Show*, she now found herself without a job because of the show's frantically abject failure to meet the competition from NBC's infuriatingly successful *Today*. Furthermore, she was in the middle of a divorce, and her father, a celebrated New York nightclub owner and operator, had lost his money in a new nightclub venture and had become desperately ill, leaving her in the role of jobless family breadwinner during an economic recession.

When her pavement-pounding failed to find her a single job opening in television, she gratefully took a job from a sympathetic friend of her father's. His public relations company needed a radio-TV division, in which one employee should be enough. With the pay at about secretarial level, the work consisted essentially of contacting radio and television producers. She loathed it but proved adept at it, as well as energetic and persistent. And she learned how to soften resistance with disarming questions.

By the spring of 1961 she was employing her energy and persistence also in looking for other work. One of the people on her long list of possibilities was Fred Freed, producer of NBC's *Today* show, who was in a state of chronic distraction over trying to maintain the show's popularity and stupefying profitability despite the burgeoning unpredictability of its star, the mercurial Dave Garroway. Feeling assured after an interview, he hired her as a writer and research assistant for a celebrated model, Anita Colby, who had recently joined the show in the hope of somehow blending newscasting with her role as national spokesperson for the S&H Green Stamp Company. With her air of cultured sophistication and her Anglican Boston accent, Colby became something of a role model for her younger assistant, who soon began showing signs of yearning to follow her example in front of the camera: "She

197

didn't make any bones about it. She told me, 'I'd love to do this someday.' I could see, when I was on the air, the way she'd stand off to the side and mouth the words she'd written for me." Colby, at 47 growing weary of the fame and fortune rat race, embarked on a practice-makes-perfect training program for her protégée, starting with an on-air report at a convocation of fashion editors. Next Walters volunteered to cover the opening of a cosmetic salon in Manhattan. She did so with a tongue-in-cheek approach, allowing the camera to watch her getting the full body-wrapped, goo-covered treatment.

And then, in the summer of 1961, a series of incidents occurred that boded well for her. First, one morning only minutes before air time, Garroway lay down on the studio floor and adamantly refused all urgent requests and strident demands to get the hell up. For the studio executives, that did it. He was replaced with John Chancellor, who immediately asked that Shad Northshield be assigned to produce the show. Since Northshield had worked well with her at CBS, she was delighted, and indeed he soon gave her reason to be, sending her off on an enviable three-week visit to Paris to cover the fall fashion shows put on by Dior and Maxime and, in the spring of 1962, on a four-week visit to India and Pakistan as part of the press corps covering First Lady Jackie Kennedy's elaborately casual goodwill trip to the mysterious, teeming East.

With the help of Jackie's social secretary, a sympathetic woman vulnerable to expressions of fear of failure, she was granted Jackie's sole television interview, a journalistic coup much appreciated at NBC. In addition, during the trip she became acquainted with a close friend of the first lady and enticed her after the trip into an interview on *Today*. Yet her on-air appearances remained sporadic, frustratingly infrequent.

And then, about a year after they had been hired, Northshield and Chancellor were asked for their keys to the washroom, evidently on the grounds that news doesn't sell unless garnished with heaps of show-biz flavoring. The new producer was novelist-playwright Al Morgan, and the new anchorman was a fellow by the name of Hugh Downs.

Morgan, although he considered her fully competent as writer and producer of occasional segments for the show, had his doubts about her being an on-air regular, chiefly because of her unobtrusive but occasionally distracting lisp-like difficulty in pronouncing her *l*'s and *r*'s. When it came to hiring a new "Today Girl," he ignored her importuning and chose someone more conspicuously in the doll category. In November 1963, however, he chose her as better able to cover the Kennedy funeral, reporting from the scene in cooperation with Downs in the Washington studio. She was, as Morgan described her performance later, "gangbusters, absolutely marvelous." This proved to be one of the opinions on which he and Downs could agree. And so he sent her to a speech therapist, later confessing that "there wasn't much he could do for her."

So once again ignoring her importuning, he asked Maureen O'Sullivan, of perennial Tarzan fame, to take over as a new "Today Girl." She accepted despite deep misgivings. When the misgivings proved prophetic and their ways parted, he finally heeded the importunings and Downs' argument that she wasn't "just a writer, but a producer, and very bright. And good-looking. Besides, she had been on the air several times." Okay, conceded Morgan, let's start her off gradually, but she's got the job.

And so, in October 1964, after her 40 long months as a writer and ad hoc producer, she was an on-air regular. Furthermore, she wasn't the "Today Girl." Her billing was "*Today* reporter Barbara Walters." She had reached her goal professionally, through hard work and self-discipline as well as talent.

OPRAH WINFREY

In the summer of 1976 the news director at WJV-TV, ABC's affiliate in Baltimore, needed another news anchor. His evening news show had just been expanded from 30 to 60 minutes. (Station bottom-liners were learning that news is a lot cheaper to report than entertainment is to present and that it can be lucrative if it's made somewhat entertaining.) In the interest of affirmative action, especially since the city was 51 percent female and 60 percent black, he should try to hire a woman or a black—but which? Oh—how about that pleasingly plump young black woman who'd been successfully news-anchoring for that station in Nashville for the past three years? A little discreet research revealed that she was 22, had left college at 19 to take the news job, and probably wasn't adverse to moving on, despite some emotional ties.

And so it was that in mid–August the new hour-long news show and Oprah Winfrey were introduced to the television gawkers of Baltimore. The news show proved reasonably popular, but not the new anchor. Not professional enough for this more sophisticated market, according to the pooh-bahs. Perhaps because of her reluctant recollections of child abuse, she was too emotional—she hadn't been able to properly interview that woman who had lost all of her seven children in a fire. She had shown emotion, even had tears in her eyes. Furthermore, there was her appearance: eyes too far apart, chin too large, nose too wide and flat, hair too thick and disorganized. She'd just have to be made over.

After an introductory session with a modiste, she was dispatched to New York for re-creation at a French beauty salon. There, after the prescriptive prodding and pummeling, something was applied to her scalp that felt like brandy flambé. This expert treatment resulted in complete baldness, except for a few hardy, lonely and incongruous wisps in front. Further, she discovered on returning to Baltimore that there wasn't a wig in all the world that would fit her properly, so she was reduced to wearing scarves in her now very private life. "I cried constantly."

200

Perhaps in an effort to make it all up to her, the station decided to improve her voice. A voice coach, that's what she needed. But the voice coach told her that her voice was perfectly okay—her problem was that she was too pleasant, too affable, too nice for television. (Off camera she has characteristically sung quietly while wandering about the television studios, greeting people warmly with smiles and hugs.) He recommended more toughness, more unpleasantness. Knowing that she couldn't change all that much, she was all the more discouraged. The station wouldn't fire her, but she knew the management was regretting her six-year contract and wondering what in the world could be done with her.

In the spring of 1977, however, a new manager arrived. Interviewing Winfrey, by now substantially back to her old self, he concluded that the best way to use her would be on a talk show. Before long she was back on the air cohosting just such a show, *People Are Talking*. The fly in the soup was that it was scheduled opposite Phil Donahue's talk show, then the highest-rated in the country.

Not a chance against Donahue—such was the critical consensus. Just a matter of time, and not much time at that. But the show caught on, with Winfrey in her element, trading observations, opinions, stories, quips with the studio audiences—listening to them attentively, responding on point. She later remembered thinking at the time, "*This* is what I should be doing—it's like *breathing!*" Thus inspired, she worked so hard that an assistant producer described her stamina as mind-boggling. She also developed a bold frankness in interviewing that became a kind of trademark. (Asking about Burt Reynolds' toupee, for instance.)

As the show's rating gradually edged ahead of Donahue's, it became a major conversation piece in the Baltimore area over the next six years, during which she discovered, among other things, that she really preferred working as a single.

At the end of those six years she received a call from WLS-TV in Chicago asking if she'd care to take over the station's *A.M. Chicago*, a rather pallid show devoted to less than probing discussions of women's homemaking and beauty concerns. Once again she would be competing with Donahue, who had moved to Chicago's WGN-TV 10 years earlier, in 1974. And once again, after she had changed the program's topics to more provocative themes, she began nipping at his heels. (He wished her well publicly, "but not in this time slot.") Thirty days after her first appearance, the shows were neck and neck, and after 90 hers had pulled ahead. Donahue moved to New York to be with his wife Marlo Thomas. In September 1985 her show was expanded from 30 to 60 minutes and given a new name, *The Oprah Winfrey Show*. She was on her way. To sustained popularity, inordinate wealth, Hollywood, a prosperous media firm (Harpo Productions), and her famous promotion of a healthier lifestyle through diet and exercise.

MALCOLM X

In late November 1963 Malcolm X, 38, was biting his tongue. A few days after the assassination of President John F. Kennedy, during a rally in Harlem he had been asked by reporters for his reaction. More emotionally than rationally, as someone whose father whites had murdered after burning down his house, he replied, "It's a case of chickens coming home to roost. Being an old farm boy myself, chickens coming home to roost never did make me sad—they've always made me glad."

It wasn't that he was rejoicing over the murder of a white man but rather that he was decrying the violence of a white society which now had turned, quite spectacularly, on one of its own. Whatever he meant, what he *said* was shocking and dismayingly newsworthy. He quite agreed. "I should have kept my big mouth shut," he later confessed to a journalist.

Indeed he should have. As a prominent, a *very* prominent minister of the Nation of Islam, that well known organization dedicated to the separation of godly blacks from devilish whites, he along with his fellow ministers had been ordered by No. 1 imam Elijah Muhammad to say nothing whatsoever about the assassination. His disobedient comment had done nothing to boost the Nation's public image. It also gave his adversaries in the Nation a golden opportunity.

For some time now he had been growing uneasy with the Nation's lack of cooperation with the burgeoning civil rights movement in the South. (The Nation's activities were conducted almost exclusively in the North.) He had been a member for nearly 12 years. He had changed his name, Malcolm Little, to Malcolm X to suit the Nation's quite reasonable contention that every black person's surname had been originated in some white master's whim during the days of chattel slavery. For many years now he had been a minister and zealous proselytizer—especially in Harlem, where he had spent his felonious youth, where self-indulgence was the name of the game, and where he nonetheless was remarkably successful peddling membership in a Nation that forbade all drinking, smoking, drugs, dating, gambling and extramarital sex.

He could hardly have been more totally committed. Yet here he was, doing nothing, for instance, to help people like Martin Luther King.

As a spokesman for the Nation he had been severely critical of King, even accusing him of being an Uncle Tom cravenly accepting the brutal treatment of white authorities. But now he was developing a growing admiration for the success of the strategy of nonviolence, especially in contrast with the Nation's disdain for all political activity. He was growing disillusioned with what he saw as its paranoid self-centeredness, its enrichment of leaders at the expense of members, its tolerance of venery at the very top. He was more and more ready to jump ship, and it was the remark about the Kennedy assassination that helped him do so, like it or not.

He wasn't the only one experiencing a change in attitude. The Nation's leaders in Chicago, including the seraphic if not divine Elijah, were becoming ever more uneasily aware that his success as proselytizer and organizer had made him ominously ambitious, threatening even to the exalted Elijah himself. The Kennedy comment was the result of an impulsive disobedience that simply couldn't be countenanced. In a preliminary move he was ordered to stop preaching, indeed to stop making any public statements, for the next 90 days.

Whatever his uncertainties about the Nation, the order left him in what he has described as "a state of emotional shock." Fortunately he had a friend named Cassius Clay, later of Muhammad Ali fame, who offered him and his wife Betty a sixth-wedding-anniversary present, their first family vacation with their three daughters—in Miami, where Clay was training for a famous confrontation with Sonny Liston.

It helped, a lot. Yet on his return he was informed that the 90 days had been merely an introduction to his permanent ouster. His distress was lessened by a feeling of some relief. He was out, but he was also out from under.

On March 12, 1964, he formally announced that he had been expelled but would continue to fight for black equality on his own. He was free now to join others in the pursuit of civil rights. He would establish a new temple in New York City, Muslim Mosque, Inc. Unlike the Nation, it would be inclusive, "to provide for the active participation of all Negroes in our political, economic, and social programs, despite their religious or non-religious beliefs."

First, however, he wanted to travel to Mecca in an effort to discover what the *real* Islam was like. He did, and he did. In Mecca he submitted to the rituals of conversion, taking the name of El Hajj El Shabazz, for he had found a religion that welcomed people of all colors, indiscriminately, including whites. Whatever might have been the plans he had on his return in May, they would be severely hampered by menacing harassment by members of the Fruit of Islam, the Nation's security force. Indeed, nothing got beyond the planning stage, for he had only nine more months to live. He was assassinated in February 1965.

BORIS YELTSIN

In early 1988 Boris Yeltsin at 57 was, and had reason to be, deeply depressed. These were the first, and worst, of his 18 months of political exile, with a devastating experience fresh in his memory.

In the previous October, as head of the Moscow city committee of the Communist Party of the Soviet Union and a nonvoting member of the Politburo, he had addressed a meeting of the Politburo's Central Committee most unconventionally. Radically, in fact. Long dissatisfied with the sluggish pace of reform in the recently unbuttoned Soviet Union, he vented his frustration in no uncertain terms. This was unprecedented. Not only was he putting a scowl on the happy face that the Soviet government officially showed to the world, but he was even subjecting that government to its first public criticism. *Glasnost* had brought a measure of free speech to the country, but it had been discreetly restricted—it was never to be targeted at the military, the secret police, or high government officialdom. And here he was, attacking Mikhail Gorbachev, general secretary of the Party and president of the Soviet Union.

Speaker after appalled speaker followed his outburst with denunciations of his intolerable behavior. Yet his offer to resign was ignored amid the pious declarations of irate loyalty. When the meeting ended, his fellow delegates, without accepting his resignation, gave every indication that he was now an all but official pariah.

His pariah status became official a few weeks later, when he was in a hospital after collapsing with a heart attack. There, overloaded with medication, especially sedatives, he was kept isolated, even from his wife. Two days after his admission, attached to an IV and thoroughly tranquilized, he had a phone call from Gorbachev inviting him to attend a Central Committee meeting that day. He protested that the doctors wouldn't even let him get out of bed. Gorbachev assured him that the doctors would be glad to help him get to the meeting.

204

They did indeed, gladly or otherwise. Weaving unsteadily from weariness and additional sedatives, he was bundled off to the meeting, at which he was fired from his Moscow city job and expelled from the Politburo. He was an easy target, being in no condition to defend himself, so that his enemies, as he has written, could "enjoy the whole process of public betrayal." After the show he was bundled back to the hospital.

He continued to receive occasional phone calls from Gorbachev. After first being urged to retire from politics completely, and after his indignant refusal, he was offered a rather obscure governmental job as head of the state committee of construction. Assuming that Gorbachev might have decided to keep him within reach as a loose cannon but also as a possible counterweight to the reactionaries, he overcame his misgivings and accepted. Remaining in Moscow, however, doubtless made his isolation more painful than if he had been dispatched to the less intensely political boondocks. He was consistently ignored, snubbed, spurned, cold-shouldered. As he has described the treatment, it was as though he had developed a communicable disease or had become a nonperson. He was plagued with severe headaches, sleeplessness, and bouts of psychological depression aggravated by his physical infirmity.

But then he discovered, or rediscovered, the people. As his health slowly improved he began walking about the city alone and was delighted by the cordial greetings he received from passersby of all descriptions. Thus inspired, and despite the grubby details of his daily job, he started thinking about the possibility of the impossible, a political comeback in a country famous for gulag disappearances. However, those were in the bad old days.

Two features of the better new days proved to be his salvation, facilitating his own considerable gumption. One was democracy, which was gradually catching on among a restless populace, and which to some extent would cause the downfall of the leader who had introduced it. The other was liberated, burgeoning television. He was subjected to ardent surveillance by the secret police, a meticulous censorship kept all mention of him out of the Soviet press, and relentless official efforts zealously prevented his being elected to *anything*. Yet in June 1988 he did manage to get elected to the Nineteenth Party Conference as a delegate from a minute but autonomous republic in the north. At the conference, which Gorbachev had called to discuss shortcomings and remedies, Yeltsin felt compelled to do just that. After bulling his way through official roadblocks to the rostrum, he launched into a vigorous speech advocating democratic reforms like the secret ballot, term limits, and open criticism of the general secretary and president. He was answered in a speech by Yegor Ligachev, Gorbachev's Man Friday, but so clumsily and virulently as to greatly enhance the target's general popularity. For the conference proceedings were broadcast nationally on television. Yeltsin thus, astonishingly, had survived his excommunication.

Three years later he would be president of the Russian republic (in the new Commonwealth of Independent States), as well as valiant foiler of a coup against Gorbachev. With the disintegration of the Soviet Union, as the Russian president he would face a hazardous future rife with problems of conspicuous affluence amid widespread destitution, his own and the people's partiality to vodka, rampant drug addiction, declining public health, growing public disaffection, and accusations of a tendency to despotism. In addition, there were ominous signs along the road ahead, like Chechnya and Gennadi Zyuganov.

How will he be remembered in history?

INDEX

Abernathy, Ralph 98
Adler, Peter Herman 161
Ali, Bardu 64
Ali, Muhammad 203
Allen, Gracie 36–37
Allen, Paul 75–76
Anderson, Eddie 94
Apollinaire, Guillaume 154
Arafat, Yasir 165
Armstrong, Louis 65
Arnez, Desi 20
Askew, Reuben 170
Assad, Hafez-el 11
Astaire, Adele 15
Astaire, Fred 100, 181
Astaire, Phyllis 16
Astor, Mary 96

Bacall, Lauren 27
Baez, Joan 71
Baker, James 39
Baldwin, James 9
Ball, Lucille 37
Barkley, Allen 192
Barry, Phillip 38
Barrymore, Lionel 74
Basie, Count (William) 65, 94
Beery, Wallace 190
Benny, Jack 94
Berman, Shelley 6
Bernstein, Carl 29
Biden, Joseph 171–172
Bogart, Humphrey 18, 19, 41, 93, 96
Bond, Julian 3

Boswell, Connee 63, 64
Botha, P. W. 128, 129
Brando, Marlon 108
Braque, Georges 154
Breen, Robert 160–161
Broder, David 49
Bruce, Lenny 118
Buchwald, Art 127
Burton, Richard 62, 107
Byrnes, James 192, 193

Caesar, Sid 5
Caldor, Louis 133–135
Campbell, Mrs. Patrick 177, 178
Cannon, Lou 169
Carmichael, Hoagy 18
Carter, Rosalyn 44
Chamberlain, Neville 189
Chancellor, John 197
Chevalier, Maurice 85
Chisholm, Shirley 109
Claire, Ina 88
Clifford, Clark 30
Clinton, Bill 9, 50–52, 172
Clinton, Hillary Rodham 47, 48
Coburn, James 62
Coca, Imogene 67
Cohan, George M. 190
Colbert, Claudette 74
Colby, Anita 196–197
Collier, Ruth 74
Colman, Ronald 182
Colson, Charles 28
Cook, Elisha, Jr. 96

207

Cooper, Gary 67
Cordiner, Ralph 169
Cosell, Howard 3
Cox, Harold 132
Crawford, Joan 16
Cronkite, Walter 27, 102, 103
Cross, Milton 78
Curley, James M. 116

Darin, Bobby 118
Davies, Marion 94
Davis, Bette 96
Davis, Peter 14
Davis, Wylie 51
Dayan, Moshe 164
"Deep Throat" 29
de Klerk, Frederik 129
Del Rio, Delores 16
DeMann, Freddy 127
DeVoe, David 136
Dietrich, Marlene 18
Dillon, Josephine 73
Dior 197
Dole, Bob 29
Dole, Elizabeth 60
Donahue, Phil 201
Douglas, William O. 192
Downs, Hugh 197
Dunham, Katherine 93

Eastland, James 132
Eden, Roger 94
Ellington, Duke 65, 93

Faulkner, William 18
Feiffer, Jules 9
Feldman, Charles 6, 17, 18
Fichandler, Zelda 107
Fleming, Ian 54
Flowers, Bertha 8, 9
Fonda, Henry 69, 71, 190
Fonda, Jane 68
Fonda, Peter 71
Fontaine, Joan 182
Foreman, George 4
Frawley, William 21
Freed, Fred 197
Frost, David 100

Gable, Clark 16
Galtieri, Leopoldo 189

Gardner, Ava 54
Garfield, John 185
Garner, James 62
Garner, John Nance 167
Garroway, David 196, 197
Garson, Greer 142
Gershwin, Ira 78
Gerstein, Richard 170
Gielgud, John 141
Gigli, Beniamino 147
Gish, Lillian 107
Godfrey, Arthur 117
Godunov, Alexander 22
Goldwater, Barry 51, 60
Gorbachev, Mikhail 204–206
Goldwyn, Sam 84, 85
Gordy, Berry, Jr. 100–101
Gould, Dave 16
Gould, Jack 31–32
Graham, Katharine 29
Graham, Sheila 54
Grant, Cary 18
Greene, Graham 191
Greenstreet, Sidney 96
Guinness, Alec 107

Hannegan, Robert 193
Harlow, Jean 191
Harris, Jed 88
Hawks, Howard 17–19
Hayden, Tom 71
Hayward, Brooke 70
Hayward, Leland 16, 17
Hempstead, David 181–182
Henderson, Fletcher 64
Henning, Carol 184
Hepburn, Katharine 191
Herbert, Victor 78
Hitchcock, Alfred 142
Hope, Bob 5, 20
Howard, Leslie 26–27
Hughes, Howard 17–19, 87, 88
Hunt, Howard 28
Huntley, Chet 31–32, 102
Hussein, King of Jordan 11
Hussein, Saddam 11
Huston, Walter 95–96

Jackson, Jimmy Lee 98
Jackson, Joseph 100–101
Jacob, Max 153

Jacobs, Jim 4
Jennings, Charles 102
Joffe, Charles 5, 6
Johnson, Bailey 7
Johnson, Van 53
Jolson, Al 77
Jordan, Dorothy 16

Kael, Pauline 123
Kahn, Louis 150
Kallir, Otto 134
Kamin, Mark 126
Kelly, Fred 112–113
Kennedy, Jacqueline 149–150, 197
Kennedy, John F. 149, 167, 202
Kennedy, Joseph P. 115–116
Kennedy, Joseph P., Jr. 115
Kennedy, Robert 132, 140, 150
Kerr, Walter 70
King, Coretta Scott 119
King, Martin Luther, Jr. 51, 97–98,
  146, 203
Knight, Gladys 100
Korda, Alexander 141
Koussevitzky, Serge 25

Lamarr, Hedy 185
Landis, Kennesaw 179
Lane, Ann 137
Lang, Fritz 191
Langham, Ria 74
Leone, Sergio 62
Ligachev, Yegor 205
Liston, Sonny 203
Logan, Joshua 70
Lorraine, Billy 35
Lorre, Peter 93, 96
Lubitsch, Ernst 85
Luce, Claire 15

McCarthy, Eugene 51
McCord, James 28, 29
McCrae, Joel 67
MacDonald, Jeanette 85
McGee, Fibber 90
McGovern, George 51
McGoohan, Patrick 54
MacLaine, Shirley 6
McLaughlin, George 179
McQueen, Steve 62
Mailer, Norman 127

Makarova, Natalia 23
Mandela, Winnie 128
Marciano, Rocky 4
Martin, Dean 158
Matisse, Henri 154
Maxime 197
May, Elaine 5
Mayer, Louis B. 94, 142, 190
Miller, Ann 87
Mitchell, John 29
Moore, Gary 5
Moore, Roger 54
Morris, Dick 47–48
Mudd, Roger 34
Muhammad, Elijah 202, 203
Murrow, Edward R. 31

Nasser, Gamal Abdel 164
Nathan, George Jean 177
Nichols, Mike 5, 83
Nivison, Josephine 91
Nixon, Richard 29, 60, 111
Northshield, Shad 198
Nugent, Frank 89–90, 191

Oberon, Merle 141, 142
Olivier, Fernande 154
O'Neill, Thomas P. 116
O'Sullivan, Maureen 197–198

Pan, Hermes 16
Parks, Rosa 119
Pegler, Westbrook 179
Peres, Shimon 164
Perkins, Anthony 70
Porter, Cole 15, 16
Powell, Dick 89
Pushkin, Alexander 22, 23

Quarry, Jerry 4

Rabin, Yitzhak 11
Raft, George 93, 96
Rather, Dan 34
Reagan, Ronald 38–39
Redgrave, Vanessa 71
Rehn, Frank 92
Reich, Robert 51
Reinhardt, Max 56–57
Remick, David 30
Reynolds, Burt 61, 201

Reynolds, Frank 103
Ribicoff, Abraham 139, 140
Richardson, Ralph 143
Ricketts, Ed 179–180
Rickey, Branch 179–180
Rickles, Don 118
Rickover, Hyman 44
Ridgely, John 19
Robards, Jason 30
Roberts, Ed 75, 76
Robertson, Adelia 173, 174
Robeson, Eslanda Goode 176–177
Robinson, Edward G. 27
Robinson, Max 103
Roche, James 140
Rodzinski, Artur 24, 25
Rogers, Ginger 16, 87
Rogers, Will 190
Rollins, Jack 5, 6
Roosevelt, Franklin 168, 192–193
Rosenblatt, Michael 126–127
Ross, Diana 101
Ross, Shirley 30
Rowan, Carl 131
Runyon, Damon 90

Sackler, Howard 108
Sahl, Mort 5
Segretti, Donald 29
Selinger, Dennis 41
Selznick, David O. 10, 142
Shamir, Yitzhak 10, 11
Shearer, Norma 74
Sherin, Ed 107, 108
Sidney, Sylvia 84, 191
Sieber, Rudolf 57
Sillman, Leonard 66–67
Simon, John 83
Sinatra, Frank 46
Spielberg, Steven 83
Stein, Gertrude 154
Stein, Leo 154
Stein, Seymour 126
Stevenson, Adlai 32
Stewart, James 66, 191
Strasberg, Lee 70
Strasberg, Susan 69–70
Sullavan, Margaret 66, 67

Tagliavina, Ferruccio 148
Taylor, Elizabeth 107
Thalberg, Irving 190
Thomas, Marlo 201
Thompson, Virgil 160–161
Threlkeld, Richard 34
Tracy, Spencer 73, 88, 185
Truman, Harry 161, 167
Truman, Margaret 192

Ustinov, Peter 107

Vadim, Roger 70–71
Vance, Vivian 21
Vanderbreggen, Cornelius 174
Van der Rohe, Mies 150
Veroni, Adua 147
Vollard, Ambroise 153
von Sternberg, Josef 57

Walesa, Anna 196
Wallace, Henry 192
Walter, Bruno 25
Walton, William 149, 150
Wanger, Walter 67, 68
Warner, Jack 19, 74
Waters, Ethel 93, 94
Webb, Chick 64
West, Mae 85–86
Westmore, Perc 18
White, Frank 47
Whiteman, Paul 77–78
Whitfield, J. C. 110
Wood, Sam 182, 191
Woodward, Bob 28, 29
Woollcott, Alexander 27
Wray, Fay 85
Wright, James 81
Wyler, William 96, 141–142

Young, Terence 53–55

Zanuck, Darryl F. 95
Ziegler, Ron 29
Zyuganov, Gennadi 206